FOR PERSONAL and

CW01099473

Our Daily Bread

2025 ANNUAL GIFT EDITION

INTRODUCTION

We're glad you've picked up a copy of the 2025 Annual Gift Edition of *Our Daily Bread*, which has been published to encourage believers in Jesus.

We hope the devotionals and feature articles will assist you in your walk with God. Several articles each month address a specific topic to help you grow in your understanding of it and in your faith in Christ.

Please share these devotionals with others who need to know more about the hope found in Jesus Christ.

If we can serve you, feel free to contact us.

The Our Daily Bread staff

COVER PHOTO: *Lofoten Islands Norway,* Denis Belitsky © Shutterstock
EDITORIAL TEAM: Paul Brinkerhoff, Tom Felten, Tim Gustafson, Regie Keller, Toria Keyes, Alyson Kieda, Becky Knapp, Monica La Rose, Julie Schwab and Peggy Willison **ACKNOWLEDGMENTS:** Scripture quotations [marked NIV] taken from the Holy Bible, New International Version Anglicised Copyright © 1979, 1984, 2011 Biblica. Used by permission of Hodder & Stoughton Ltd, an Hachette UK company. All rights reserved. 'NIV' is a registered trademark of Biblica UK trademark number 1448790.

ourdailybread.org • europe@odb.org

Printed in Europe.   ISBN: 978-1-913135-87-4

THE MYSTERY OF SUFFERING

Life is marked by events of suffering, both great and small. Some are the byproduct of a natural disaster impacting entire communities with loss, grief and sorrow. Others are the fruit of human evil that has a profound effect on the world. Still others are intensely private, affecting an individual person or a single family. In all these cases, a common thread is found—the struggle to understand suffering and why it happens.

The book of Job describes the intense suffering of Job. If you read up to chapter 38, when God finally speaks, you expect some kind of definitive answer to the problem of human suffering. Instead, the story takes a sharp turn. God doesn't give answers, He just asks questions—science questions, in fact, covering the fields of zoology, astronomy and meteorology, revealing His ultimate sovereignty over all creation.

Job stood before almighty God in dumbfounded silence. He wanted to know "Why?" but God responded with "Who". The lesson for us is this: if God can run the universe in such a spectacular way, we can trust His love and wisdom with the inexplicable and puzzling mysteries of life. We don't know what God will do in the future for us or for our loved ones who are struggling, but we know we can trust Him.

When you're facing the mystery of suffering, read the final chapters of Job beginning with chapter 38. God, the ultimate Comforter, can be trusted.

Adapted from When You Don't Know What to Say *by Roy Clark. © 2007 Our Daily Bread Ministries. Read more at **DiscoverySeries.org/Q0729**.*

★ The suffering we experience in this world is painful and hard to understand. Yet, we know that God can use it to bring about good. This month we're looking at how suffering can lead us to hope in Him and His promises. The topic is featured in the devotions for **January 1, 8, 15** and **22**.

Rejoice in the Lord always. I will say it again:
Rejoice! [PHILIPPIANS 4:4]

CHOOSE JOY

Keith was feeling down as he trudged through the produce aisle. His hands trembled from the first signs of Parkinson's disease. *How long before his quality of life began to slide? What would this mean for his wife and children?* Keith's gloom was shattered by laughter. Over by the potatoes, a man pushed a giggling boy in a wheelchair. The man leaned over and whispered to his son, who couldn't stop grinning. He was noticeably worse off than Keith, yet he and his dad were finding joy where they could.

Writing from prison or under house arrest as he awaited the outcome of his trial, the apostle Paul seemingly had no right to be joyful (PHILIPPIANS 1:12–13). The emperor was Nero, a wicked man who had a growing reputation for violence and cruelty, so Paul had reason to be concerned. He also knew there were preachers who were taking advantage of his absence to gain glory for themselves. They thought they could "stir up trouble" for the apostle while he was imprisoned (V. 17).

Yet Paul chose to rejoice (VV. 18–21), and he told the Philippians to follow his example: "Rejoice in the Lord always. I will say it again: Rejoice!" (4:4). Our situation might seem bleak, yet Jesus is with us now, and He's guaranteed our glorious future. Christ, who walked out of His tomb, will return to raise His followers to live with Him. As we begin this new year, may we rejoice!

MIKE WITTMER

What personal suffering or injustice causes you to languish in your sorrow? How might the truth of Jesus bring you joy?

Father, raise my eyes above my circumstances. I look to You alone for joy.

BIBLE IN A YEAR | GENESIS 1–3; MATTHEW 1

I baptise you with water. But one who is
more powerful than I will come. [LUKE 3:16]

CHANGED LIVES

"**W**ithout God, I could do nothing," proclaims a gospel
song, which continues, "I'm leaning and depending on Jesus." We might nod at the lyrics and sing
along, but perhaps we could ponder how much we really live
out our faith in this wholehearted fashion. Do we depend on
Jesus fully? Do we know in our head and our heart that our sins
are forgiven?

As we consider what or Whom we depend on, we can learn
from John the Baptist. He explodes onto the scene in the manner of Old Testament prophets as he calls people to repent. His
message strikes the hearts of those assembled, and they ask what
they should do (LUKE 3:10). His reply illustrates the fruit that comes
from love for one's neighbour. When the people start to wonder if
he could be the Messiah, he quickly points to the coming of Jesus,
who will baptise "with the Holy Spirit and fire" (V. 16).

God gives us the power to change. When we repent, He
washes us clean from our wrongdoing and fills us with His Spirit.
We no longer are bound with shame over our sins but are set
free. We can love God and our neighbour as we depend on the
strength and love of Jesus, walking with Him day by day.

Know that God helps us to live by His power and sets us free
from our sins.　　　　　　　　　　　　　　　*AMY BOUCHER PYE*

> **How do you think John the Baptist would tell you to
> prepare the way for the Lord? How can you depend on
> Jesus as you ask Him to make you more like Him?**
>
> *Saving Jesus, thank You for working within me through
> Your Spirit, cleansing me from wrongdoing and helping me
> to produce fruit. Make me more like You.*

BIBLE IN A YEAR | GENESIS 4–6; MATTHEW 2

LORD, I wait for you; you will answer,
Lord my God. [PSALM 38:15]

RESCUE MISSION

Volunteers at a farm animal rescue organisation in Australia found a wandering sheep weighed down by about thirty-five kilos of filthy, matted wool. Rescuers suspected the sheep had been forgotten and lost in the bush for at least five years. Volunteers soothed him through the uncomfortable process of shearing away his heavy fleece. Once freed from his burden, Baarack ate. His legs grew stronger. He became more confident and content as he spent time with his rescuers and the other animals at the sanctuary.

The psalmist David understood the pain of being weighed down with heavy burdens, feeling forgotten and lost, and desperate for a rescue mission. In Psalm 38, David cried out to God. He had experienced isolation, betrayal and helplessness (VV. 11–14). Still, he prayed with confidence: "LORD, I wait for you; you will answer, Lord my God" (V. 15). David didn't deny his predicament or minimise his inner turmoil and physical ailments (VV. 16–20). Instead, he trusted that God would be near and answer him at the right time and in the right way (VV. 21–22).

When we feel weighed down by physical, mental or emotional burdens, God remains committed to the rescue mission He planned from the day He created us. We can count on His presence when we cry out to Him: "Come quickly to help me, my Lord and my Saviour" (V. 22).   *XOCHITL DIXON*

> *How has God revealed His faithfulness when you've felt weighed down? How has God used others to comfort and support you?*
>
> *Gracious God, help me to encourage others who feel weighed down, lost, or forgotten.*

BIBLE IN A YEAR | GENESIS 7-9; MATTHEW 3

I am making a way in the wilderness and
streams in the wasteland. [ISAIAH 43:19]

NEW VISION

Wearing my new eyeglasses as I stepped into the sanctuary, I sat down and spotted a friend sitting directly
across the aisle on the other side of the church. As I
waved at her, she looked so near and clear. It felt like I could
reach out and touch her even though she was several yards
away. Later, as we talked following the service, I realised she was
in the same seat she always sat in. I simply could see her better
because of an upgraded prescription in my new spectacles.

God, speaking through the prophet Isaiah, knew that the
Israelites stuck in Babylonian captivity would need a new prescription—a new view. He told them. "I am doing a new thing!
. . . I am making a way in the wilderness" (ISAIAH 43:19). And His
message of hope included the reminders that He had "created"
them, "redeemed" them, and would be with them. "You are
mine," He encouraged them (V. 1).

In whatever you're facing today, the Holy Spirit can provide
better vision for you to put the old behind you and look for the
new. By God's love (V. 4), it's popping up all around you. Can you
see what He's doing in the midst of your pain and bondage?
Let's put on our new spiritual glasses to see the new that God is
doing even in our wilderness moments.   *KATARA PATTON*

> **What new things do you see cropping up even in your
> wilderness? How can adjusting your vision help you focus
> on the new rather than the past?**
>
> *God of new beginnings, thank You for all Your promises.
> Help me to see the new that You bring about even in my
> wilderness moments.*

BIBLE IN A YEAR | GENESIS 10–12; MATTHEW 4

I am going there to prepare a place for you.
[JOHN 14:2]

A NESTING PLACE

Sand martins—small birds related to swallows—dig their nests into riverbanks. Land development in South East England reduced their habitat, and the birds had fewer and fewer places to nest when they returned from their winter migration each year. Local conservationists sprang into action and built an enormous artificial sandbank to house them. With the help of a sand-sculpting firm, they moulded sand to create a space for the birds to take up residence for years to come.

This gracious act of compassion vividly depicts the words Jesus used to console His disciples. After telling them He'd be leaving and that they wouldn't be able to go with Him until later (JOHN 13:36), He offered them the assurance that He'd "prepare a place for [them]" in heaven (14:2). Though they were rightly saddened that Jesus said He would leave them soon and that they could not follow Him, He encouraged them to look on this holy errand as part of His preparation to receive them—and us.

Without Jesus' sacrificial work on the cross, the "many rooms" of the Father's house wouldn't be able to receive us (V. 2). Having gone before us in preparation, Christ assures us He'll return and take those who trust in His sacrifice to be with Him. There we'll take up residence with Him in a joyous eternity.

KIRSTEN HOLMBERG

**When have you felt you weren't 'at home' in this life?
What do you most look forward to about heaven?**

Thank You, Jesus, for preparing a place for me in heaven with You.

BIBLE IN A YEAR | GENESIS 13-15; MATTHEW 5:1-26

Be fruitful and increase in number; fill the
earth and subdue it. [GENESIS 1:28]

MADE FOR ADVENTURE

I recently made a wonderful discovery. Following a dirt path
into a cluster of trees near my home, I found a hidden home-
made playground. A ladder made of sticks led up to a lookout, swings made from old cable spools hung from branches,
and there was even a suspension bridge slung between boughs.
Someone had turned some old wood and rope into a creative
adventure!

Swiss doctor Paul Tournier believed that we were made for
adventure because we're made in God's image (GENESIS 1:26–27).
Just as God ventured forth to invent a universe (VV. 1–25), just as
He took the risk of creating humans who could choose good or
evil (3:5–6) and just as He called us to "be fruitful and increase in
number; fill the earth and subdue it" (1:28), we too have a drive
to invent, take risks and create new things as we fruitfully rule
the earth. Such adventures may be large or small, but they're
best when they benefit others. I bet the makers of that playground would get a kick out of people finding and enjoying it.

Whether it's inventing new music, exploring new forms of
evangelism or rekindling a marriage that's grown distant, adventures of all kinds keep our heart beating. What new task or
project is tugging at you right now? Perhaps God is leading you
to a new adventure.   *SHERIDAN VOYSEY*

> **How else do you see God being adventurous in Scripture?**
> **How can His adventures inspire our own?**
>
> *Adventurous God, send me on a new adventure out of love*
> *for You and others!*

BIBLE IN A YEAR | GENESIS 16–17; MATTHEW 5:27–48

"Who are you, Lord?" Saul asked.
[ACTS 9:5]

WHO ARE YOU, LORD?

At sixteen years old, Luis Rodriguez had already been in jail for selling drugs. Now, arrested for attempted murder, he was in prison again—looking at a life sentence. But God spoke into his guilty circumstances. Behind bars, young Luis remembered his early years when his mother had faithfully taken him to church. He now felt God tugging at his heart. Luis eventually repented of his sins and came to Jesus.

In the book of Acts, we meet a zealous Jewish man named Saul, who was also called Paul. He was guilty of aggravated assault on believers in Jesus and had murder in his heart (ACTS 9:1). There's evidence he was a kind of gang leader, and part of the mob at the execution of Stephen (7:58). But God spoke into Saul's guilty circumstances—literally. On the street leading into Damascus, Saul was blinded by a light, and Jesus said to him, "Why do you persecute me?" (9:4). Saul asked, "Who are you, Lord?" (V. 5), and that was the beginning of his new life. He came to Jesus.

Luis Rodriguez served time but eventually was granted parole. Since then, he's served God, devoting his life to prison ministry.

God specialises in redeeming the worst of us. He tugs at our hearts and speaks into our guilt-drenched lives. Maybe it's time we repent of our sins and come to Jesus.   *KENNETH PETERSEN*

> **What guilt are you experiencing or have experienced?**
> **How do you sense God is calling or has called you back to Himself?**
>
> *Jesus, I've strayed from you, but I feel You tugging at my heart. Forgive me of my sins, I pray.*

BIBLE IN A YEAR | GENESIS 18-19; MATTHEW 6:1-18

In all these things we are more than conquerors through him who loved us. [ROMANS 8:37]

MORE THAN CONQUERORS

When my husband coached our son's football team, he rewarded the players with an end-of-year party and acknowledged their improvement over the season. One of our youngest players, Jack, approached me during the event. "Didn't we lose the game today?"

"Yes," I said. "But we're proud of you for doing your best."

"I know," he said. "But we lost. Right?"

I nodded.

"Then why do I feel like a winner?" Jack asked.

Smiling, I said, "Because you are a winner."

Jack had thought that losing a game meant he was a failure even when he'd done his best. As believers in Jesus, our battle is not confined to a sports field. Still, it's often tempting to view a tough season of life as a reflection of our worth.

The apostle Paul affirmed the connection between our present suffering and our future glory as God's children. Having given Himself for us, Jesus continues to work on our behalf during our ongoing battle with sin and transforms us to His likeness (ROMANS 8:31–32). Though we'll all experience hardship and persecution, God's unwavering love helps us persevere (VV. 33–34).

As His children, we may be tempted to allow struggles to define our worth. However, our ultimate victory is guaranteed. We may stumble along the way, but we'll always be "more than conquerors" (VV. 35–39).　　　　　　　　　　　*XOCHITL DIXON*

> **When has your confidence in God's love helped you press on? How has He affirmed your value as His beloved child even after a great loss?**
>
> *Father, thank You for helping me rise up through trials in victorious praise.*

BIBLE IN A YEAR | GENESIS 20–22; MATTHEW 6:19–34

If someone . . . preaches a [false] Jesus other
than the Jesus we preached, . . . you [wrongly]
put up with it. [2 CORINTHIANS 11:4]

THE RIGHT JESUS

The buzz in the room faded to a comfortable silence as
the book club leader summarised the novel the group
would discuss. My friend Joan listened closely but didn't
recognise the plot. Finally, she realised she had read a non-fiction book with a similar title to the work of fiction the others
had read. Although she enjoyed reading the *wrong* book, she
couldn't join her friends as they discussed the *right* book.

The apostle Paul didn't want the Corinthian believers in Jesus
to believe in a wrong Jesus. He pointed out that false teachers
had infiltrated the church and presented a different 'Jesus' to
them, and they had swallowed the lies (2 CORINTHIANS 11:3–4).

Paul denounced the heresy of these phony teachers. In his
first letter to the church, however, he'd reviewed the truth about
the Jesus of Scripture. This Jesus was the Messiah who "died for
our sins . . . was raised on the third day . . . and then [appeared]
to the Twelve," and finally to Paul himself (1 CORINTHIANS 15:3–8).
This Jesus had come to earth through a virgin named Mary and
was named Immanuel (God with us) to affirm His divine nature
(MATTHEW 1:20–23).

Does this sound like the Jesus you know? Understanding and
accepting the truth written in the Bible about Him assures us
that we're on the spiritual path that leads to heaven.

JENNIFER BENSON SCHULDT

***How do you know that you believe the truth about Jesus?
What might you need to investigate to make sure you
understand what the Bible says about Him?***

Dear God, help me to walk in the light of Your truth.

BIBLE IN A YEAR | GENESIS 23–24; MATTHEW 7

Do not fear, for I have redeemed you.
[ISAIAH 43:1]

THE GOD WHO REDEEMS

As part of a sermon illustration, I walked towards the beautiful painting an artist had been creating on the platform and made a dark streak across the middle of it. The congregation gasped in horror. The artist simply stood by and watched as I defaced what she'd created. Then, selecting a new brush, she lovingly transformed the ruined painting into an exquisite work of art.

Her restorative work reminds me of the work God can perform in our lives when we've made a mess of them. The prophet Isaiah rebuked the people of Israel for their spiritual blindness and deafness (ISAIAH 42:18–19), but then he proclaimed the hope of God's deliverance and redemption: "Do not fear, for I have redeemed you" (43:1). He can do the same for us. Even after we've sinned, if we confess our sins and turn to God, He forgives and restores us (VV. 5–7; SEE 1 JOHN 1:9). We can't bring beauty out of the mess, but Jesus can. The good news of the gospel is that He has redeemed us by His blood. The book of Revelation assures us that in the end, Christ will dry our tears, redeem our past, and make all things new (REVELATION 21:4–5).

We have a limited vision of our story. But God who knows us "by name" (ISAIAH 43:1) will make our lives more beautiful than we could ever imagine. If you've been redeemed by faith in Jesus, your story, like the painting, has a glorious ending.

GLENN PACKIAM

How have you messed up? What has God provided for your restoration and redemption?

Dear Jesus, thank You for never giving up on me. I surrender to You and ask that You please redeem what I've ruined.

BIBLE IN A YEAR | GENESIS 25–26; MATTHEW 8:1–17

My God sent his angel, and he shut the
mouths of the lions. [DANIEL 6:22]

OUT OF THE LIONS' DEN

When Taher and his wife, Donya, became believers in Jesus, they knew they risked persecution in their home country. Indeed, one day Taher was blindfolded, handcuffed, imprisoned and charged with apostasy. Before he appeared at trial, he and Donya agreed that they wouldn't betray Jesus.

What happened at the sentencing amazed him. The judge said, "I don't know why, but I want to take you out of the whale's and lion's mouth." Then Taher "knew that God was acting"; he couldn't otherwise explain the judge referencing two passages in the Bible (SEE JONAH 2, DANIEL 6). Taher was released from prison and the family later found exile elsewhere.

Taher's surprising release echoes the story of Daniel. A skilled administrator, he was going to be promoted, which made his colleagues jealous (DANIEL 6:3-5). Plotting his downfall, they convinced King Darius to pass a law against praying to anyone other than the king—which Daniel ignored. King Darius had no choice but to throw him to the lions (V. 16). But God "rescued Daniel" and saved him from death (V. 27), even as He saved Taher through the judge's surprising release.

Many believers today suffer for following Jesus, and sometimes they are even killed. When we face persecution, we can deepen our faith when we understand that God has ways we can't even imagine. Know that He's with you in whatever battles you face.   *AMY BOUCHER PYE*

> **How do you respond to the story of Taher and Donya's
> commitment to Christ? How can you trust in the
> unlimited power of God?**
>
> *Saving God, help me to trust in You when the obstacles
> feel insurmountable.*

BIBLE IN A YEAR | GENESIS 27-28; MATTHEW 8:18-34

I knew that this was the word of the LORD;
so I bought the field. [JEREMIAH 32:8–9]

A RISKY INVESTMENT

The BBC's Dragon's Den has aired some unusual ideas over the years. Such as the *Easyxchair*—an armchair that doubles as a gym! Yet the programme has also featured investment opportunities that seemed risky but turned out to be excellent. Some years back, for instance, the investors rejected one hopeful, saying: "The public don't want to order a takeaway online." Yet today that's the main way people get take-out.

God told Jeremiah to make what seemed like a foolish investment: "Buy [the] field at Anathoth in the territory of Benjamin" (JEREMIAH 32:8). This was no time to be buying fields, however; the country was on the verge of being ransacked. "The army of the king of Babylon was then besieging Jerusalem" (V. 2), and whatever field Jeremiah purchased would soon be Babylon's.

Yet God intended a future no one else could envision: "This is what the LORD Almighty, the God of Israel, says: Houses, fields and vineyards will again be bought in this land" (V. 15). God saw more than ruins and desolation. Instead, God promised a future of restoration.

At times we may discern God leading us to make what feels like a risky investment. When we've tested what we sense is from God, we can trust that He can bring about remarkable transformations. Our obedience can reflect the gift of God's eternal investment in us—and the redemption to come (V. 15).   *CHRIS WALE*

How might God be calling you to invest in someone or something? Who can you ask to help you discern God's leading?

God, it's a good thing You see the future because sometimes all I see is ruin and disaster. Show me where to go and how to give myself, for Your glory.

BIBLE IN A YEAR | GENESIS 29–30; MATTHEW 9:1–17

I have become all things to all people so that
by all possible means I might save some.
[1 CORINTHIANS 9:22]

GOOD NEWS FOR ALL

Mary Sumner (1828–1921), founder of the Mother's Union, was so nervous about speaking at her first meeting that she asked her clergyman husband to step in. But his gentle encouragement and her passion to help mothers from all kinds of backgrounds helped her overcome her fears. The meetings helped mothers support each other while Mary taught them how to know and live well for Christ.

A prayer she wrote and prayed daily reflects her heart: "All this day, O Lord, let me touch as many lives as possible for You." Mary's prayer affirmed her belief that the good news of Jesus is for all people. In this she followed the Apostle Paul, who wrote, "I have become all things to all people so that by all possible means I might save some" (1 CORINTHIANS 9:22). While staying true to Jesus, Paul accommodated himself to the various people he engaged with: Jews, God-fearers or unbelievers; the confident, broken or demoralised (SEE VV. 20–23). Compelled by Christ's love, Paul gave generously of himself all for the sake of the gospel (V. 23).

Seeing individuals as Jesus sees them inspires us to reach all kinds of people: those we don't usually associate with at work. The neighbour who's still a stranger. The unknown friends we could make in the group we've just joined. No matter how different we might feel, we can share the blessing of Christ with them.   *ANNE LE TISSIER*

> *What holds you back from engaging with others? What*
> *experiences or interests could help you build bridges with*
> *people you don't know?*

> *Heavenly Father, please help me to love people who are*
> *different to me. As I grow to know them, help me to bring*
> *them Your truth, love and support.*

BIBLE IN A YEAR | GENESIS 31–32; MATTHEW 9:18–38

Save me, LORD, from lying lips and from
deceitful tongues. [PSALM 120:2]

A NEW BEGINNING

"**C**hristian consciousness begins in the painful realisation that what we had assumed was the truth is in fact a lie," Eugene Peterson wrote in his powerful reflections on Psalm 120. Psalm 120 is the first of the "psalms of ascent" (PSALMS 120–134) sung by pilgrims on their way to Jerusalem. And as Peterson explored this in *A Long Obedience in the Same Direction*, these psalms also offer us a picture of the spiritual journey towards God.

That journey can only begin with profound awareness of our need for something different. As Peterson puts it, "A person has to be thoroughly disgusted with the way things are to find the motivation to set out on the Christian way. . . . [One] has to get fed up with the ways of the world before he, before she, acquires an appetite for the world of grace."

It's easy to become discouraged by the brokenness and despair we see in the world around us—the pervasive ways our culture often shows callous disregard for the harm being done to others. Psalm 120 laments this honestly: "I am for peace; but when I speak, they are for war" (V. 7).

But there's healing and freedom in realising that our pain can also awaken us to a new beginning through our only help, the Saviour who can guide us from destructive lies into paths of peace and wholeness (121:2). As we enter this new year, may we seek Him and His ways.　　　　　　　*MONICA LA ROSE*

How have you become accustomed to destructive ways?
How does the gospel invite you into ways of peace?

Loving God, help me yearn for and work for Your ways of
peace through the power of Your Spirit.

BIBLE IN A YEAR | GENESIS 33–35; MATTHEW 10:1–20

I will rejoice in the LORD, I will be joyful in
God my Saviour. [HABAKKUK 3:18]

FROM LAMENT TO PRAISE

Monica prayed feverishly for her son to return to God.
She wept over his wayward ways and even tracked him
down in the various cities where he chose to live. The
situation seemed hopeless. Then one day it happened: her son
had a radical encounter with God. He became one of the greatest theologians of the church. We know him as Augustine, Bishop of Hippo.

"How long, LORD?" (HABAKKUK 1:2). The prophet Habakkuk
lamented God's inaction regarding the people in power who
perverted justice (V. 4). Think of the times we've turned to God in
desperation—expressing our laments due to injustice, a seemingly hopeless medical journey, ongoing financial struggles or
children who've walked away from God.

Each time Habakkuk lamented, God heard his cries. As we
wait in faith, we can learn from the prophet to turn our lament
into praise, for he said, "I *will* rejoice in the LORD, I *will* be joyful
in God my Saviour" (3:18 ITALICS ADDED). He didn't understand
God's ways, but he trusted Him. Both lament and praise are acts
of faith, expressions of trust. We lament as an appeal to God
based on His character. And our praise of Him is based on who
He is—our amazing, almighty God. One day, by His grace, every
lament will turn to praise.   *GLENN PACKIAM*

> **What are your laments today? How can you turn
> them into praise?**

> *Dear Jesus, remind me of who You are and of what
> You've done in my life.*

BIBLE IN A YEAR | GENESIS 36-38; MATTHEW 10:21-42

Blessed are those who hunger and thirst
for righteousness, for they will be filled.
[MATTHEW 5:6]

THE 'CHEWING' YEARS

My wife recently gave me a Labrador retriever puppy we named Max. One day when Max was spending time with me in my study, I was concentrating at my desk and heard the sound of paper ripping behind me. I turned to find a guilty-looking puppy with a book wide open and a page dangling from his mouth.

Our veterinarian tells us that Max is going through his "chewing years". As puppies lose their milk teeth and permanent ones grow, they soothe their gums by chewing almost anything. We have to watch Max carefully to ensure he isn't gnawing on something that could harm him, and we point him to healthy alternatives.

Max's urge to chew—and my responsibility to watch him—cause me to think about what we 'chew on' in our minds and hearts. Do we carefully consider what we are feeding our eternal souls when we read or surf the web or watch TV? The Bible encourages us, "Like newborn babies, crave pure spiritual milk, so that by it you may grow up in your salvation, now that you have tasted that the Lord is good" (1 PETER 2:2–3). We need to fill ourselves daily with God's Word and truth if we are to thrive as followers of Christ. Only then can we grow to maturity in Him.   *JAMES BANKS*

> **What 'hungers' are seeking your attention today? How could you take a step towards hungering for more of God's Word?**

> *Loving Lord, help me to hunger for You and Your Word and to stay away from that which harms me. Fill me with Your goodness today.*

BIBLE IN A YEAR | GENESIS 39–40; MATTHEW 11

Your brother will rise again.
[JOHN 11:23]

NEVER LATE

As a foreign visitor to a small West African town, my pastor made sure to arrive on time for a 10 a.m. Sunday service. Inside the church building, however, he found the meeting room empty. So he waited. One hour. Two hours. Finally, at about 12:30 p.m., when the local pastor arrived after his long walk there—followed by some choir members and a gathering of friendly town people—the service began "in the fullness of time," as my pastor later said. "The Spirit welcomed us, and God wasn't late." My pastor understood the culture was different there for its own good reasons.

Time seems relative, but God's perfect, on-time nature is affirmed throughout the Scriptures. Thus, after Lazarus got sick and died, Jesus arrived four days later, with Lazarus' sisters asking why. "Lord," Martha said to Jesus, "if you had been here, my brother would not have died" (JOHN 11:21). We may think the same, wondering why God doesn't hurry to fix our problems. Better instead to wait by faith for His answers and power.

As theologian Howard Thurman wrote, "We wait, our Father, until at last something of thy strength becomes our strength, something of thy heart becomes our heart, something of thy forgiveness becomes our forgiveness. We wait, O God, we wait." Then, as with Lazarus, when God responds, we're miraculously blessed by what wasn't, after all, a delay.   *PATRICIA RAYBON*

What are you waiting for God to do or provide on your behalf? How can you wait by faith?

For you, Father, I wait. Grant me Your strength and faithful hope in my waiting.

BIBLE IN A YEAR | GENESIS 41–42; MATTHEW 12:1–23

The Sovereign LORD says: Repent! Turn from
your idols and renounce all your detestable
practices! [EZEKIEL 14:6]

HEART PROBLEM

"**D**o you see it, brother Tim?" My friend, a Ghanaian
pastor, flashed his torchlight on a carved object leaning against a mud hut. Quietly he said, "That is the
village idol." Each Tuesday evening, Pastor Sam travelled into
the bush to share the Bible in this remote village.

In the book of Ezekiel, we see how idolatry plagued the people of Judah. When Jerusalem's leaders came to see the prophet Ezekiel, God told him, "These men have set up idols in their
hearts" (EZEKIEL 14:3). God wasn't merely warning them against
idols carved of wood and stone. He was showing them that idolatry is a problem of the *heart*. We all struggle with it.

Bible teacher Alistair Begg describes an idol as "anything
other than God that we regard as essential to our peace, our
self-image, our contentment or our acceptability." Even things
that have the appearance of being noble can become idols to us.
When we seek comfort or self-worth from anything other than
the living God, we commit idolatry.

"Repent!" God said. "Turn from your idols and renounce all
your detestable practices!" (V. 6). Israel proved incapable of doing this. Thankfully, God had the solution. Looking forward to the
coming of Christ and the gift of the Holy Spirit, He promised, "I will
give you a new heart and put a new spirit in you" (36:26). We can't
do this alone.   *TIM GUSTAFSON*

When stress hits you, where do you turn for comfort?
What might you need to turn away from today?

*Father, show me the idols in my heart. Then help me
destroy them and live in Your love.*

BIBLE IN A YEAR | GENESIS 43–45; MATTHEW 12:24–50

But I tell you, love your enemies.
[MATTHEW 5:44]

BUT I'M TELLING YOU

❝I❞ know what they're saying. But I'm telling you . . ." As a boy, I heard my mother give that speech a thousand times. The context was always peer pressure. She was trying to teach me not to follow the herd. I'm not a boy any longer, but herd mentality's still alive and kicking. A current example is this phrase: "Only surround yourself with positive people." Now while that phrase may be commonly heard, the question we must ask is: "Is that Christ-like?"

"But I'm telling you . . ." Jesus uses that lead-in a number of times in Matthew 5. He knows full well what the world is constantly telling us. But His desire is that we live differently. In this case, He says, "Love your *enemies* and pray for those who persecute you" (V. 44). Later in the New Testament, the apostle Paul uses the word "enemies" to describe guess who? That's right: *us*—"while we were God's enemies" (ROMANS 5:10). Far from some "do as I say, not as I do" sentiment, Jesus backed up His words with actions. He loved us, and gave His life for us.

What if Christ had only made room in His life for 'positive people'? Where would that leave us? Thanks be to God that His love is no respecter of persons. For God so loved the world, and in His strength we are called to do likewise.　　　*JOHN BLASE*

When's the last time someone extended love to you when you weren't 'positive'? What's a tangible way today that you can show love to an enemy?

Father, it's tempting to surround myself with only those who love me. But that's not living, at least not the kind of living You desire for me. Help me to love even my enemies.

BIBLE IN A YEAR | GENESIS 46–48; MATTHEW 13:1–30

[Love] burns like blazing fire, like a mighty flame.
[SONG OF SONGS 8:6]

LOVE LIKE BLAZING FIRE

Poet, painter and printmaker William Blake enjoyed a forty-five-year marriage with his wife, Catherine. From their wedding day until his death in 1827, they worked side by side. Catherine added colour to William's sketches, and their devotion endured years of poverty and other challenges. Even in his final weeks as his health failed, Blake kept at his art, and his final sketch was his wife's face. Four years later, Catherine died clutching one of her husband's pencils in her hand.

The Blakes' vibrant love offers a reflection of the love discovered in the Song of Songs. And while the Song's description of love certainly has implications for marriage, early believers in Jesus believed it also points to Jesus' unquenchable love for all His followers. The Song describes a love "as strong as death," which is a remarkable metaphor since death is as final and unescapable a reality as humans will ever know (8:6). This strong love "burns like blazing fire, like a mighty flame" (V. 6) And unlike fires we're familiar with, these flames can't be doused, not even by a deluge. "Many waters cannot quench love," the Song insists (V. 7).

Who among us doesn't desire true love? The Song reminds us that whenever we encounter genuine love, God is the ultimate source. And in Jesus, each of us can know a profound and undying love—one that burns like a blazing fire.   *WINN COLLIER*

Where have you encountered strong love? How does Jesus' love encourage you?

Dear God, please help me to receive Your love and share it with others.

Be completely humble and gentle; be
patient, bearing with one another in love.
[EPHESIANS 4:2]

COFFEE BREATH

I was sitting in my chair one morning years ago when my youngest came downstairs. She made a beeline for me, jumping up onto my lap. I gave her a fatherly squeeze and a gentle kiss on the head, and she squealed with delight. But then she furrowed her brow, crinkled her nose and shot an accusatory glance at my coffee mug. "Daddy," she announced solemnly. "I love you, and I like you, but I don't like your smell."

My daughter couldn't have known it, but she spoke with grace and truth: she didn't want to hurt my feelings, but she felt compelled to tell me something. And sometimes we need to do that in our relationships.

In Ephesians 4, Paul zones in on how we relate to each other—especially when telling difficult truths. "Be completely humble and gentle; be patient, bearing with one another in love" (V. 2). Humility, gentleness and patience form our relational foundation. Cultivating those character qualities as God guides us will help us "[speak] the truth in love" (V. 15) and seek to communicate "what is helpful for building others up according to their needs" (V. 29).

No one likes being confronted about weaknesses and blind spots. But when something about us 'smells', God can use faithful friends to speak into our lives with grace, truth, humility and gentleness.

ADAM R. HOLZ

When has someone gently confronted you? What do you think is most important when you lovingly address a weakness you see in others?

Father, help me to humbly receive correction, and help me to offer it with love, grace and gentleness.

BIBLE IN A YEAR | EXODUS 1–3; MATTHEW 14:1–21

He reached down from on high and took
hold of me. [PSALM 18:16]

REACHING OUT

I n a recent post, blogger Bonnie Gray recounted the moment
when overwhelming sadness began to creep into her heart.
"Out of the blue," she stated, "during the happiest chapter in
my life, . . . I suddenly started experiencing panic attacks and depression." Gray tried to find different ways to address her pain,
but she soon realised that she wasn't strong enough to handle
it alone. "I hadn't wanted anyone to question my faith, so I kept
quiet and prayed that my depression would go away. But God
wants to heal us, not shame us or make us hide from our pain."
Gray found healing in the solace of His presence; He was her
anchor amid the waves that threatened to overwhelm her.

When we're in a low place and filled with despair, God is there
and will sustain us too. In Psalm 18, David praised God for deliv-
ering him from the low place he was in after nearly being defeated by his enemies. He proclaimed, "[God] reached down from
on high and took hold of me; he drew me out of deep waters"
(V. 16). Even in moments when despair seems to consume us like
crashing waves in an ocean, God loves us so much that He'll
reach out to us and help us, bringing us into a "spacious place"
of peace and security (V. 19). Let's look to Him as our refuge when
we feel overwhelmed by the challenges of life.   *KIMYA LODER*

When have you felt overwhelmed by trials?
How did God sustain you?

*Heavenly Father, there are times when my burdens
become too much to carry. Thank You for continuously
reaching out to me, sustaining me and granting me Your
peace, strength and wisdom.*

BIBLE IN A YEAR | EXODUS 4-6; MATTHEW 14:22-36

Rejoice with me; I have found my lost sheep.
[LUKE 15:6]

LOST, FOUND, JOY

"They call me 'the ringmaster'. So far this year I've found 167 lost rings."

During a walk on the beach with my wife, Cari, we struck up a conversation with an older man who was using a metal detector to scan an area just below the surf line. "Sometimes rings have names on them," he explained, "and I love seeing their owners' faces when I return them. I post online and check to see if anyone contacted lost and found. I've found rings missing for years." When we mentioned that I enjoy metal detecting as well but didn't do it frequently, his parting words were, "You never know unless you go!"

We find another kind of 'search and rescue' in Luke 15. Jesus was criticised for caring about people who were far from God (VV. 1–2). In reply, He told three stories about things that were lost and then found—a sheep, a coin and a son. The man who finds the lost sheep "joyfully puts it on his shoulders and goes home. Then he calls his friends and neighbours together and says, 'Rejoice with me' " (LUKE 15:5–6). All the stories are ultimately about finding lost people for Christ, and the joy that comes as they're found in Him.

Jesus came "to seek and to save the lost" (19:10), and He calls us to follow Him in loving people back to God (SEE MATTHEW 28:19). The joy of seeing others turn to Him awaits. We'll never know unless we go.   *JAMES BANKS*

***What joy have you seen when people turn to God?
How will you point others to Jesus' love today?***

*Thank You, Jesus, for finding and loving me! Please send
me in Your joy to another who needs You today.*

BIBLE IN A YEAR | EXODUS 7-8; MATTHEW 15:1-20

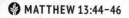
The kingdom of heaven is like treasure.
[MATTHEW 13:44]

NO LOSS

My friend Ruel attended a school reunion held in a former classmate's home. The waterfront mansion could accommodate two hundred attendees, and it made Ruel feel small.

"I've had many happy years of pastoring remote rural churches," Ruel told me, "and even though I know I shouldn't, I couldn't help but feel envious of my classmate's material wealth. My thoughts strayed to how different life might be if I'd used my degree to become a businessman instead."

"But I later reminded myself there's nothing to feel envious about," Ruel continued with a smile. "I invested my life in serving God, and the results will last for eternity." I'll always remember the peaceful look on his face as he said those words.

Ruel drew peace from Jesus' parables in Matthew 13:44–46. He knew that God's kingdom is the ultimate treasure. Seeking and living for His kingdom might take various forms. For some, it might mean full-time ministry, while for others, it may be living out the gospel in a secular workplace. Regardless of how God chooses to use us, we can continue to trust and obey His leading, knowing, like the men in Jesus' parables, the value of the imperishable treasure we've been given. Everything in this world has infinitely less worth than all we gain by following God (1 PETER 1:4–5).

Our life, when placed in His hands, can bear eternal fruit.

KAREN HUANG

What have you had to live without for the sake of following God? How does Matthew 13:44–46 encourage you?

Father, let each day of my life be a celebration of the treasure I've found in You.

BIBLE IN A YEAR | EXODUS 9–11; MATTHEW 15:21–29

We always carry around in our body the death of Jesus, so that the life of Jesus may also be revealed in our body. [2 CORINTHIANS 4:10]

RESILIENCE FOR TODAY

In his book *Tortured for Christ*, Richard Wurmbrand described being imprisoned for fourteen years in Romania for speaking openly about Jesus. "Whoever was caught [preaching to other prisoners] received a severe beating. A number of us decided to pay the price . . . so we accepted [the guards'] terms."

We may not experience imprisonment or torture, but our culture doesn't always have much respect for what we believe. We may be ignored, mocked and rejected—even by loved ones. That's why we need the same resilience as Wurmbrand to keep going.

Centuries earlier, Paul explained why he endured hardships and persecution (2 CORINTHIANS 4:8–9): to reveal "the life of Jesus" within him (V. 10). Paul's intimacy with Jesus couldn't ever be thwarted; His presence provided the courage Paul needed to keep preaching to "more and more people," which caused "thanksgiving to overflow to the glory of God" (V. 15). Despite his trials, Paul knew that inwardly he was "being renewed day by day" (V. 16).

As with Paul, the authorities tried to take everything away from Wurmbrand. "But," the prisoner said, "they could not take my Jesus from me." The Lord is here with us too, and He is the source of our resilience. He is why "we do not lose heart" (V. 16), even when we face troubles for serving Him. He guides us steadfastly towards "an eternal glory that far outweighs them all" (V. 17).   *CHRIS WALE*

What situations or relationships cause you to lose heart? How does it encourage you that Jesus inwardly strengthens and renews you?

Jesus, You know the challenges I face when it comes to living out my faith openly. Help me to keep my heart set on You, so that even when I face hardships or persecution, people will see You living in me.

BIBLE IN A YEAR | EXODUS 12–13; MATTHEW 16

Bear with each other and forgive one another.
[COLOSSIANS 3:13]

LOVE THAT FORGIVES

Eighty years of marriage! My husband's great-uncle Pete and great-aunt Ruth celebrated this remarkable milestone on 31 May, 2021. After a chance meeting in 1941 when Ruth was still in secondary school, the young couple were so eager to get married that they eloped the day after Ruth finished full-time education. Pete and Ruth believe God brought them together and has guided them all these years.

Reflecting on eight decades of marriage, Pete and Ruth both agree that one key to sustaining their relationship has been the decision to choose forgiveness. Anyone in a healthy relationship understands that we all regularly need forgiveness for the ways we hurt each other, whether through an unkind word, a broken promise or a forgotten task.

In a section of Scripture written to help believers in Jesus live together in unity, Paul refers to the essential role forgiveness plays. After urging his readers to choose "compassion, kindness, humility, gentleness and patience" (COLOSSIANS 3:12), Paul adds the encouragement to "forgive one another if any of you has a grievance" (V. 13). Most importantly, all their interactions with each were to be guided by love (V. 14).

Relationships that model the characteristics outlined by Paul are a blessing. May God help all of us work to cultivate healthy relationships characterised by love and forgiveness.

LISA M. SAMRA

> *How have you experienced healing through forgiving or being forgiven? How are relationships strengthened through practicing both forgiveness and accountability?*

Jesus, help me to forgive others just as You've forgiven me.

BIBLE IN A YEAR | EXODUS 14–15; MATTHEW 17

He will not always accuse, nor will he
harbour his anger forever. [PSALM 103:9]

MERCY FOR YOU AND ME

One of consequences of the COVID-19 pandemic was the docking of cruise ships and the quarantining of passengers. One article I read included interviews of some of the tourists. Commenting about how being quarantined provided more opportunities for conversations, one passenger joked how his spouse—who possessed an excellent memory—was able to bring up every transgression he had ever committed, and sensed she wasn't done yet!

Accounts like this might make us smile, remind us of our humanness and serve to caution us if we're prone to hold too tightly to the things we should release. Yet what helps us to be kindly disposed to those who hurt us? Glimpses of our great God, as He's portrayed in passages like Psalm 103:8–12.

One paraphrase of verses 8–10 is noteworthy: "GOD is sheer mercy and grace; not easily angered, he's rich in love. He doesn't endlessly nag and scold, nor hold grudges forever. He doesn't treat us as our sins deserve, nor pay us back in full for our wrongs." Asking for God's help as we prayerfully read Scripture can cause us to have second thoughts about ill-conceived payback or plans to punish. And it can prompt prayers for ourselves and for those we may be tempted to harm by withholding grace, mercy and forgiveness.   *ARTHUR JACKSON*

> **Who have you been tempted to harm because of the hurt they've caused you? Who can you ask to pray for you?**
>
> *God of mercy, kindness and forgiveness, please help me to extend grace and mercy to those who've caused me pain.*

BIBLE IN A YEAR | EXODUS 16–18; MATTHEW 18:1–20

Each of you should give what you have
decided in your heart to give . . . for God
loves a cheerful giver. [2 CORINTHIANS 9:7]

THE PINK COAT

Brenda was walking towards the shopping centre exit when
a flush of pink from a display window caught her eye. She
turned and stood spellbound before a "candy-floss-colour-
ed coat." *Oh, how Holly would love it!* Finances had been tight for
her co-worker friend who was a single mother, and while Brenda
knew Holly needed a warm coat, she was also confident that her
friend would never lay down cash on such a purchase for herself.
After wavering ever so slightly, Brenda smiled, reached for her
wallet and arranged for the coat to be shipped to Holly's home.
She added an anonymous card, "You are so very loved." Brenda
practically danced to her car.

Joy is a by-product of God-nudged giving. As Paul instructed
the Corinthians in the art of generosity, he said, "Each of you
should give what you have decided in your heart to give, not
reluctantly or under compulsion, for God loves a cheerful giver"
(2 CORINTHIANS 9:7). He also noted, "Whoever sows generously
will also reap generously" (V. 6).

Sometimes we slip cash into the offering plate. At other times
we donate online to a worthy ministry. And then there are moments when God leads us to respond to the need of a friend with a
tangible expression of His love. We offer a bag of groceries, a tank
of petrol . . . or even the gift of a perfectly pink coat. *ELISA MORGAN*

> ***Who might you show God's love to today? How can your
> generosity bubble up in joy as a return gift to you?***
>
> *Loving Father, You gave me the gift of Your Son, and so I
> want to give to others. May I respond to Your gentle nudge
> to meet the needs of another.*

BIBLE IN A YEAR | EXODUS 19-20; MATTHEW 18:21-35

Let us then approach God's throne of grace with confidence, so that we may receive mercy and find grace to help us in our time of need. [HEBREWS 4:16]

SEVEN MINUTES OF TERROR

When the Mars rover *Perseverance* landed on that red planet on 18 February, 2021, those monitoring its arrival endured "seven minutes of terror". As the spacecraft ended its 292-million-mile journey, it went through a complex landing procedure it had to do on its own. Signals from Mars to Earth take several minutes, so NASA couldn't hear from *Perseverance* during the landing. Not being in contact was frightening for the team who had put so much effort and resources into the mission.

Sometimes we may experience our own times of fear when we feel we're not hearing from God—we pray but we don't get answers. In Scripture, we find people getting answers to prayer quickly (SEE DANIEL 9:20–23) and those not getting answers for a long time (SEE HANNAH'S STORY IN 1 SAMUEL 1:10–20). Perhaps the most poignant example of a delayed answer—one that surely struck terror in the hearts of Mary and Martha—was when they asked Jesus to help their sick brother Lazarus (JOHN 11:3). Jesus delayed, and their brother died (VV. 6–7, 14–15). Yet four days later, Christ answered by resurrecting Lazarus (VV. 43–44).

Waiting for answers to our prayers can be difficult. But God can comfort and help as we "approach [His] throne of grace with confidence, . . . [that] we may receive mercy and find grace to help us in our time of need" (HEBREWS 4:16). *DAVE BRANON*

What are you praying for, but the answer doesn't seem to be coming? How can God increase your faith as you wait on Him?

Loving God, You know what's on my heart. Please help me trust You as I await Your answer.

BIBLE IN A YEAR | EXODUS 21–22; MATTHEW 19

They will run and not grow weary, they will
walk and not be faint. [ISAIAH 40:31]

RUNNING ON EMPTY

❝I just don't think I can do this anymore," my friend said through her tears as she discussed the overwhelming sense of hopelessness she faced as a nurse in a global health crisis. "I know that God has called me to nursing, but I'm overwhelmed and emotionally drained," she confessed. Seeing that a cloud of exhaustion had come over her, I responded, "I know you feel helpless right now, but ask God to give you the direction you're seeking and the strength to persevere." At that moment, she decided to intentionally seek God through prayer. Soon after, my friend was invigorated with a new sense of purpose. Not only was she emboldened to continue nursing, but God also gave her the strength to serve even more people by travelling to hospitals around the country.

As believers in Jesus, we can always look to God for help and encouragement when we feel overburdened because "He will not grow tired or weary" (ISAIAH 40:28). The prophet Isaiah states that our Father in heaven "gives strength to the weary and increases the power of the weak" (V. 29). Though God's strength is everlasting, He knows that we'll inevitably have days when we're physically and emotionally consumed (V. 30). But when we look to God for our strength instead of trying to sprint through life's challenges alone, He'll restore and renew us and give us the resolve to press on in faith. *KIMYA LODER*

When have you tried to handle overwhelming situations alone? How might you look to God for help?

Dear God, thank You for helping me when the challenges of life seem unbearable.

BIBLE IN A YEAR | EXODUS 23-24; MATTHEW 20:1-16

In his hand is the life of every creature and
the breath of all mankind. [JOB 12:10]

IN HIS HAND

When I glimpse a palette of vivid colours painted across the sky or take in the delicate design of a daffodil, I ponder God the Creator. Beauty can awe us as we see His imprint in nature. Even when we are surrounded by a mass of concrete with no green in sight, we may hear the melodious birdsong and know that God is our Maker.

Job pointed to God as Creator not in wonder, but in what seems like exasperation. Job had been tested to the extreme by God—and his friends and their comments didn't help him. Job responds to them that they should "ask the animals" or "let the fish in the sea" inform them "that the hand of the LORD has done this" (JOB 12:7–9). Job was distraught by the trials that descended on him, and although he was troubled and confused by them, he remained convinced that God could be seen in His creation: "In his hand is the life of every creature" (V.10).

This Old Testament story reminds me that when we gaze at a stunning sunset with tears streaming because of pain or some injustice, yet we can trust in God. Though we suffer now, one day He will welcome us to a place of no more tears and no more crying (REVELATION 21:4). As we wait for that wonderful day, He will give us the strength to persevere, even as He did for Job.

AMY BOUCHER PYE

> **Whether life feels sunny or stormy for you, or somewhere in between, how do you sense God's imprint? Why might you seek to open your eyes and heart to this reality?**
>
> *Marvellous Maker, in Your hand is the life and breath of every creature on this earth. Help me to wonder at Your creation and give thanks to You.*

BIBLE IN A YEAR | EXODUS 25–26; MATTHEW 20:17–34

A RIGHT-SIDE-UP KINGDOM

In the Sermon on the Mount, Jesus presents the foundational ideas that describe life in His kingdom. Because these landmark ideas are so counter-cultural to the way life is pursued in our world, scholars have referred to His teaching as the presentation of an upside-down King for an upside-down kingdom.

However, it's our world that's upside-down. It's the value system and mindset of the surrounding culture that's turned the world's thinking on its head.

We need a serious corrective to our upside-down perspective, and Jesus' opening statements of blessing—known as the Beatitudes (MATTHEW 5:3–12)—are almost shocking in the way they challenge our thinking and values. What Jesus calls blessed, this world would call foolish. After all, who would describe the poor, grieving or persecuted as the *blessed*? Well, Jesus would. And He did:

> *Blessed are the poor in spirit, for theirs is the kingdom of heaven.*
>
> *Blessed are those who mourn, for they will be comforted.*
>
> *Blessed are the meek, for they will inherit the earth.*
>
> *Blessed are those who hunger and thirst for righteousness, for they will be filled.*
>
> *Blessed are the merciful, for they will be shown mercy.*
>
> *Blessed are the pure in heart, for they will see God.*

Blessed are the peacemakers, for they will be called children of God.

Blessed are those who are persecuted because of righteousness, for theirs is the kingdom of heaven.

Blessed are you when people insult you, persecute you and falsely say all kinds of evil against you because of me. Rejoice and be glad, because great is your reward in heaven, for in the same way they persecuted the prophets who were before you.

These statements of blessing don't constitute a path into relationship with the King or citizenship in His kingdom. They describe the person already living under the influence of the one true King. So, for example, the mourners aren't blessed because they mourn (v. 4). They're blessed because God will respond to their mourning with comfort. It's not a statement of transaction but of hope and expectation. In the midst of their grief, they know that God is the God of all comfort.

In the right-side-up kingdom of Jesus, He assures us that His responses to whatever we encounter will always be more than enough to carry us through. When we see that our state of blessedness comes not from life's circumstances but rather by the faithfulness of the King who cares for His people, we can begin to live life right-side-up.

Bill Crowder, Our Daily Bread *author*

★ What does it mean to live out the "Blessed are . . ." statements Jesus presented in the Sermon on the Mount? This month we're looking at the Beatitudes found in Matthew 5:3–12 and considering the characteristics that God chooses to bless. The topic is featured in the devotions for **February 1**, **8**, **15** and **22**.

Blessed are those who mourn.
[MATTHEW 5:4]

BLESSING IN THE TEARS

I received an email from a young man who explained that his father (only sixty-three) was in the hospital in a critical condition, hanging on to life. Though we'd never met, his dad's work and mine shared many intersections. The son, trying to cheer his father, asked me to send a video message of encouragement and prayer. Deeply moved, I recorded a short message and a prayer for healing. I was told that his dad watched the video and gave a hearty thumbs-up. Sadly, a couple days later, I received another email telling me that he had died. He held his wife's hand as he took his final breath.

My heart broke. Such love, such devastation. The family lost a husband and father far too soon. Yet it's surprising to hear Jesus insist that it's precisely these grieving ones who are blessed: "Blessed are those who mourn," Jesus says (MATTHEW 5:4). Jesus isn't saying suffering and sorrow are good, but rather that God's mercy and kindness pour over those who need it most. Those overcome by grief due to death or even their own sinfulness are most in need of God's attention and consolation—and Jesus promises us "they will be comforted" (V. 4).

God steps towards us, His loved children (V. 9). He blesses us in our tears.   *WINN COLLIER*

In what places do you encounter sorrow in your story and in others' stories? How does Jesus' promise of blessing alter how you view this grief?

God, I am awash in grief and sorrow. Please help me to experience Your blessing even in the tears.

BIBLE IN A YEAR | EXODUS 27-28; MATTHEW 21:1-22

The student is not above the teacher, but everyone who is fully trained will be like their teacher. [LUKE 6:40]

LIKE OUR GREAT TEACHER

In a viral video, a three-year-old white belt karate student imitated her instructor. With passion and conviction the little girl said the student creed with her leader. Then, with poise and attentiveness, the little ball of cuteness and energy imitated everything her teacher said and did—at least she did a pretty good job!

Jesus once said, "The student is not above the teacher, but everyone who is fully trained will be like their teacher" (LUKE 6:40). He told His disciples that to imitate Him included being generous, loving, non-judgemental (VV. 37–38), and discerning about whom they followed: "Can the blind lead the blind? Will they not both fall into a pit?" (V. 39). His disciples needed to discern that this standard disqualified the Pharisees who were blind guides—leading people to disaster (MATTHEW 15:14). And they needed to grasp the importance of following their Teacher. Thus, the aim of Christ's disciples was to become like Jesus Himself. So it was important for them to pay careful attention to Christ's instruction about generosity and love and apply it.

As believers striving to imitate Jesus today, let's give our lives over to our Master Teacher so we can become like Him in knowledge, wisdom and behaviour. He alone can help us reflect His generous, loving ways.

MARVIN WILLIAMS

What parts of Jesus' life are you seeking to imitate these days? When is it most difficult for you to imitate Christ, the Master Teacher?

Jesus, my Great Teacher, help my discipline and attentiveness to be worthy of You!

BIBLE IN A YEAR | EXODUS 29–30; MATTHEW 21:23–46

The foreigner residing among you
must be treated as your native-born.
[LEVITICUS 19:34]

WE ARE STRANGERS

Everything felt drastically different in their new country—new language, schools, customs, traffic and weather. They wondered how they would ever adjust. People from a nearby church gathered around them to help them in their new life in a new land. Patti took the couple shopping at a local food market to show them what was available and how to purchase items. As they wandered around the market, their eyes widened and they smiled broadly when they saw their favourite fruit from their homeland—pomegranates. They bought one for each of their children and even placed one in Patti's hands in gratefulness. The small fruit and new friends brought big comfort in their strange, new land.

God, through Moses, gave a list of laws for His people, which included a command to treat foreigners among them "as your native-born" (LEVITICUS 19:34). "Love them as yourself," God further commanded. Jesus called this the second greatest commandment after loving God (MATTHEW 22:39). For even God "watches over the foreigner" (PSALM 146:9).

Besides obeying God as we help new friends adapt to life in our country, we may be reminded that we too in a real sense are "strangers on earth" (HEBREWS 11:13). And we'll grow in our anticipation of the new heavenly land to come.   *ANNE CETAS*

Who might God want you to look after? In what ways has He gifted you to spread His love to others?

Compassionate God, I understand something of what it feels like to be a stranger in this world. Lead me to be an encourager of other foreigners and strangers.

BIBLE IN A YEAR | EXODUS 31–33; MATTHEW 22:1–22

Don't call me Naomi. . . . Call me Mara, because the Almighty has made my life very bitter. [RUTH 1:20]

WHAT'S YOUR NAME?

Jen remarried after her first husband died. The children of her new husband never accepted her, and now that he's passed away too, they hate her for remaining in their childhood home. Her husband left a modest sum to provide for her; his kids say she's stealing their inheritance. Jen is understandably discouraged, and she's grown bitter.

Naomi's husband moved the family to Moab, where he and their two sons died. Years later, Naomi returned to Bethlehem empty-handed, except for her daughter-in-law Ruth. The town was stirred and asked, "Can this be Naomi?" (RUTH 1:19). She said they shouldn't use that name, which means "my pleasant one". They should call her "Mara," which means "bitter," because "I went away full, but the LORD has brought me back empty" (VV. 20–21).

Is there a chance your name is Bitter? You've been disappointed by friends, family or declining health. You deserved better. But you didn't get it. Now you're bitter.

Naomi came back to Bethlehem bitter, but she came back. You can come home too. Come to Jesus, the descendant of Ruth, born in Bethlehem. Rest in His love.

In time, God replaced Naomi's bitterness with the joyful fulfilment of His perfect plan (4:13–22). He can replace your bitterness too. Come home to Him.   *MIKE WITTMER*

What name describes you? What does it mean for you to live out the name that describes who you are in Jesus?

Father, I'm coming home to find my rest in Your Son.

BIBLE IN A YEAR | EXODUS 34–35; MATTHEW 22:23-46

The dust returns to the ground it came from,
and the spirit returns to God who gave it.
[ECCLESIASTES 12:7]

I CAN ONLY IMAGINE

I settled into the church pew behind a woman as the worship team began playing "I Can Only Imagine." Raising my hands, I praised God as the woman's sweet soprano voice harmonised with mine. After telling me about her health struggles, we decided to pray together during her upcoming cancer treatments.

A few months later, Louise told me she feared dying. Leaning onto her hospital bed, I rested my head next to hers, whispered a prayer, and quietly sang our song. I can only imagine what it was like for Louise when she worshipped Jesus face-to-face just a few days later.

The apostle Paul offered comforting assurance for his readers who were facing death (2 CORINTHIANS 5:1). The suffering experienced on this side of eternity may cause groaning, but our hope remains anchored to our heavenly dwelling—our eternal existence with Jesus (VV. 2–4). Though God designed us to yearn for everlasting life with Him (VV. 5–6), His promises are meant to impact the way we live for Him now (VV. 7–10).

As we live to please Jesus while waiting for Him to return or call us home, we can rejoice in the peace of His constant presence. What will we experience the moment we leave our earthly bodies and join Jesus in eternity? We can only imagine!

XOCHITL DIXON

When have you been worried about or discouraged by facing death or losing a loved one? How does God's promise of everlasting life encourage you?

Loving God, thank You for promising to be with me on earth and for all eternity.

BIBLE IN A YEAR | EXODUS 36–38; MATTHEW 23:1-22

While Joseph was there in the prison,
the LORD was with him; he showed him
kindness. [GENESIS 39:20–21]

THE LONELIEST MAN

On 20 July 1969, Neil Armstrong and Buzz Aldrin stepped out of their lunar landing module and became the first humans to walk on the surface of the moon. But we don't often think about the third person on their team, Michael Collins, who was flying the command module for *Apollo 11*.

After his teammates clambered down the ladder to test the lunar surface, Collins waited alone on the far side of the moon. He was out of touch with Neil, Buzz and everyone on earth. NASA's mission control commented, "Not since Adam has any human known such solitude as Mike Collins."

There are times when we feel completely alone. Imagine, for instance, how Joseph, Jacob's son, felt when he was taken from Canaan to Egypt after his brothers sold him (GENESIS 37:23–28). Then he was thrust into further isolation by being thrown in prison on false charges (39:19–20).

How did Joseph survive in prison in a foreign land with no family anywhere nearby? Listen to this: "While Joseph was there in the prison, the LORD was with him" (VV. 20–21). Four times we're reminded of this comforting truth in Genesis 39.

Do you feel alone or isolated from others? Hold on to the truth of God's presence, promised by Jesus Himself: "Surely I am with you always" (MATTHEW 28:20). With Jesus as your Saviour, you're never alone. *DAVE BRANON*

***When do you feel most alone? How does God remind you
that He's with you in your times of isolation?***

*Dear heavenly Father, please help me know, as You've promised
in the Scriptures, that You're with me as You were with Joseph.*

BIBLE IN A YEAR | EXODUS 39–40; MATTHEW 23:23–39

As a shepherd looks after his scattered flock . . . ,
so will I look after my sheep. [EZEKIEL 34:12]

THE GOOD SHEPHERD

When Pastor Warren heard that a man in his church had deserted his wife and family, he asked God to help him meet the man as if by accident so they could chat. And that's just what God did! When Warren walked into a restaurant, he spotted the gentleman in a nearby booth. "Got some room for another hungry man?" he asked, and soon they were sharing deeply and praying together.

As a pastor, Warren was acting as a shepherd for those in his church community, even as God through the prophet Ezekiel said He would tend His flock. God promised to look after His scattered sheep, rescuing them and gathering them together (EZEKIEL 34:12–13). He would "tend them in a good pasture" and "search for the lost and bring back the strays"; He would "bind up the injured and strengthen the weak" (VV. 14–16). God's love for His people reverberates through each of these images. Though Ezekiel's words anticipate God's future actions, they reflect the eternal heart of the God and Shepherd who would one day reveal Himself in Jesus.

No matter our situation, God reaches out to each of us, seeking to rescue us and sheltering us in a rich pasture. He longs for us to follow the Good Shepherd, He who lays down His life for His sheep (SEE JOHN 10:14–15). *AMY BOUCHER PYE*

> *How does Jesus, the Good Shepherd, care for you? How could you offer Him any wounds that need tending or weakness you'd like strengthened?*

Dear God, You love me even when I go astray and wander. Help me to stay always in Your sheepfold, that I might receive Your love and care.

BIBLE IN A YEAR | LEVITICUS 1–3; MATTHEW 24:1–28

If we confess our sins, he is faithful and just
and will forgive us our sins. [1 JOHN 1:9]

GOD'S ARMS ARE OPEN

frowned at my phone and sighed. Worry wrinkled my brow. A friend and I had had a serious disagreement over an issue with our children, and I knew I needed to call her and apologise. I didn't want to do it because our viewpoints were still in conflict, yet I knew I hadn't been kind or humble the last time we discussed the matter.

Anticipating the phone call, I wondered, *What if she doesn't forgive me? What if she doesn't want to continue our friendship?* Just then, lyrics to a song came to mind and took me back to the moment when I confessed my sin in the situation to God. I felt relief because I knew God had forgiven me and released me from guilt.

We can't control how people will respond to us when we try to work out relational problems. As long as we own up to our part, humbly ask for forgiveness and make any changes needed, we can let God handle the healing. Even if we have to endure the pain of unresolved 'people problems', peace with Him is always possible. God's arms are open, and He is waiting to show us the grace and mercy we need. "If we confess our sin, He is faithful and just and will forgive us our sins and purify us from all unrighteousness" (1 JOHN 1:9). *JENNIFER BENSON SCHULDT*

How does forgiveness create peace? What steps will you take in God's power towards reconciliation with someone this week?

Dear God, remind me of Your unending grace. Help me to be humble and to commit all my relationships to You.

BIBLE IN A YEAR | LEVITICUS 4–5; MATTHEW 24:29–51

Anyone who has seen me has seen the
Father. [JOHN 14:9]

SEEING JESUS

At four months old, Leo had never seen his parents. He'd been born with a rare condition that left his vision blurred. For him, it was like living in dense fog. But then eye doctors fitted him with a special set of glasses.

Leo's father posted the video of Mum placing the new glasses over his eyes for the first time. We watch as Leo's eyes slowly focus. A smile spreads wide across his face as he truly sees his mum for the first time. Priceless. In that moment, little Leo could see clearly.

John reports a conversation Jesus had with His disciples. Philip asked Him, "Show us the Father" (JOHN 14:8). Even after all this time together, Jesus' disciples couldn't recognise who was right in front of them. He replied, "Don't you believe that I am in the Father, and that the Father is in me?" (V. 10). Earlier Jesus had said, "I am the way and the truth and the life" (V. 6). This is the sixth of Jesus' seven "I am" statements. He's telling us to look through these "I am" lenses and see who He truly is—God Himself.

We're a lot like the disciples. In difficult times, we struggle and develop blurred vision. We fail to focus on what God has done and can do. When little Leo put on the special glasses, he could see his parents clearly. Perhaps we need to put on our God-glasses so we can clearly see who Jesus really is.   *KENNETH PETERSEN*

What are some ways in which your vision of Jesus may have become cloudy? How can you look to Him again with clear vision?

Jesus, please help me turn my eyes on You. Show me clearly Your path for me.

BIBLE IN A YEAR | LEVITICUS 6-7; MATTHEW 25:1-30

He is my refuge and my fortress, my
God, in whom I trust. [PSALM 91:2]

COME HOME TO GOD

One early evening while I was jogging near a construction
site in our neighbourhood, a skinny, dirty kitten meowed
at me plaintively and followed me home. Today, Mickey is
a healthy, handsome adult cat, enjoying a comfortable life in our
household and deeply loved by my family. Whenever I jog on the
road where I found him, I often think, *Thank You, God. Mickey
was spared from living on the streets. He has a home now.*

Psalm 91 speaks of those who "[dwell] in the shelter of the
Most High" (V. 1), making their home with God. The Hebrew
word for *dwells* here means "to remain, to stay permanently".
As we remain in Him, He helps us live according to His wisdom
and to love Him above all (V. 14; JOHN 15:10). God promises us the
comfort of being with Him for eternity, as well as the security
of His being with us through earthly hardship. Although trouble
may come, we can rest in His sovereignty, wisdom and love, and
in His promises to protect and deliver us.

When we make God our refuge, we live "in the shadow of
the Almighty" (PSALM 91:1). No trouble can touch us except that
which His infinite wisdom and love allow. This is the safety of
God as our home.   *KAREN HUANG*

***What does being home in God mean? How might your
response to hardship change if you chose to live in the
shelter of the Most High?***

Heavenly Father, thank You for the home I have in You.

Christ Jesus came into the world to
save sinners—of whom I am the worst.
[1 TIMOTHY 1:15]

AN UNDESERVED GIFT

When my friend gave me a gift recently, I was surprised.
I didn't think I deserved such a nice present from her.
She'd sent it after hearing about some work stress I
was experiencing. Yet she was going through just as much stress,
if not more, than I was, with an ageing parent, challenging children, upheaval at work and strain in her marriage. I couldn't believe she had thought of me before herself, and her simple gift
brought me to tears.

In truth, we're all recipients of a gift that we could never deserve. Paul put it this way: "Christ Jesus came into the world to
save sinners—of whom I am the worst" (1 TIMOTHY 1:15). Although
he "was once a blasphemer and persecutor and a violent man,
. . . the grace of our Lord was poured out on [him] abundantly"
(VV. 13–14). The risen Jesus gave Paul a deep understanding of
the free gift of grace. As a result, he learned what it meant to be
an undeserving recipient of that gift and he became a powerful
instrument of God's love and told many people about what God
had done for him.

It's only through God's grace that we receive love instead of
condemnation, and mercy instead of judgement. Today, let's
celebrate the undeserved grace that God has given and be
on the lookout for ways to demonstrate that grace to others.

KAREN PIMPO

How have you lost sight of the miraculous gift of grace?
What would it look like to be motivated by grace once again?

Dear God, help me understand more fully what it means to
extend Your gift of grace to others.

BIBLE IN A YEAR | LEVITICUS 11–12; MATTHEW 26:1–25

Even though I walk through the darkest valley,
I will fear no evil, for you are with me. [PSALM 23:4]

HOPE IN THE VALLEY

William Carey is known as the "father of modern missions". But when he first arrived in India in 1792, he was quickly besieged by illness, loneliness and poverty. Then he was deserted by his missionary partner, one of his sons died of dysentery, and his wife's mental health deteriorated so severely that she threatened him with a knife.

"I am in a strange land with no Christian friend, a large family and nothing to supply their wants," Carey wrote. "This is indeed the valley of the shadow of death to me."

Carey's dark valley was impossible to navigate, humanly speaking. Yet he could write, "But I rejoice that I am here notwithstanding; and God is here." Carey's hope echoed David's when he composed Psalm 23: "Even though I walk through the darkest valley, I will fear no evil, for you are with me" (PSALM 23:4).

Hope in life's valleys is found in the Shepherd who walks through them with us. He promises that whatever valley we're facing, it will come to an end; one day we will finally sit at the table He has prepared for us in His home (VV. 5–6).

If you're walking through a valley today, you can get a sense of that glorious future as you draw close to your Shepherd, the source of all reassurance. Seasons of darkness can become seasons of hope when we affirm, "You are with me" (V. 4).

CHRIS WALE

Which promises or assurances in Psalm 23 bring you special hope and comfort? How can they help you draw closer to your Shepherd today?

Good Shepherd, I thank You that You are with me. No matter what I face or go through, You will walk each step and each moment with me.

BIBLE IN A YEAR | LEVITICUS 13; MATTHEW 26:26–50

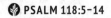
The LORD is with me; I will not be afraid.
[PSALM 118:6]

WHEN HARD PRESSED

Many years ago, a friend told me how intimidated she was while trying to cross a street where several roads intersected. "I'd never seen anything like this; the rules I'd been taught for crossing the street seemed ineffective. I was so frightened that I'd stand on the corner, wait for the bus, and ask the bus driver if he'd please allow me to ride to the other side of the street. It would take a long time before I successfully learned to navigate this intersection both as a pedestrian and later as a driver."

As complicated as a dangerous traffic intersection can be, navigating life's complexities can be even more menacing. Although the psalmist's specific situation in Psalm 118 is uncertain, we know it was difficult and just right for prayer: "When hard pressed, I cried to the LORD" (V. 5), the psalmist exclaimed. And his confidence in God was unmistakable: "The LORD is with me; I will not be afraid. . . . The LORD is with me; he is my helper" (VV. 6–7).

It's not unusual to be fearful when we need to change jobs or schools or housing. Anxieties arise when health declines, relationships change or money disappears. But these challenges needn't be interpreted as abandonment by God. When hard pressed, may we find ourselves prayerfully pressing into His presence.   *ARTHUR JACKSON*

What difficulty has brought you closer to God? With whom can you share your experience of His gracious help?

Gracious Father, please help me to trust You when I'm hard pressed.

BIBLE IN A YEAR | LEVITICUS 14; MATTHEW 26:51–75

As a bridegroom rejoices over his bride, so
will your God rejoice over you. [ISAIAH 62:5]

REJOICING LOVE

Brendan and Katie beamed at each other. Looking at the
pure joy on their faces, you would have never guessed the
difficult ways so many of their wedding plans had been
dramatically altered due to COVID-19 restrictions. Even with
only twenty-five family members present, joy and peace radi-
ated from the two as they said their vows because of their love
for each other and expressed their gratefulness for God's love
sustaining them.

The image of a bride and groom delighting over each other is
the picture the prophet Isaiah painted to describe the type of
delight and love God has for His people. In a beautifully poetic
description of God's promised deliverance, Isaiah reminded his
readers that the salvation God offered them reflected the reality
of living in a broken world—comfort for the broken-hearted, joy
for those who mourn and provision for the needs of His people
(ISAIAH 61:1–3). God offered help to His people because, just like
a bride and groom celebrate their love for each other, "so will
your God rejoice over you" (62:5).

It's a remarkable truth that God delights in us and wants a
relationship with us. Even when we struggle because of the effects of living in a broken world, we have a God who loves us,
not begrudgingly, but with a rejoicing, lasting love that "endures
forever" (PSALM 136:1).   *LISA M. SAMRA*

**What images remind you of God's love?
How does His rejoicing love bring you joy?**

Loving God, thank You for rejoicing over me in love.

Do not merely listen to the word, and so deceive yourselves. Do what it says. [JAMES 1:22]

A LIFE TO BE LIVED

Hartley's Jam. Perhaps you've seen it in the supermarket or have a jar in your cupboard. Strawberry is my favourite! But the nineteenth-century origins of this British household name may surprise you.

William Hartley built his successful business on principles from God's word. "Religion" Hartley said, "is a life to be lived." He didn't just read his Bible, he responded by following James' teaching to "Do what it says" (JAMES 1:22). As Hartley humbly let "the word planted in" him take hold of his heart (V. 21), it shaped his lifestyle and perspective and affected how he ran his business. His integrity led to quality products at a reasonable price. And he worked hard to serve his staff by investing his profits into their needs and community.

Religion isn't just a knowledge of God, it's a personal relationship with Jesus that shows itself in how we live. James describes God's word as a "mirror" that reflects the image of God's grace and compassion to us, which in turn transforms our responses to others (SEE VV. 23–24). Like Hartley, we can see each new venture as an opportunity to serve others with the love we have received.

Whether we're leaders or followers, owners or employees, and whether we have an upfront or unseen role, faith is something we live out. Our relationship with Jesus can bless those we encounter today (SEE V. 27).   *ANNE LE TISSIER*

When are you tempted to keep your faith hidden?
How does Hartley's integrity, work ethic and care for
others' needs inspire you to put your faith into action?

Creator God, inspire me to respond to what I read in your
word, that I will convey Your presence and truth to the lives
that connect with mine.

BIBLE IN A YEAR | LEVITICUS 17–18; MATTHEW 27:27–50

In him was life, and that life was the
light of all mankind. [JOHN 1:4]

REFLECTING HIS LIGHT

To capture the beauty of reflective light in his landscape oil
paintings, artist Armand Cabrera works with a key artistic
principle: "Reflected light is never as strong as its source
light." He observes that novice painters tend to exaggerate reflected light. He says, "Reflected light belongs to the shadow
and as such it must support, not compete with the lighted areas
of your painting."

We hear similar insight in the Bible concerning Jesus as
"the light of all mankind" (JOHN 1:4). John the Baptist "came as
a witness to testify concerning that light, so that through him
all might believe" (V. 7). The gospel writer tells us, "He himself
[John] was not the light; he came only as a witness to the light"
(V. 8).

As with John, we're chosen by God to reflect Christ's light to
those living in the shadows of an unbelieving world. This is our
role, as one source says, "perhaps because unbelievers are not
able to bear the full blazing glory of His light first hand."

Cabrera teaches his art students that "anything that has direct light falling on it in a scene becomes a source of light itself." Similarly, with Jesus as "the true light that gives light to
everyone" (V. 9), we can shine as witnesses. As we reflect Him,
may the world be amazed to see His glory shine through us.

PATRICIA RAYBON

***How do you reflect the light of Christ? How can you shine
His transforming light in the shadows?***

*Shine on me, beautiful Light of God. Please help me to
shine Your light in the shadows of an unbelieving world.*

BIBLE IN A YEAR | LEVITICUS 19-20; MATTHEW 27:51-66

All of us have become like one who is
unclean, and all our righteous acts are like
filthy rags. [ISAIAH 64:6]

CLEANSED COMPLETELY

Recently, my wife and I were cleaning our house before
having guests over. I noticed some dark stains on our
white kitchen tile floor—the kind that required getting on
my knees to scrub.

But I soon had a sinking realisation: the more I scrubbed, the
more I noticed *other* stains. Each stain I eliminated only made
the others that much more obvious. Our kitchen floor suddenly
seemed *impossibly* dirty. And with each moment, I realised, *No
matter how hard I work, I can never get this floor completely clean.*

Scripture says something similar about self-cleansing—our
best efforts at dealing with sin on our own always fall short.
Seeming to despair of God's people, the Israelites, ever experiencing His salvation (ISAIAH 64:5), the prophet Isaiah wrote, "All
of us have become like one who is unclean, and all our righteous
acts are like filthy rags" (V. 6).

But Isaiah knew there is always hope through God's goodness.
So he prayed, "You, LORD, are our Father. We are the clay, you
are the potter" (V. 8). He knew that God alone can cleanse what
we cannot, until the deepest stains are "white as snow" (1:18).

We can't scrub away the smudges and smears of sin on our
souls. Thankfully, we can receive salvation in the One whose
sacrifice allows us to be cleansed completely (1 JOHN 1:7).

ADAM R. HOLZ

> *Why is it hard to accept God's forgiveness? Why do you
> think you're tempted to try to deal with sin on your own?*
>
> *Father, help me to rest in Your forgiveness instead of trying
> to earn what You've already freely given.*

BIBLE IN A YEAR │ LEVITICUS 21–22; MATTHEW 28

Pray in the Spirit on all occasions with all kinds of prayers and requests.
[EPHESIANS 6:18]

PRAYER CARDS

During a writing conference where I served as a faculty member, Tamy handed me a postcard with a handwritten prayer on the back. She explained that she read the faculty biographies, wrote specific prayers on each card and prayed as she delivered them to us. In awe over the details in her personal message to me, I thanked God for encouraging me through Tamy's gesture. Then I prayed for her in return. When I struggled with pain and fatigue during the conference, I pulled out the postcard. God refreshed my spirit as I reread Tamy's note.

The apostle Paul recognised the life-affirming impact of prayer for others. He urged believers to prepare for battle "against the spiritual forces of evil in the heavenly realms" (EPHESIANS 6:12). He encouraged ongoing and specific prayers, while emphasising the need to intervene for one another in what we call intercessory prayer. Paul also requested bold prayers on his behalf. "Pray also for me, that whenever I speak, words may be given me so that I will fearlessly make known the mystery of the gospel, for which I am an ambassador in chains" (VV. 19–20).

As we pray for one another, the Holy Spirit comforts us and strengthens our resolve. He affirms that we need Him and one another, assuring us that He hears every prayer—silent, spoken or scribbled on a prayer card—and He answers according to His perfect will. *XOCHITL DIXON*

How has God ministered to you through the intercessory prayers of others? Who can you encourage with a prayer card today?

Dear God, please help me approach You with confident prayers for myself and others.

BIBLE IN A YEAR | LEVITICUS 23-24; MARK 1:1-22

If my people . . . will humble themselves
. . . , then I will hear from heaven.
[2 CHRONICLES 7:14]

REVIVAL COMES

Aurukun is a small town in northern Australia—its Aboriginal population drawn from seven clans. While the gospel came to Aurukun a century ago, eye-for-eye retribution sometimes remained. In 2015, clan tensions grew, and when a murder happened, payback required someone from the offender's family to die in return.

But something remarkable happened in early 2016. The people of Aurukun started seeking God in prayer. Repentance followed, then mass baptisms, as revival began sweeping the town. People were so joyful they danced in the streets, and instead of enacting payback, the family of the murdered man forgave the offending clan. Soon 1,000 people were in church each Sunday—in a town of just 1,300!

We see revivals like this in Scripture, as in Hezekiah's day when crowds joyfully returned to God (2 CHRONICLES 30), and on the day of Pentecost when thousands repented (ACTS 2:38–47). While revival is God's work, done in His time, history shows prayer precedes it. "If my people . . . will humble themselves and pray and seek my face and turn from their wicked ways," God told Solomon, "I will forgive their sin and will heal their land" (2 CHRONICLES 7:14).

As the people of Aurukun found, revival brings joy and reconciliation to a town. How our own cities need such transformation! Father, bring revival to us too.   *SHERIDAN VOYSEY*

While there's no 'formula' for revival, what do you think helps lead to it? How can you respond to God today to help revival come?

Dear Father, please bring revival to our land, starting with me.

BIBLE IN A YEAR | LEVITICUS 25; MARK 1:23–45

[God] will not forget your work and the love you
have shown him as you have helped his people
and continue to help them. [HEBREWS 6:10]

GOD SEES US

A Scottish explorer was the first Westerner to witness "the
smoke that thunders". Staring in awe at this mighty tor-
rent of water, he renamed it "Victoria Falls". David Livingstone (1813–73) wasn't just an explorer but a missionary in
Africa. He spent many years sharing his faith and fighting against
slavery, writing in a letter sent back home that "the gospel is the
power of God" to bring real change.

Like the thunderous impact of standing before Victoria Falls,
we might be a bit awestruck by heroes of the faith such as Livingstone. In fact, they can leave us wondering, *But what if my
life is quiet rather than dynamic? What if my serving is unseen?*

The letter of Hebrews encourages us with the promise that God
"will not forget your work and the love you have shown him as you
have helped his people and continue to help them" (HEBREWS 6:10).
God sees and remembers everything done in His name. This truth
can spur us on to "show this same diligence to the very end" in
everything that we do (V. 11), whether it feels dynamic or not.

To work meaningfully we don't need to preach to multitudes,
free prisoners or discover new lands. No matter what acts of service we do today, let's "imitate those who through faith and patience inherit what has been promised" (V. 12). Everything done
in Jesus' name is seen and celebrated in heaven.   *CHRIS WALE*

> **What service do you do for God? How does knowing He
> doesn't forget your acts encourage you, especially if your
> work goes unnoticed?**

> *Loving God, my service to You is far from perfect but I also
> know that You see and value me. Thank You for equipping
> me to serve.*

BIBLE IN A YEAR | LEVITICUS 26–27; MARK 2

But David remained in Jerusalem.
[2 SAMUEL 11:1]

DEATH ZONE

In 2019, a climber saw his last sunrise from the peak of Mount Everest. He survived the dangerous ascent, but the high altitude squeezed his heart, and he passed away on the trek down. One medical expert warns climbers not to think of the summit as their journey's end. They must get up and down quickly, remembering "they're in the Death Zone."

David survived his dangerous climb to the top. He killed lions and bears, slew Goliath, dodged Saul's spear and pursuing army, and conquered Philistines and Ammonites to become king of the mountain.

But David forgot he was in the death zone. At the peak of his success, as "the LORD gave David victory wherever he went" (2 SAMUEL 8:6), he committed adultery and murder. His initial mistake? He lingered on the mountaintop. When his army set out for new challenges, he "remained in Jerusalem" (11:1). David once had volunteered to fight Goliath; now he relaxed in the accolades of his triumphs.

It's hard to stay grounded when everyone, including God, says you're special (7:11–16). But we must. If we've achieved some success, we may appropriately celebrate the accomplishment and accept congratulations, but we must keep moving. We're in the death zone. Come down the mountain. Humbly serve others in the valley—asking God to guard your heart and your steps.

MIKE WITTMER

Are you climbing your mountain or near the top? How might you avoid the pitfalls that come with success?

Father, grant me success, and protect me from its excess.

BIBLE IN A YEAR | NUMBERS 1–3; MARK 3

He humbled himself by becoming
obedient to death—even death on a cross!
[PHILIPPIANS 2:8]

BE HUMBLE DAY

I'm often amused by the unofficial holidays people come up with. February alone has a Sticky Bun Day, a Sword Swallowers Day, even a Dog Biscuit Appreciation Day! Today has been labelled Be Humble Day. Universally recognised as a virtue, humility is certainly worth celebrating. But interestingly, this hasn't always been the case.

Humility was considered a weakness, not a virtue, in the ancient world, which prized *honour* instead. Boasting about one's achievements was expected, and you sought to raise your status, never lower it. Humility meant inferiority, like a servant to a master. But all this changed, historians say, at Jesus' crucifixion. There, the One who was "in very nature God" gave up His divine status to become "a servant" and "humbled himself" to die for others (PHILIPPIANS 2:6–8). Such a praiseworthy act forced humility to be redefined. By the end of the first century, even secular writers were calling humility a virtue because of what Christ had done.

Every time someone is praised for being humble today, the gospel is being subtly preached. For without Jesus, humility wouldn't be seen as good, and a Be Humble Day would be unthinkable. Christ relinquished His status for us, revealing through all history the humble nature of God. *SHERIDAN VOYSEY*

***What would the world be like if humility was still a
weakness? In what relationships can you imitate Jesus'
humility today?***

*I praise You, Jesus, for being the Humble One. And I desire
to humble myself to You today as my only fitting response!*

BIBLE IN A YEAR | NUMBERS 4–6; MARK 4:1–20

You would have asked him and he would
have given you living water. [JOHN 4:10]

WATER OF LIFE

Andrea's home life was unstable, and she left at fourteen,
finding a job and living with friends. Yearning for love and
affirmation, she later moved in with a man who introduced her to drugs, which she added to the alcohol she already
drank regularly. But the relationship and the substances didn't
satisfy her longings. She kept searching, and after several years
she met some believers in Jesus who reached out to her, offering to pray with her. A few months later, she finally found the
One who would quench her thirst for love—Jesus.

The Samaritan woman at the well whom Jesus approached
for water found her thirst satisfied too. She was there in the
heat of the day (JOHN 4:5–7), probably to avoid the stares and
gossip of other women, who would have known her history
of multiple husbands and her current adulterous relationship
(VV. 17–18). When Jesus approached her and asked her for a
drink, he bucked the social conventions of the day, for He, as
a Jewish teacher, would not normally have associated with a
Samaritan woman. But He wanted to give her the gift of living
water that would lead her to eternal life (V. 10). He wanted to
satisfy her thirst.

When we receive Jesus as our Saviour, we too drink of this
living water. We can then share a cup with others as we invite
them to follow Him.   *AMY BOUCHER PYE*

**How do you think the woman at the well felt when Jesus
asked her for some water? What does it mean to you to
receive His living water?**

*Father God, You welcome all who are thirsty to come to the
waters and drink. Satisfy my thirst through Your living water.*

BIBLE IN A YEAR | NUMBERS 7-8; MARK 4:21-41

From the ends of the earth I call to you . . .
as my heart grows faint. [PSALM 61:2]

PRAYING IN DIFFICULT TIMES

Author and theologian Russell Moore described noticing the eerie silence in the orphanage where he adopted his boys. Someone later explained that the babies had stopped crying because they learned that no one would respond to their cries.

When we face difficult times, we too can feel that no one hears. And worst of all, we can feel that God Himself doesn't listen to our cries or see our tears. But He does! And that's why we need the language of petition and protest found especially in the book of Psalms. The psalmists petition for God's help and also protest their situation to Him. In Psalm 61, David brings his petitions and protests before his Creator, stating, "I call to you, I call as my heart grows faint; lead me to the rock that is higher than I" (V. 2). David cries out to God because he knows that only He is his "refuge" and "strong tower" (V. 3).

Praying the petitions and protests of the psalms is a way of affirming God's sovereignty and appealing to His goodness and faithfulness. They're proof of the intimate relationship we can experience with God. In difficult moments, we can all be tempted to believe the lie that He doesn't care. But He does. He hears us and is with us.   *GLENN PACKIAM*

> *How does it encourage you to know that God hears*
> *your desperate prayers? What petitions and protests*
> *will you share with Him today?*

> *Dear Jesus, help me to offer You my petitions, protests*
> *and praise.*

BIBLE IN A YEAR | NUMBERS 9–11; MARK 5:1-20

Day after day, . . . [the apostles] never
stopped teaching and proclaiming the good
news that Jesus is the Messiah. [ACTS 5:42]

KEEP TALKING ABOUT JESUS!

In an interview, a musician who's a believer in Christ recalls a time he was urged to "stop talking about Jesus" so much. Why? It was suggested that his band could be more famous and raise more money to feed the poor if he stopped saying his work was all about Jesus. After thinking it through, he decided, "The entire point of my music is to share my faith in Christ. . . . No way [am I] going to be silent." He said his "burning calling [is] to share the message of Jesus."

Under much more threatening circumstances, the apostles received a similar message. They'd been jailed and miraculously delivered by an angel, who told them to continue telling others about their new life in Christ (ACTS 5:19–20). When the religious leaders learned of the apostles' escape and that they were still proclaiming the gospel, they reprimanded them: "We gave you strict orders not to teach in [Jesus'] name" (V. 28).

Their reply: "We must obey God rather than human beings!" (V. 29). As a result, the leaders flogged the apostles and "ordered them not to speak in the name of Jesus" (V. 40). The apostles rejoiced that they were worthy of suffering for Jesus' name, and "day after day . . . never stopped teaching and proclaiming the good news" (V. 42). May God help us to keep following their example!

ALYSON KIEDA

If you've ever been told to stop talking about Jesus, what was your response? What are some ways you can tell others about Him?

Dear God, thank You for the example of the apostles and others who were bold witnesses for You. Please give me courage to follow their lead.

BIBLE IN A YEAR | NUMBERS 12–14; MARK 5:21–43

I desire to do your will, my God; your law is
within my heart. [PSALM 40:8]

IS IT A SIGN?

The offer looked good, and was exactly what Peter needed.
After being laid off, this sole breadwinner of a young family had prayed desperately for a job. "Surely this is God's
answer to your prayers," his friends suggested.

Reading about the prospective employer, however, Peter felt
uneasy. The company invested in suspicious businesses and had
been flagged for corruption. In the end, Peter rejected the offer,
though it was painful to do so. "I believe God wants me to do
the right thing," he shared with me. "I just have to trust He will
provide for me."

Peter was reminded of the account of David meeting Saul in a
cave. It seemed like he was being given the perfect opportunity
to kill the man hunting him down, but David resisted. "The LORD
forbid that I should do such a thing . . . for he is the anointed
of the LORD," he reasoned (1 SAMUEL 24:6). David was careful to
distinguish between his own interpretation of events and God's
command to obey His instruction and do the right thing.

Instead of always trying to look for 'signs' in certain situations,
let's look to God and His truth for wisdom and guidance to discern what lies before us. He will help us do what's right in His
eyes.   *LESLIE KOH*

*What could help you discern between a personal
interpretation of events and what God would want you
to do? Whom can you turn to for godly advice?*

*God, my Provider, grant me the wisdom to discern
opportunities before me and the faith to follow Your way,
that I might always do what pleases You.*

BIBLE IN A YEAR | NUMBERS 15–16; MARK 6:1–29

All the widows stood around [Peter], crying and showing him the robes and other clothing that Dorcas had made. [ACTS 9:39]

SEEING A NEED

In the last few days of my dad's life, one of the nurses dropped by his room and asked me if she could give him a shave. As Rachel gently pulled the razor across his face, she explained, "Older men of his generation like to have a neat shave every day." Rachel had seen a need and acted on her instinct to show kindness, dignity and respect to someone. The tender care she provided reminded me of my friend Julie who still paints her elderly mother's nails because it's important to her mum that she "looks pretty".

Acts 9 tells us about a disciple named Dorcas (also known as Tabitha) who showed kindness by providing handmade clothing for the poor (VV. 36, 39). When she died, her room was filled with friends who tearfully mourned this kind woman who loved helping others.

But Dorcas' story didn't end there. When Peter was brought to where her body lay, he knelt and prayed. In God's power, he called her by name, saying, "Tabitha, get up" (V. 40). Amazingly, Dorcas opened her eyes and rose to her feet. When her friends realised she was alive, word spread quickly through the town and "many people believed in the Lord" (V. 42).

And how did Dorcas spend the next day of her life? Probably exactly as she had before—seeing the needs of people and meeting them.

CINDY HESS KASPER

Whom do you know that always seems to find ways to help others? What can you do to become more aware of others' needs?

Father, open my eyes each day to see the hurting and needy people around me. Open my heart to do what I can to show them what God's love looks like.

BIBLE IN A YEAR | NUMBERS 17–19; MARK 6:30–56

Then the LORD opened the donkey's mouth.
[NUMBERS 22:28]

A BABOON, A DONKEY, AND ME

Jack knew how to put trains on the right track. In nine years of work, he never missed a track switch as locomotives drew near the Uitenhage, South Africa, station, indicating by their whistles the direction they were to go.

Jack was also a chacma baboon. He was cared for by railway signalman James Wide, and Jack in turn took care of James. Wide had lost both his legs in a fall between moving rail cars. He trained Jack to help him with tasks around the house and soon Jack assisted him at work also, learning how to respond to the incoming trains' signals by pulling corresponding levers for their tracks.

The Bible tells of another animal that helped someone in a surprising way—Balaam's donkey. Balaam was a pagan prophet serving a king who intended to harm Israel. As Balaam was riding his donkey enroute to assist the king, "the LORD opened the donkey's mouth" and it spoke to Balaam (NUMBERS 22:28). The donkey's speech was part of the way God opened "Balaam's eyes" (V. 31), warned him of imminent danger and kept him from harming His people.

A railway baboon? A talking donkey? Why not? If God can use these amazing animals for good purposes, it's not at all far-fetched to believe He can use you and me as well. Looking to Him and seeking His strength, we can accomplish more than we ever thought possible.   *JAMES BANKS*

**Whom have you seen God use unexpectedly? What will
you do to make yourself available to Him today?**

*I want to serve You, God! Use my hands, my feet, my
mouth, whatever You like! Help me to live for You today.*

BIBLE IN A YEAR | NUMBERS 20-22; MARK 7:1-13

REST IS A GIFT FROM GOD

Tossing and turning in bed, I fretted over my list of weekly tasks. Family, friends and even people I barely knew depended on me. For the fourth night in a row, I watched the clock change to three a.m. before I fell asleep. The alarm I'd set for six a.m. shocked me into starting my day. I snapped at my husband. Barking orders at my son, I rushed him into the car. I don't remember driving to his school. But I'll never forget watching his teacher close the classroom door before I headed outside and collapsed from exhaustion onto the playground.

A friend drove me home and promised to care for my son until my husband returned from work. My neighbour prayed over me and stayed close by until I woke up . . . eight hours later.

God knows His children worry, fear and sometimes try to do too much. He also knows how desperately we need down time to rejuvenate physically, emotionally, mentally and spiritually.

In Psalm 62, David says his "soul finds rest *in* God" (V. 1). For this holistic revitalisation, David needed to be silent and still as he leaned into God's proven trustworthiness as our all-sufficient hope-giver, deliverer and protector (VV. 5–7). Urging others to trust in God "at all times" by approaching Him with honest prayers, David demonstrates bold dependence on God and His power (VV. 8, 12).

God didn't design us to be weighed down by worry or the need to meet everyone's needs. He does, however, prove His dependability. When we trust His constant presence and His power, we can worship Him by resting. What a priceless gift from God!

Xochitl Dixon, *Our Daily Bread* author

★ In our busy world, we can overlook the value and importance of rest. But it's an important part of God's design and purpose for us. This month, we're looking at rest and considering what it means to experience this gift from Him. The topic is addressed in the devotions for **March 1, 15, 22** and **31**.

Come to me, all you who are weary
and burdened, and I will give you rest.
[MATTHEW 11:28]

FINDING REST IN JESUS

The restless soul is never satisfied with wealth and success. A deceased music icon could testify to this truth. He had nearly forty of his albums appear in various top-ten charts and just as many number one singles. But he also had multiple marriages and spent time in prison. Even with all his achievements, he once lamented: "There's a restlessness in my soul that I've never conquered, not with motion, marriages or meaning. . . . It's still there to a degree. And it will be till the day I die." Sadly, he could have found rest in his soul *before* his life ended.

Jesus invites all those, like this musician, who have become weary from toiling in sin and its consequences to come to Him personally: "Come to me," He says. When we receive salvation in Jesus, He will take the burdens from us and "give [us] rest" (MATTHEW 11:28). The only requirements are to believe in Him and then to learn from Him how to live the abundant life He provides (JOHN 10:10). Taking on the yoke of Jesus' discipleship results in our finding "rest for [our] souls" (MATTHEW 11:29).

When we come to Jesus, He doesn't abbreviate our accountability to God. He gives peace to our restless souls by providing us a new and less burdensome way to live in Him. He gives us true rest. 　　　　*MARVIN WILLIAMS*

In what ways do you feel weary and burdened right now? What's it like to experience the promised rest Jesus offers?

Jesus, let my restless soul find peace and rest in You alone.

BIBLE IN A YEAR | NUMBERS 23–25; MARK 7:14–37

Blessed is the one . . . who meditates on his law day and night. [PSALM 1:1–2]

A REFRESHING OASIS

When Andrew and his family went on safari in Kenya, they had the pleasure of watching a variety of animals frequenting a small lake that appeared in the scrabbly landscape. Giraffes, wildebeests, hippopotamuses and waterfowl all travelled to this life-giving source of water. As Andrew observed their comings and goings, he thought how the "Bible is like a divine watering hole"—not only is it a source of guidance and wisdom but it's a refreshing oasis where people from all walks of life can quench their thirst.

Andrew's observation echoed the psalmist who called people "blessed" when they delight in and meditate on God's law, a term used in the Old Testament to describe His instruction and commandments. Those who meditate on the Scriptures are "like a tree planted by streams of water, which yields its fruit in season" (PSALM 1:3). Just as a tree's roots reach down into the soil to find the source of refreshment, people who truly believe in and love God will root themselves deeply in Scripture and find the strength they need.

Submitting ourselves to God's wisdom will keep our foundations embedded in Him; we won't be "like chaff that the wind blows away" (V. 4). When we ponder what God has given to us in the Bible, we gain nourishment that can lead to our bearing fruit that lasts.

AMY BOUCHER PYE

> **How does the Bible provide a foundation for the way you live? What can help you meditate on Scripture throughout the day?**
>
> *Loving God, You've given me the gift of Your words in the Bible. Help me to treasure them with gratitude and wonder.*

BIBLE IN A YEAR | NUMBERS 26–27; MARK 8:1–21

While we were still sinners, Christ died
for us. [ROMANS 5:8]

THIS LOVE IS REAL

" I felt like the rug had been pulled from under me," Jojie said. "The shock of the discovery was like a physical blow." She'd found out that her fiancé was seeing
someone else. Jojie's previous relationship had ended similarly.
So when she later heard about God's love at a Bible study, she
couldn't help wondering: *Is this another scam? Will I get hurt if
I believe God when He says He loves me?*

Like Jojie, we may have experienced troubled relationships
that left us feeling wary—or even afraid—of trusting someone's
promise of love. We may even feel this way about God's love,
wondering where the catch is. There is, however, no catch. "God
demonstrates his own love for us in this: while we were still sinners, Christ died for us" (ROMANS 5:8).

"Eventually, I realised God had already proven His love," Jojie
says, "by dying for me." My friend discovered that since our sinful state separated us from God, He reached out to us by giving
Jesus to die on our behalf (ROMANS 5:10; 1 JOHN 2:2). Because of
this, our sins are forgiven, and we can look forward to eternity
with Him (JOHN 3:16).

Whenever we wonder whether we can truly trust God's love,
let's remember what Christ did for us on the cross. We can trust
His promises of love, knowing that He's faithful.   *KAREN HUANG*

> **When or why have you found it difficult to trust God's
> love? How can knowing Jesus died for you change
> your response?**

> *Dear Jesus, thank You for the great love You showed me
> by dying for me. Let Your love change me, heal me and
> direct my relationships.*

BIBLE IN A YEAR | NUMBERS 28-30; MARK 8:22-38

[Josiah] would not listen to what
Necho had said at God's command.
[2 CHRONICLES 35:22]

LISTENING TO GOD

Back when I was driving to university and back home again, the road to our house seemed painfully dull. Because it was long and straight, I found myself driving faster than I should have more than once. First, I was given a warning. Then I received a speeding ticket. Then I was caught a third time in the very same place.

Refusing to listen can have unfortunate consequences. One tragic example of this is from the life of Josiah, a good and faithful king. When Necho, the king of Egypt, marched through Judah's territory to help Assyria in battle against Babylon, Josiah went out to counter him. Necho sent messengers telling Josiah, "God has told me to hurry; so stop opposing God, who is with me" (2 CHRONICLES 35:21). God really did send Necho, but Josiah "would not listen to what Necho had said at God's command but went to fight him on the plain of Megiddo" (V. 22). Josiah was fatally injured in the battle, "and all Judah and Jerusalem mourned for him" (V. 24).

Josiah, who loved God, discovered that insisting on his own way without taking the time to listen to Him or His wisdom through others never ends well. May God give us the humility we need to always check ourselves and take His wisdom to heart. *JAMES BANKS*

What do you need God's wisdom for in your life?
What will you do to listen to Him today?

Ever wise and loving God, help me to be humble and to listen for Your wisdom today. Thank You that when I ask for wisdom, You give "generously . . . without finding fault" (JAMES 1:5).

BIBLE IN A YEAR │ NUMBERS 31-33; MARK 9:1-29

You know me, LORD.
[JEREMIAH 12:3]

GOD KNOWS US

I recently saw a photograph of Michelangelo's sculpture *Moses*, in which a close-up view showed a small bulging muscle on Moses' right arm. This muscle is the extensor digiti minimi, and the contraction only appears when someone lifts their little finger. Michelangelo, known as a master of intricate details, paid close attention to the human bodies he sculpted, adding intimate features nearly everyone else would miss. Michelangelo knew the human body in ways few other sculptors have, but the details he carved into granite were his attempts to reveal something deeper—the soul, the interior life of human beings. And of course, there, Michelangelo always fell short.

Only God knows the deepest realities of the human heart. Whatever we see of one another, no matter how attentive or insightful it might be, is only a shadow of the truth. But God sees deeper than the shadows. "You know me, LORD," the prophet Jeremiah said; "you see me" (12:3). God's knowledge of us isn't theoretical or cerebral. He doesn't observe us from a distance. Rather, He peers into the hidden realities of who we are. God knows the depths of our interior lives, even those things we struggle to understand ourselves.

No matter our struggles or what's going on in our hearts, God sees us and truly knows us.　　　　　　　*WINN COLLIER*

> ***What makes you feel alone, isolated or unseen? How does it change things to realise that God knows you?***
>
> *Dear God, this world can be a lonely place, but I'm astounded at how truly You know me. It fills me with wonder and joy.*

BIBLE IN A YEAR | NUMBERS 34–36; MARK 9:30–50

God heard the boy crying.
[GENESIS 21:17]

ALL ALONE?

Sue's family was falling apart before her eyes. Her husband had suddenly left their home, and she and her children were confused and angry. She asked him to go for marriage counselling with her, but he wouldn't because he claimed the problems were hers. Panic and hopelessness set in when she realised he might never come back. Would she be able to care for herself and her children alone?

Hagar, a servant of Abraham and Sarah, faced those thoughts as well. Impatient for God to give them a son as promised (GENESIS 12, 15), Sarah gave Hagar to her husband, and Hagar gave birth to Ishmael (16:1–4, 15). However, when God fulfilled His promise and Sarah gave birth to Isaac, family tensions erupted and Abraham sent Hagar away with their son Ishmael with just some water and food (21:8–21). Can you imagine her desperation? Soon they ran out of provisions in the desert. Not knowing what to do and not wanting to see her son die, Hagar put Ishmael under a bush and walked a distance away. They both began to sob. But "God heard the boy crying" (V. 17). He heard their cries, provided for their needs and was with them.

Times of desperation when we feel all alone cause us to cry out to God. What a comfort to know that during those moments and throughout our lives, He hears us, provides for us and stays near to us. *ANNE CETAS*

How has God provided for you when you've felt alone?
How have you responded to Him?

I'm grateful, God, that I never really walk alone.
Help me in my desperation.

BIBLE IN A YEAR | DEUTERONOMY 1-2; MARK 10:1-31

When you have turned back,
strengthen your brothers. [LUKE 22:32]

NEVER TOO FAR

Raj had trusted Jesus as Saviour in his youth, but soon afterwards, he drifted from the faith and led a life apart from God. Then one day, he made the decision to renew his relationship with Jesus and go back to church—only to be scolded by a woman who berated him for being absent for all these years. The scolding added to Raj's sense of shame and guilt for his years of drifting. *Am I beyond hope?* he wondered. Then he recalled how Christ had restored Simon Peter (JOHN 21:15–17) even though he'd denied Him (LUKE 22:34, 60–61).

Whatever scolding Peter might have expected, all he received was forgiveness and restoration. Jesus didn't even mention Peter's denial, but instead gave him a chance to reaffirm his love for Christ and take care of His followers (JOHN 21:15–17). Jesus' words before Peter disowned Him were being fulfilled: "When you have turned back, strengthen your brothers" (LUKE 22:32).

Raj asked God for that same forgiveness and restoration, and today he's not only walking closely with Jesus but serving in a church and supporting other believers as well. No matter how far we've strayed from God, He's always ready not only to forgive us and welcome us back but also to restore us so we can love, serve and glorify Him. We're never too far from God: His loving arms are wide open.   *LESLIE KOH*

> **What fears might you have about turning back to God?**
> **How can knowing His heart of forgiveness help you to**
> **return to Him?**

*Father, thank You for Your endless mercy and patience with
me. Thank You that I can trust in Your everlasting love.*

BIBLE IN A YEAR | DEUTERONOMY 3–4; MARK 10:32–52

I found the one my heart loves. I held him and would not let him go. [SONG OF SONGS 3:4]

THE END OF THE SEARCH

While browsing in a charity shop, Hannah, my daughter, spotted a wedding dress. She tried it on. The whole shop froze. It was perfect. "Mum?" she beamed at me, "What do you think?"

Mean mother that I am, I made her spend a whole hour looking at photos of it on her phone to be absolutely certain this was the one. An hour and five minutes later, we emerged as the proud owners. A pang of sadness hit me, however, because now we would never have the excitement of going wedding dress shopping. Fun though it would have been, we didn't need to keep searching for the perfect item which we'd already found.

Solomon describes the end of an even more important search: "for the one my heart loves" (SONG OF SONGS 3:1). Although he was thinking of the love between couples, there are echoes here of our spiritual searching, which ends when we find Christ. "I found the one my heart loves. I held him and would not let him go" (V. 4).

Sometimes the excitement and soul-satisfaction of knowing Jesus fades over time. We search again for a new thrill. But like the lovers in this passage, once we've found Jesus, our search has stopped. Instead, we can echo the passionate single-mindedness of holding Him and never letting go!

If you feel like you're lacking something today, cling even tighter to Jesus. There's endless fulfilment and joy to be found in getting to know the One our hearts love. *DEBBI FRALICK*

What do you find yourself searching for at the moment? How does clinging to Jesus bring satisfaction to even your deepest needs?

Jesus, You are the One my heart loves. Help me experience the excitement and satisfaction of living each day in Your presence.

BIBLE IN A YEAR | DEUTERONOMY 5-7; MARK 11:1-18

Write [these commandments] on the
doorframes of your houses and on your gates.
[DEUTERONOMY 6:9]

COMFORT ON DOORFRAMES

A s I scanned my social media feed in the aftermath of a nearby and devastating flood, I came across a friend's post. After realising her home would have to be gutted and rebuilt, my friend's mum encouraged her to look for God even in the heart-wrenching work of cleaning up. My friend later posted pictures of Bible verses she uncovered on the exposed door frames of the home, apparently written at the time the home had been built. Reading the Scriptures on the wooden planks gave her comfort.

The tradition of writing Bible verses on doorframes may stem from God's command to Israel. God instructed the Israelites to post His commands on doorframes as a way of remembering who He is. By writing the commandments on their hearts (DEUTERONOMY 6:6), teaching them to their children (V. 7), using symbols and other means to recall what God commands (V. 8) and placing the words on doorframes and entry ways (V. 9), the Israelites had constant reminders of God's words. They were encouraged to never forget what He had said or their covenant with Him.

Displaying God's words in our homes as well as planting their meaning in our hearts can help us to build a foundation that relies on His faithfulness as revealed in Scripture. And He can use those words to bring us comfort even in the midst of tragedy or heart-wrenching loss.

KATARA PATTON

> **When has Scripture comforted you the most? How are
> the truths of Scripture the foundation for your life?**
>
> *Heavenly Father, thank You for Scripture that guides my
> path. Remind me to build my foundation on it.*

BIBLE IN A YEAR | DEUTERONOMY 8–10; MARK 11:19-33

And you will go out and frolic like
well-fed calves. [MALACHI 4:2]

FREEDOM!

When I would care for a wonderful black Labrador Retriever, one of my favourite tasks was releasing her from the chain that kept her attached to the outbuilding. I would cry, "Freedom!" and I was sure she understood my meaning as she bounded about, running with wild abandon and frolicking in the grass. Her delight felt palpable.

The prophet Malachi speaks of the sheer joy that those who love and revere the Lord will experience on the "day [that] is coming" (MALACHI 4:1). These words shine with encouragement in an Old Testament book that also reverberates with judgement, such as when Malachi says, "the arrogant and every evildoer will be stubble" (V. 1). The Israelites had let their worship of the only true God wane, and no longer were they observing the prescribed customs in the Temple that they had rebuilt after its destruction. They had given their hearts over to idols and other gods.

Being trapped in our sinful behaviour can feel like a prison, but when we repent and confess our wrongdoing, we too can experience the joy of release like an animal bursting out of its stall. We feel a sense of freedom and promise, knowing that no longer are we bound by deceit or lies. We can bounce with jubilation as we praise the God who has cancelled our sentence. We are free!　　　　　　　　　　　　　　　　　*AMY BOUCHER PYE*

> **When have you experienced a sense of freedom after you've received God's forgiveness? How do you like to express wonder and joy over your salvation?**

> *Saviour and Redeemer, thank You for loving me enough to set me free from the sins that entangle me. Help me to turn from them and to become more like You.*

BIBLE IN A YEAR | DEUTERONOMY 11–13; MARK 12:1–27

David would take up his lyre and play.
Then relief would come to Saul.
[1 SAMUEL 16:23]

MUSICAL MEDICINE

When five-year-old Bella was hospitalised for cancer, she received music therapy as part of her treatment. Many people have experienced the powerful effect of music on mood without understanding exactly why, but researchers have recently documented a clinical benefit. Music is now being prescribed for cancer patients like Bella, and those suffering from Parkinson's disease, dementia and trauma.

King Saul reached for a musical prescription when he was feeling tormented. His attendants saw his lack of peace and suggested they find someone to play the lyre for him in the hope it would make him "feel better" (1 SAMUEL 16:16). They sent for Jesse's son David, and Saul was pleased with him and asked that he "remain in [his] service" (V. 22). David played for Saul in his moments of unrest, bringing him relief from his anguish.

We may only just be discovering scientifically what God has known all along about how music can affect us. As the Author and Creator of both our bodies and music itself, He provided a prescription for our health that's readily accessible to all, regardless of the era in which we live or how easy it is to visit a doctor. Even when there's no way to listen, we can sing to God in the midst of our joys and struggles, making music of our own (PSALM 59:16; ACTS 16:25).   *KIRSTEN HOLMBERG*

> ***How has God used music to soothe you? How can you
> bring music to someone as David did to Saul?***
>
> *Father, thank You for creating music and using it to soothe
> my heart and mind during times of struggle.*

BIBLE IN A YEAR | DEUTERONOMY 14-16; MARK 12:28-44

If it is possible, as far as it depends on you,
live at peace with everyone. [ROMANS 12:18]

FRIENDS AND ENEMIES

Scholar Kenneth E. Bailey spoke of the leader of an African
nation who'd learned to maintain an unusual posture in
the international community. He'd established a good relationship with both Israel and the nations surrounding it. When
someone asked him how his nation maintained this fragile balance, he responded, "We choose our friends. We do not encourage our friends to choose our enemies [for us]."

That is wise—and genuinely practical. What that African country modelled on an international level is what Paul encouraged
his readers to do on a personal level. In the midst of a lengthy
description of the characteristics of a life changed by Christ, he
wrote, "If it is possible, as far as it depends on you, live at peace
with everyone" (ROMANS 12:18). He goes on to reinforce the importance of our dealings with others by reminding us that even
the way we treat our enemies (VV. 20–21) reflects our trust in and
dependence upon God and His ultimate care.

To live in peace with everyone may not always be possible (after all, Paul does say "if"). But our responsibility as believers in
Jesus is to allow His wisdom to guide our living (JAMES 3:17–18) so
that we engage those around us as peacemakers (MATTHEW 5:9).
What better way could there be to honour the Prince of Peace?

BILL CROWDER

> ***Where do you struggle to live at peace? How could
> being an intentional peacemaker interject grace into
> that conflict?***

> *Loving Father, I was Your enemy and You called me
> friend. Enable me to be a peacemaker so I can show
> that same grace to others.*

BIBLE IN A YEAR | DEUTERONOMY 17–19; MARK 13:1–20

Let us run with perseverance the race
marked out for us. [HEBREWS 12:1]

RUNNING FOR WHAT MATTERS

It was impossible not to shed a tear at my friend Ira's status update. Posted in 2022 only days after she'd left her home in Kyiv, the besieged capital of Ukraine, she shared a past image of herself lifting her country's flag after completing a running event. She wrote, "We are all running to the best of our abilities a marathon called life. Let's run it these days even better than that. With something that never dies in our hearts." In the following days, I saw the many ways my friend continued to run that race, as she kept us updated on how to pray for and support those suffering in her country.

Ira's words brought new depth to the call in Hebrews 12 for believers to "run with perseverance" (V. 1). That call follows chapter 11's moving account of the heroes of faith, the "great cloud of witnesses" (12:1) who'd lived with courageous, persistent faith—even at risk to their lives (11:33–38). Even though they "only saw . . . and welcomed [God's promises] from a distance" (V. 13), they were living for something eternal, for something that never dies.

All believers in Jesus are called to live that same way. Because the *shalom*—the flourishing and peace—of God's kingdom is worth giving our all for. And because it's Christ's example and power that sustains us (12:2–3).   *MONICA LA ROSE*

What examples have you seen of courageous faith? How does Jesus' example give you hope?

Dear God, words fail me when I see Your people's faith and courage in heart-breaking circumstances. Give me the courage to follow You like that.

BIBLE IN A YEAR | DEUTERONOMY 20–22; MARK 13:21–37

The heavens declare the glory of God . . . their
voice goes out into all the earth. [PSALM 19:1–4]

ENCOUNTERING GOD THROUGH CREATION

Submerging her shoulders in near-freezing water, the swimmer's 'Oo-oo-oohs' and 'Aa-a-a-ahs' sing-songed through the crisp, winter air. The ancient practice of swimming in open water surged during the Covid pandemic in the UK—I shiver just thinking about it! But the words of another rosy-cheeked wild swimmer captured my imagination: "We're outside, connecting with nature. Once you're in there, you can sigh so, so deeply. We always look for the kingfisher . . . It's lovely."

Connecting with nature, suggests the Psalmist, heightens our awareness of God. Creation declares the truth and beauty of its Creator (PSALM 19:1). Day and night, the skies display God's glorious majesty: "their voice goes out into all the earth" (VV. 2–4). And just as the radiant light of the sun touches all, no one is hidden from God's loving care—a care displayed throughout His created world (VV. 4–6).

Wherever we are, we can all connect with God through nature— even by gazing out of the window at the sky, opening our hearts to His revelations. Listening to birdsong stills our racing thoughts, inviting His restoration. Appreciating God's sunset brushstrokes on our homeward commute reassures us of His presence. Seasonal changes prompt thoughts of what God is nurturing within us. A daisy prising its way through tarmac promises that we can fulfil our God-given potential, despite apparent obstacles.

Endless gifts in creation are ours to receive from God today. Amazing!

ANNE LE TISSIER

In what ways has God used nature to convey His love, presence or inspiration to you in the past? Why not pause, take a deep breath and enjoy meeting with God in His creation today?

Creator God, thank You for the gift of this world to help me to know You better.

BIBLE IN A YEAR | DEUTERONOMY 23–25; MARK 14:1–26

Be still, and know that I am God.
[PSALM 46:10]

STILL BEFORE GOD

The first photograph of a living person was taken by Louis Daguerre in 1838. The photo depicts a figure on an otherwise empty avenue in Paris in the middle of an afternoon. But there's an apparent mystery about it; the street and pavements should have been bustling with the traffic of carriages and pedestrians at that time of day, yet none can be seen.

The man wasn't alone. People and horses were *there* on the busy Boulevard du Temple, the popular area where the photo was taken. They just didn't show up in the picture. The exposure time to process the photograph (known as a Daguerreotype) took seven minutes to capture an image, which had to be motionless during that time. It appears that the man on the pavement was the sole person photographed because he was the only one standing *still*—he was having his boots shined.

Sometimes stillness accomplishes what motion and effort can't. God tells His people in Psalm 46:10, "Be still and know that I am God." Even when nations are "in uproar" (V. 6) and "the earth" shakes (V. 2), those who quietly trust in Him will discover in Him "an ever-present help in trouble" (V. 1).

The Hebrew verb rendered "be still" can also be translated "cease striving". When we rest in God instead of relying on our limited efforts, we discover Him to be our unassailable "refuge and strength" (V. 1).   *JAMES BANKS*

How will you 'show up' for God by being still before Him today? Where do you need to trust Him more?

Heavenly Father, please help me to trust in You and to rest in the quiet awareness of Your unfailing love.

BIBLE IN A YEAR | DEUTERONOMY 26–27; MARK 14:27–53

I stand at the door and knock.
[REVELATION 3:20]

WE'RE NOT ALONE

In Fredric Brown's short story thriller "Knock", he wrote, "The last man on Earth sat alone in a room. There was a knock on the door." Yikes! Who could that be, and what do they want? What mysterious being has come for him? The man is not alone.

Neither are we.

The church in Laodicea heard a knock on their door (REVELATION 3:20). What supernatural Being had come for them? His name was Jesus, "the First and the Last . . . the Living One" (1:17-18). His eyes blazed like fire, and His face "like the sun shining in all its brilliance" (V. 16). When His best friend, John, caught a glimpse of His glory, he "fell at his feet as though dead" (V. 17). Faith in Christ begins with the fear of God.

We're not alone, and this is also comforting. Jesus "is the radiance of God's glory and the exact representation of his being, sustaining all things by his powerful word" (HEBREWS 1:3). Yet Christ uses His strength not to slay us but to love us. Hear His invitation, "If anyone hears my voice and opens the door, I will come in and eat with that person, and they with me" (REVELATION 3:20). Our faith begins with fear—Who is at the door?—and it ends in a welcome and strong embrace. Jesus promises to always stay with us, even if we're the last person on earth. Thank God, we're not alone.   *MIKE WITTMER*

Why can't we separate Christ's power from His love?
Why are both vitally important?

Dear Jesus, I welcome You into my heart and life.

"Do not I fill heaven and earth?"
declares the Lord. [JEREMIAH 23:24]

EVERYWHERE

Stories abound about St. Patrick, including the tale of him driving out all the snakes from Ireland. But these legends, written long after his death, are most likely entertaining tales. Yet what we *do* know of this fifth-century man of God is remarkable. Despite having been a captive in Ireland for six years, Patrick later obeyed the Lord's calling to return and preach the gospel there. "Daily I expect to be murdered or betrayed or reduced to slavery if the occasion arises," he wrote. "But I fear nothing . . . I have cast myself into the hands of Almighty God, who reigns everywhere."

Knowing that God "reigns everywhere" brings tremendous reassurance, especially in times of trial. God spoke this message to His people in Jerusalem when they were under threat. Within their camp their leaders were corrupt and the prophets were making up visions from God (V. 25); on the horizon lay the threat of Babylon's army. Yet God declared Himself to be "nearby" despite the corrupt leaders and "far away" despite Babylon's power (JEREMIAH 23:23). "Do not I fill heaven and earth?" God asked them (V. 24).

God still "reigns everywhere." We might be experiencing trials and hardship, but we can take courage in God's promise that He reigns over everything. In all the situations we'll encounter today we know He is still our King and that He will exercise His love and saving grace.   *CHRIS WALE*

What reassurance does God's eternal reign give you?
How can you remind yourself that He is still King, even
when your circumstances don't make sense?

Thank You, heavenly Father, that You reign over me and
over the whole world. Help me to serve You and to partner
with You in extending Your love and goodness.

BIBLE IN A YEAR | DEUTERONOMY 30-31; MARK 15:1-25

If we confess our sins, he is faithful and just
and will forgive us our sins. [1 JOHN 1:9]

WEEDING OUT SINS

When I noticed a sprig budding next to the garden hose by our porch, I ignored the seemingly harmless eyesore. How could a little weed possibly hurt our lawn? But as the weeks passed, that nuisance grew to be the size of a small bush and began taking over our garden. Its stray stalks arched over a portion of our walkway and sprouted up in other areas. Admitting its destructive existence, I asked my husband to help me dig out the wild weeds by the roots and then protect our garden with weed killer.

When we ignore or deny its presence, sin can invade our lives like unwanted overgrowth and darken our personal space. Our sinless God has no darkness in Him . . . at all. As His children, we're equipped and charged to face sins head-on so we can "walk in the light, as he is in the light" (1 JOHN 1:7). Through confession and repentance, we experience forgiveness and freedom from sin (VV. 8–10) because we have a great advocate—Jesus (2:1). He willingly paid the ultimate price for our sins—His lifeblood—and "not only for ours but also for the sins of the whole world" (V. 2).

When our sin is brought to our attention by God, we can choose denial, avoidance or deflection of responsibility. But when we confess and repent, He weeds out sins that harm our relationships with Him and others.   *XOCHITL DIXON*

> **How does knowing your sins are offences against God change your view about repentance? What sins have taken root and need to be weeded out of your life?**
>
> *Loving Father, please uproot the sins from my life so I can grow closer to You and others.*

BIBLE IN A YEAR | DEUTERONOMY 32–34; MARK 15:26–47

Placing his hands on Saul, [Ananias] said, "Brother Saul, the Lord . . . has sent me." [ACTS 9:17]

BROTHER SAUL

"Lord, please send me anywhere but there." That was my prayer as a teenager before embarking on a year as a foreign exchange student. I didn't know where I would be going, but I knew where I *didn't* want to go. I didn't speak that country's language, and my mind was filled with prejudices against its customs and people. So I asked God to send me elsewhere.

But God in His infinite wisdom sent me precisely where I asked not to go. I'm so glad He did! Forty years later, I still have dear friends in that land. When I got married, my best man Stefan came from there. When he got married, I flew there to return the favour. And we're planning another visit soon.

Beautiful things happen when God causes a change of heart! Such a transformation is illustrated by just two words: "Brother Saul" (ACTS 9:17).

Those words were from Ananias, a believer God called to heal Saul's sight immediately after his conversion (VV. 10–12). Ananias resisted at first because of Saul's violent past, praying: "I have heard many reports about this man and all the harm he has done to your holy people" (V. 13).

But Ananias was obedient and went. And because he had a change of heart, Ananias gained a new brother in faith, Saul became known as Paul, and the good news of Jesus spread with power. True change is always possible through Him! *JAMES BANKS*

How have you sensed God calling you to have a change of heart? How can you encourage a new believer today?

Jesus, thank You for changing my heart with Your love. Help me to extend it to others.

BIBLE IN A YEAR | JOSHUA 1–3; MARK 16

I am like a weaned child with its mother; like a weaned child I am content. [PSALM 131:2]

CATCHING CONTENTMENT

I n a doctor's advice column, he responded to a reader named Brenda, who lamented that her ambitious pursuits had left her discontented. His words were blunt. Humans aren't designed to be happy, he said, "only to survive and reproduce." We're cursed to chase the "teasing and elusive butterfly" of contentment, he added, "not always to capture it."

I wonder how Brenda felt reading those nihilistic words and how different she may have felt had she read Psalm 131 instead. In its words, David gives us a guided reflection on how to find contentment. He begins in a posture of humility, putting his kingly ambitions aside, and while wrestling life's big questions is important, he puts those aside too (V. 1). Then he quiets his heart before God (V. 2), entrusting the future into His hands (V. 3). The result is beautiful: "like a weaned child with its mother," he says, "I am content" (V. 2).

In a broken world like ours, contentment will at times feel elusive. In Philippians 4:11–13, the apostle Paul said contentment is something to be *learned*. But if we believe we're only designed to "survive and reproduce," contentment will surely be an uncatchable butterfly. David shows us another way: catching contentment through quietly resting in God's presence.

SHERIDAN VOYSEY

When do you most feel content? How could you set aside unhurried time to be quietly present with God today?

Dear God, I rest in You, the deepest well of my truest contentment.

BIBLE IN A YEAR | JOSHUA 4–6; LUKE 1:1–20

Though outwardly we are wasting away, yet
inwardly we are being renewed day by day.
[2 CORINTHIANS 4:16]

SPIRITUAL RENEWAL

Chinese medicine has practised pearl powder exfoliation
for thousands of years, using ground pearls to scrub away
dead cells resting at the top of the skin. In Romania, re-
juvenating therapeutic mud has become a widely sought-after
exfoliant that's purported to make skin youthful and glowing. All
over the world, people use body care practices they believe will
renew even the dullest of skin.

The tools we've developed to maintain our physical bodies, however, can only bring us temporary satisfaction. What
matters more is that we remain spiritually healthy and strong.
As believers in Jesus, we're given the gift of spiritual renewal
through Him. The apostle Paul wrote, "Though outwardly we
are wasting away, yet inwardly we are being renewed day by
day" (2 CORINTHIANS 4:16). The challenges we face daily can weigh
us down when we hold on to things like fear, hurt and anxiety.
Spiritual renewal comes when we "fix our eyes not on what is
seen, but on what is unseen" (V. 18). We do this by turning our
daily worries over to God and praying for the fruit of the Holy
Spirit—including love, joy and peace—to emerge anew in our
lives (GALATIANS 5:22–23). When we release our troubles to God
and allow His Spirit to radiate through us each day, He restores
our souls.   *KIMYA LODER*

**How can you ask God to renew your spirit? How does the
work of the Holy Spirit encourage you today?**

*Jesus, each day I face obstacles that try to break my spirit.
Sometimes I feel defeated, but I know that through You my
spirit can be renewed.*

BIBLE IN A YEAR | JOSHUA 7-9; LUKE 1:21-38

God had finished the work . . . so on the
seventh day he rested from all his work.
[GENESIS 2:2]

PERMISSION TO REST

We sat on some rocks on the beach, my friend Susy and I, watching the foam send up sea spray in arched curls. Looking at the incoming waves crashing one after another against the rocks, Susy announced, "I love the ocean. It keeps moving so I don't have to!"

Isn't it interesting how some of us feel we need 'permission' to pause from our work to rest? Well, that's just what our good God offers us! For six days, God spun the earth into existence, creating light, land, vegetation, animals and humans. Then on the seventh day, He rested (GENESIS 1:31–2:2). In the Ten Commandments, God listed His rules for healthy living to honour Him (EXODUS 20:3–17), including the command to remember the Sabbath as a day of rest (VV. 8–11). In the New Testament we see Jesus healing all the sick of the town (MARK 1:29–34) and then early the next morning retreating to a solitary place to pray (V. 35). Purposefully, our God both worked and rested.

The rhythm of God's provision in work and His invitation to rest reverberates around us. Spring's planting yields growth in summer, harvest in autumn, and rest in winter. Morning, noon, afternoon, evening, night. God orders our lives for both work and rest, offering us permission to do both.   *ELISA MORGAN*

*How would you assess the balance in your life between
work and rest? When and how might you pause each day
to reflect on God's example of rhythm and rest?*

*Dear God, thank You that You made me to follow after Your
heart, to both work and rest for Your glory and my good.*

The law of the LORD is perfect,
refreshing the soul. [PSALM 19:7]

WHY DO THIS?

As I was helping my twelve-year-old grandson, Logan, with some tough algebra-type homework, he told me of his dream of becoming an engineer. After we returned to figuring out what to do with the *x*'s and *y*'s in his assignment, he said, "When am I ever going to use this stuff?"

I couldn't help but smile, saying, "Well, Logan, this is exactly the stuff you'll use if you become an engineer!" He hadn't realised the connection between algebra and his hoped-for future.

Sometimes we view Scripture that way. When we listen to sermons and read certain parts of the Bible, we may think, "When am I ever going to use this?" The psalmist David had some answers. He said God's truths found in Scripture are effective for "refreshing the soul", "making wise the simple" and "giving joy to the heart" (PSALM 19:7–8). The wisdom of Scripture, found in the first five books of the Bible as referred to in Psalm 19 (as well as all of Scripture), helps us as we daily rely on the Spirit's leading (PROVERBS 2:6).

And without the Scriptures, we'd lack the vital way God has provided for us to experience Him and better know His love and ways. Why study the Bible? Because "the commands of the LORD are radiant, giving light to the eyes" (PSALM 19:8). *DAVE BRANON*

Why is the wisdom found in Scripture relevant for you today? How can you grow in your understanding of it?

Loving God, please make Your Word a light to my path. Help me to use the wisdom of Scripture to direct my steps and grow to love You more.

BIBLE IN A YEAR | JOSHUA 13–15; LUKE 1:57–80

I commit you to God and to the word of his grace, which can build you up and give you an inheritance among all those who are sanctified. [ACTS 20:32]

RECOGNISING GOD'S VOICE

After years of research, scientists have learned that wolves have distinct voices that help them communicate with each other. Using a specific sound analysis code, one scientist realised that various volumes and pitches in a wolf's howl enabled her to identify specific wolves with 100 percent accuracy.

The Bible provides many examples of God recognising the distinct voices of His beloved creations. He called Moses by name and spoke to him directly (EXODUS 3:4–6). The psalmist David proclaimed, "I call out to the LORD, and he answers me from his holy mountain" (PSALM 3:4). The apostle Paul also emphasised the value of God's people recognising His voice.

When bidding farewell to the Ephesian elders, Paul said the Spirit had "compelled" him to head to Jerusalem. He confirmed his commitment to follow God's voice, though he didn't know what to expect upon his arrival (ACTS 20:22). The apostle warned that "savage wolves" would "arise and distort the truth," even from within the church (VV. 29–30). Then, he encouraged the elders to remain diligent in discerning God's truth (V. 31).

All believers in Jesus have the privilege of knowing that God hears and answers us. We also have the power of the Holy Spirit who helps us recognise God's voice, which is always in alignment with the words of Scripture.   *XOCHITL DIXON*

What false teaching has God helped you combat as you studied Scripture? When has He used the Bible to encourage you?

God, when the noise of the world around me threatens to make me wander from You, please help me recognise and obey Your voice.

BIBLE IN A YEAR | JOSHUA 16–18; LUKE 2:1–24

Because of the LORD's great love we are not consumed, for his compassions never fail. They are new every morning; great is your faithfulness. [LAMENTATIONS 3:22–23]

THE REBOOT OF GRACE

O ver the last several decades, a new word has entered our movie vocabulary: *reboot*. In cinematic parlance, a reboot takes an old story and jumpstarts it. Some reboots retell a familiar tale, like a superhero story or a fairy tale. Other reboots take a lesser-known story and retell it in a new way. But in each case, a reboot is a bit like a fresh start; it's a chance to breathe new life into the old.

There's another story that involves reboots—the gospel story. In it, Jesus invites us to His offer of forgiveness, as well as abundant and eternal life (JOHN 10:10). And in the book of Lamentations, Jeremiah reminds us that God's love for us makes every day a 'reboot' of sorts: "Because of the LORD's great love we are not consumed, for his compassions never fail. They are new every morning; great is your faithfulness" (3:22–23).

God's grace invites us to embrace each day as a fresh opportunity to experience His faithfulness. Whether we're struggling with the effects of our own mistakes or going through other hardships, God's Spirit can breathe forgiveness, new life and hope into each new day. Every day is a reboot of sorts, an opportunity to follow the lead of the great Director, who is weaving our story into His bigger one.   *ADAM R. HOLZ*

> *How do you think reflecting upon and remembering God's faithfulness in the midst of trials changes your perspective on them? How has God's forgiveness and grace brought a reboot to your life?*

Father, thank You that Your grace and forgiveness invite me to start over, fresh, every morning.

BIBLE IN A YEAR | JOSHUA 19–21; LUKE 2:25–52

Jonathan made a covenant with David because
he loved him as himself. [1 SAMUEL 18:3]

THE TELLING ROOM

Northern Spain produced a beautiful way of expressing communion and friendship. With the countryside full of handmade caves, after each harvest some farmers would sit in a room built above a cave and take an inventory of their various foods. As time passed, the room became known as the "telling room"—a place of communion where friends and families would gather to share their stories, secrets and dreams. If you needed the intimate company of safe friends, you would head for the telling room.

Had they lived in northern Spain, the deep friendship shared by Jonathan and David might have led them to create a telling room. When King Saul became so jealous that he wanted to kill David, Jonathan, Saul's oldest son, protected and befriended him. The two became "one in spirit" (1 SAMUEL 18:1). And Jonathan "loved him as himself" (VV. 1, 3) and—though he was heir apparent to the throne—recognised David's divine selection to be king. He gave David his robe, sword, bow and belt (V. 4). Later, David declared that Jonathan's deep love for him as a friend was wonderful (2 SAMUEL 1:26).

As believers in Jesus, may He help us build our own relational "telling rooms"—friendships that reflect Christ-like love and care. Let's take the time to linger with friends, open our hearts, and live in true communion with one another in Him.

MARVIN WILLIAMS

What kinds of commitments have you made to your friends?
How can you express your love to them this week?

Dear God, please help me to pursue vulnerable, loving and authentic friendships.

BIBLE IN A YEAR | JOSHUA 22-24; LUKE 3

The prayer of a righteous person is powerful
and effective. [JAMES 5:16]

GOD IS LISTENING

Charles, an actor and martial artist, honoured his mother on her hundredth birthday by sharing how instrumental she'd been in his spiritual transformation. "Mum has been an example of perseverance and faith," he wrote. She raised three boys on her own during the Great Depression; suffered the death of two spouses, a son, a stepson and grandchildren; and endured many surgeries. "[She] has prayed for me all my life, through thick and thin." He continued, "When nearly losing my soul to Hollywood, she was back home praying for my success and salvation." He concluded, "I thank [my mum] for helping God to make me all I can and should be."

The prayers of Charles' mother helped him to find salvation—and a godly wife. She prayed fervently for her son, and God heard her prayers. We don't always get our prayers answered the way we'd like, so we cannot use prayer as a magic wand. However, James assures us that "the prayer of a righteous person is powerful and effective" (5:16). Like this mum, we're to continue to pray for the sick and those in trouble (VV. 13–15). When, like her, we commune with God through prayer, we find encouragement and peace and the assurance that the Spirit is at work.

Does someone in your life need salvation or healing or help? Lift your prayers to God in faith. He's listening.   *ALYSON KIEDA*

***When have you seen God answer your fervent prayers?
Who continues to be in your prayers?***

Dear Father, help me to continually be in prayer and not to give up. Thank You for Your love that helps me persevere.

Do not be anxious about anything, but in every situation, by prayer and petition, with thanksgiving, present your requests to God. [PHILIPPIANS 4:6]

STRESS TO PEACE

Moving house often ranks as one of the biggest stressors in life. We moved to our current home after I'd lived in my previous one for nearly twenty years. I'd lived alone in that first home for eight years before I got married. Then my husband moved in, along with all his things. Later, we added a child, and that meant even more stuff.

Our moving day to the new house wasn't without incident. Five minutes before the movers arrived, I was still finishing up a book manuscript. And the new home had several sets of stairs, so it took double the time and twice as many movers as planned.

But I wasn't feeling stressed out by the events of that day. Then it hit me: I'd spent many hours finishing writing a book—one filled with Scripture and biblical concepts. By God's grace, I'd been poring over the Bible, praying and writing to meet my deadline. So, I believe the key was my immersion in Scripture and in prayer.

Paul wrote, "Do not be anxious about anything, but in every situation, by prayer and petition, with thanksgiving, present your requests to God" (PHILIPPIANS 4:6). When we pray—and "rejoice in" God (V. 4)—we refocus our mind from the problem to our Provider. We may be asking God to help us deal with a stressor, but we're also connecting with Him, which can provide a peace "which transcends all understanding" (V. 7).   *KATARA PATTON*

What stressful situations do you need God to give you peace in today? How can praying with thanksgiving transform your mind?

Provider and Protector, I give my concerns to You. May Your peace guard my mind and heart.

BIBLE IN A YEAR | JUDGES 4–6; LUKE 4:31–44

Your life is now hidden with Christ in God.
[COLOSSIANS 3:3]

ONE SOCK?

Toby, our five-year-old, loves his fluffy green socks with dragon faces on the toes. But one morning he cried, "I've only got one sock!" Cue the whole family embarking on a house-wide search-and-rescue mission, pulling out drawers, tipping out toy boxes and turning rooms upside down. But without success. Finally, Toby pulled off his dragon sock—to reveal the other one! He had cheekily put both socks onto the same foot, creating the perfect hiding place. We were exasperated and amused in equal measure!

Sometimes we wish we could find such a clever way to hide ourselves—tucked away and completely covered up. But Paul assures us that we *do* have such a refuge: "your life is now hidden with Christ in God" (COLOSSIANS 3:2–3). This profound, mind-boggling truth means that we are covered by Christ, even when we feel ashamed or unworthy. His story is now our story: we have already been "raised with Christ", since "[we] died" with Him by faith (VV. 2–3). His destiny is our destiny: "You also will appear with him in glory" (V. 4).

Be reassured! Whatever we face today, we're not left exposed or alone. Jesus has hidden us safely in Himself. Without wanting to trivialise such a profound truth, we're not unlike that one sock tucked into another—from heaven's viewpoint, all that's seen of our lives is Christ covering us with His story and His righteousness.   *CHRIS WALE*

When you're struggling, what refuge do you tend to run to?
What does being perfectly hidden in Christ mean to you?

Covering Jesus, thank You for being my perfect hiding place. I choose to take refuge in You today, knowing that You will meet all my needs.

BIBLE IN A YEAR | JUDGES 7–8; LUKE 5:1–16

I do not do the good I want to do, . . .
I keep on doing [evil]. [ROMANS 7:19]

TO DO OR NOT TO DO

When I was a kid, a decommissioned World War II tank was put on display in a park near my home. Multiple signs warned of the danger of climbing on the vehicle, but a couple of my friends immediately scrambled up. Some of us were a bit reluctant, but eventually we did the same. One boy refused, pointing to the posted signs. Another jumped down quickly as an adult approached. The temptation to have fun outweighed our desire to follow rules.

There's a heart of childish rebellion lurking within all of us. We don't like being told what to do or not to do. Yet we read in James that when we know what is right and don't do it—it is sin (4:17). In Romans, the apostle Paul wrote: "I do not do the good I want to do, but the evil I do not want to do—this I keep on doing. Now if I do what I do not want to do, it is no longer I who do it, but it is sin living in me that does it" (7:19–20).

As believers in Jesus, we may puzzle over our struggle with sin. But too often we depend solely on our own strength to do what's right. One day, when this life is over, we'll be truly dead to sinful impulses. Until then, however, we can rely on the power of the One who's death and resurrection won the victory over sin.

CINDY HESS KASPER

> **What sins are the biggest struggle for you? How can you rely more on God's power to overcome their stronghold?**
>
> *Loving God, please help me to choose to do what's right. My heart's desire is to reflect Your perfect character and holy ways.*

You will keep in perfect peace those whose minds are steadfast, because they trust in You. [ISAIAH 26:3]

REST ASSURED IN GOD

Researchers in Fujian, China, wanted to help intensive care unit (ICU) patients sleep more soundly. They measured the effects of sleep aids on test subjects in a simulated ICU environment, complete with bright, hospital-grade lighting and audio recordings of machines beeping and nurses talking. Their research showed that tools like sleep masks and ear plugs improved their subjects' rest. But they acknowledged that for truly sick patients in a real ICU, peaceful sleep would still be hard to come by.

When our world is troubled, how can we find rest? The Bible's clear: there's peace for those who trust in God, regardless of their circumstances. The prophet Isaiah wrote about a future time when the ancient Israelites would be restored after hardship. They would live securely in their city, because they knew that God made it safe (ISAIAH 26:1). They would trust that He was actively working in the world around them to bring good—"He humbles those who dwell on high," raising up the oppressed, and bringing justice (VV. 5–6). They would know that "the LORD himself, is the Rock eternal," and they could trust Him forever (V. 4).

"You will keep in perfect peace those whose minds are steadfast," wrote Isaiah, "because they trust in you" (V. 3). God can provide peace and rest for us today as well. We can rest in the assurance of His love and power, no matter what's going on around us.   *KAREN PIMPO*

What threatens to overwhelm you today? How can you remind yourself of God's power and love?

Dear God, I trust You and choose to rest assured in Your love today.

BIBLE IN A YEAR | JUDGES 11–12; LUKE 6:1–26

FROM BITTERNESS TO FORGIVENESS

I didn't mean to grow up bitter. But my skin colour made me a target. In school, one teacher even called me "Nobody." The result? Bitterness. I knew Jesus, but I also knew hurt. Its sting fertilised my bitterness which, like a weed "springs up and causes trouble" (HEBREWS 12:15 ESV).

So, while I loved God and believed He loved me, my bitterness stood between us. I'd forgotten the Bible's call to "make every effort to live in peace with everyone and to be holy; without holiness no one will see the Lord" (V. 14).

Instead, I was obsessed with racial hatred, ignoring Paul's call to "get rid of all bitterness, rage and anger, brawling and slander, along with every form of malice" (EPHESIANS 4:31). But how? God reveals three ways:

Take your bitterness to Him. Ask Him to banish it. In reply, I heard God say, "Forgive." But how?

Ask God to teach you. In fact, forgiveness isn't an act, it's a process. As scholar Lewis Smedes explained, forgiveness doesn't excuse offenders; it means "we are ready to be healed." How?

Rely on the Holy Spirit's great power. Then His work in us becomes His witness. Indeed, "But you will receive power when the Holy Spirit comes on you; and you will be my witnesses . . . to the ends of the earth (ACTS 1:8).

As God does His work in us, a bitter root can bloom—in Christ—into a beautiful flower. True, our 'soil' will always need weeding. But God's love can turn our bitter sin into grace.

Patricia Raybon, *Our Daily Bread* author

★ Scripture reveals that believers in Jesus are to forgive as God in Christ has forgiven us. But what does this look like, especially when it's hard to forgive? The topic is addressed in the devotions for **April 1, 8, 15** and **22**.

Oh, what joy for those . . . whose sin is put
out of sight! [PSALM 32:1 (NLT)]

MORE THAN SKIN DEEP

José, a young believer in Jesus, was visiting his brother's church. As he entered the sanctuary prior to the service, his brother's face fell when he saw him. José's tattoos, covering both arms, were visible since he was wearing a T-shirt. His brother told him to go home and put on a long-sleeved shirt, for many of José's tattoos reflected the ways of his past. José suddenly felt dirty. But another man overheard the brothers' interaction and brought José to the pastor, telling him what had happened. The pastor smiled and unbuttoned his shirt, revealing a large tattoo on his chest—something from his own past. He assured José that because God had made him pure from the inside out, he didn't need to cover his arms.

David experienced the joy of being made pure by God. After confessing his sin to Him, the king wrote, "Oh, what joy for those whose disobedience is forgiven, whose sin is put out of sight!" (PSALM 32:1 NLT). He could now "shout for joy" with others "whose hearts are pure!" (V. 11 NLT). The apostle Paul later quoted Psalm 32:1–2 in Romans 4:7–8, a passage declaring that faith in Jesus leads to salvation and a pure standing before Him (SEE ROMANS 4:23–25).

Our purity in Jesus is much more than skin deep, for He knows and purifies our hearts (1 SAMUEL 16:7; 1 JOHN 1:9). May we rejoice in His purifying work today.   *TOM FELTEN*

***What past sins have you struggled with? What does it
mean to be transformed and purified by faith in Jesus?***

*Jesus, thank You for forgiving my sins and making
me pure within.*

BIBLE IN A YEAR | JUDGES 13–15; LUKE 6:27–49

I tell you, . . . if they keep quiet, the stones
will cry out. [LUKE 19:40]

BLUESTONE CHURCH BELLS

Bluestone is a fascinating variety of rock. When struck, certain bluestones will ring with a musical tone. Maenclochog, a Welsh village whose name means "bell" or "ringing stones", used bluestones as church bells until the eighteenth century. Interestingly, the ruins of Stonehenge, in England, are built of bluestone, causing some to wonder if that landmark's original purpose was musical. Some researchers claim that the bluestone at Stonehenge was brought from near Maenclochog, nearly two hundred miles away, because of their unique acoustic properties.

Musical ringing stones are yet another of the wonders of God's great creation, and they remind us of something Jesus said during His Palm Sunday entry into Jerusalem. As the people praised Jesus, the religious leaders demanded Him to rebuke them. " 'I tell you,' he replied, 'if they keep quiet, the stones will cry out' " (LUKE 19:40).

If bluestone can make music, and if Jesus made mention of even the stones bearing witness to their Creator, how might we express our own praise to the One who made us, loves us and rescued us? He is worthy of all worship. May the Holy Spirit stir us to give Him the honour He deserves. All of creation praises Him.

BILL CROWDER

**How many ways can you think of in which creation praises
God? How can you join in daily worship of our Creator?**

*Creator God, You are deserving of all worship, praise and
gratitude. When my heart grows hard and I lose sight of Your
worthiness, remind me that all creation sings Your praise.*

BIBLE IN A YEAR | JUDGES 16–18; LUKE 7:1-30

🔖 **2 CORINTHIANS 12:9-10**

THURSDAY | 3 APRIL

I will boast all the more gladly about my weaknesses, so that Christ's power may rest on me. [2 CORINTHIANS 12:9]

FINDING STRENGTH IN GOD

Football player Christian Pulisic faced several injuries that influenced his career. After learning he wouldn't be in the starting line-up of the Champions League semi-finals game, he was disappointed, but he described how God had revealed Himself to him. "As always, I reach out to God, and He gives me strength," he said. "I feel like I always have Someone who's with me. I don't know how I would do any of this without that feeling." Pulisic ultimately made a momentous impact when he was substituted later in the game. He initiated a clever play that led to the match-winning goal and secured their spot in the final. These experiences taught him a valuable lesson: we can always view our weaknesses as opportunities for God to reveal His immeasurable power.

The world teaches us to rely on our own strength when encountering problems. However, biblical wisdom teaches us that God's grace and power give us strength in the most trying circumstances (2 CORINTHIANS 12:9). Therefore, we can move in confidence, recognising that we never face trials alone. Our "weaknesses" become opportunities for God to reveal His power, strengthening and supporting us (VV. 9–10). We can then use our struggles to offer praise to God, giving thanks for His goodness and sharing these encounters with others so that they can come to experience His love.

KIMYA LODER

When have you tried to overcome a struggle on your own? How can you look to God for strength?

Dear heavenly Father, thank You for being the source of my strength and guiding me each day.

BIBLE IN A YEAR | JUDGES 19–21; LUKE 7:31–50

Remain in me, as I also remain in you.
[JOHN 15:4]

AT HOME IN JESUS

Several years ago, we brought home an adult black cat named Juno from the local animal shelter. Truthfully, I only wanted help thinning our mice population, but the rest of the family wanted a pet. The shelter gave us rigorous instructions on how to establish a feeding routine that first week so Juno would learn our house was his home, the place he belonged and where he'd always have food and safety. This way, even if Juno might roam, he would always eventually come home.

If we don't know our true home, we're forever tempted to roam in vain search for goodness, love and meaning. If we want to find our true life, however, Jesus said, "Abide in me" (JOHN 15:4 ESV). Biblical scholar Frederick Dale Bruner highlights how *abide* (like a similar word, *abode*) evokes a sense of family and home. So Bruner translates Jesus' words this way: "Stay at home in me."

To drive this idea home, Jesus used the illustration of branches attached to a vine. Branches, if they want to live, must always stay at home, tenaciously fixed (*abiding*) where they belong.

There are many voices beckoning us with hollow promises to fix our problems or provide us with some new 'wisdom' or exhilarating future. But if we're to truly live, we must remain in Jesus. We must stay at home. *WINN COLLIER*

> **What pulls you away from your home in Jesus? How has Jesus shown Himself to be your true source of life?**
>
> *Jesus, I like to roam. I'm pulled in all kinds of directions. But I want to stay at home with You. You're my life. Help me to abide in You.*

BIBLE IN A YEAR | RUTH 1-4; LUKE 8:1-25

Whoever wants to be my disciple must deny
themselves and take up their cross and follow me.
[MATTHEW 16:24]

MORE THAN A LITTLE PIECE

We all leave a bit of ourselves behind when we move to a new place. But to become a long-term resident of Villas Las Estrellas, Antarctica, a cold and desolate place, leaving a piece of yourself behind is a literal thing. With the nearest hospital 625 miles away, a person will be in serious trouble if their appendix bursts. So every citizen must first undergo an appendectomy before moving there.

Drastic, right? But it's not as drastic as becoming a resident of the kingdom of God. Because people want to follow Jesus on their own terms and not His (MATTHEW 16:25–27), He redefines what it means to be a disciple. He said, "Whoever wants to be my disciple must deny themselves and take up their cross and follow me" (V. 24). This includes being prepared to let go of anything that competes with Him and His kingdom. And as we take up our cross, we declare a willingness to undergo social and political oppression and even death for the sake of devotion to Christ. Along with *letting go* and *taking up*, we're also to *take on* a willingness to truly follow Him. This is a moment-by-moment posture of following His lead as He guides us into service and sacrifice.

Following Jesus means so much more than leaving a little piece of our lives behind. As He helps us, it's about submitting and surrendering our whole lives—including our bodies—to Him alone.   *MARVIN WILLIAMS*

What does it mean for you to follow Jesus?
How is He asking you to sacrifice your life for Him?

Dear Jesus, help me give up anything that competes with
You and Your kingdom.

BIBLE IN A YEAR | 1 SAMUEL 1–3; LUKE 8:26-56

The Son of Man did not come to be
served, but to serve. [MATTHEW 20:28]

THE CHALLENGE TO SERVE

Although just thirteen years old, DeAvion took up a challenge to serve others. He and his mum had heard a story about a man who called on kids to mow fifty lawns for free during their summer holidays. Their focus was to assist the elderly, single mums, people with disabilities—or anyone who just needed help. The founder created the challenge to teach the importance of work ethic and giving back to the community. Despite the heat and the availability of other activities a teenager could pursue in the summer, DeAvion chose to serve others and completed the challenge.

The challenge to serve comes to believers in Jesus as well. The evening before He would die for all people, Jesus ate dinner with His friends (JOHN 13:1–2). He was well aware of the suffering and death He would soon encounter, yet He got up from the meal, wrapped a towel around Himself and began to wash His disciples' feet (VV. 3–5). "Now that I, your Lord and Teacher, have washed your feet, you also should wash one another's feet," He said (V. 14).

Jesus, the humble Servant and our example, cared for people: He healed the blind and sick, taught the good news of His kingdom and gave His life for His friends. Because Christ loves you, ask Him who He wants you to serve this week.   *ANNE CETAS*

> **What about God's love and compassion means the
> most to you? How can you use your gifts and talents
> to serve others?**
>
> *Dear God, show me how to love others with the same
> love You have for me.*

BIBLE IN A YEAR | 1 SAMUEL 4–6; LUKE 9:1–17

His sweat was like drops of blood falling
to the ground. [LUKE 22:44]

DROPS OF RED

Walking through the Scottish National Gallery, I was drawn to the strong brushwork and vibrant colours of one of many *Olive Trees* paintings by Dutch artist Vincent van Gogh. Many historians believe the work was inspired by Jesus' experience in the garden of Gethsemane on the Mount of Olives. What especially caught my eye on the canvas of the painting were the small red splotches of paint among the ancient trees.

Known as the Mount of Olives because of all the olive trees located on the mountainside, Jesus went there to pray on the night that He predicted His disciple Judas would betray Him. Jesus was overwhelmed with anguish knowing the betrayal would result in His crucifixion. As He prayed, "his sweat was like drops of blood falling to the ground" (LUKE 22:44). Jesus' agony was evident in the garden as He prepared for the pain and humiliation of a public execution that would result in the physical shedding of His blood on that Good Friday long ago.

The red paint on Van Gogh's painting reminds us that Jesus had to "suffer many things and be rejected" (MARK 8:31). While suffering is part of His story, however, it no longer dominates the picture. Jesus' victory over death transforms even our suffering, allowing it to become only a part of the beautiful landscape of our lives He's creating.   *LISA M. SAMRA*

*Why is it important for you to remember Jesus' suffering?
How does His example help you when you suffer?*

*Jesus, thank You for being willing to suffer, even to death,
so that I might receive eternal life.*

BIBLE IN A YEAR | 1 SAMUEL 7-9; LUKE 9:18-36

Both were running, but the other disciple
outran Peter and reached the tomb first.
[JOHN 20:4]

RUNNING TO JESUS

O n a trip to Paris, Ben and his friends found themselves at
one of the renowned museums in the city. Though Ben
wasn't a student of art, he was in awe as he looked upon
the painting titled *The Disciples Peter and John Running to the
Sepulchre on the Morning of the Resurrection* by Eugène Bur-
nand. Without words, the looks on the faces of Peter and John
and the position of their hands speak volumes, inviting onlook-
ers to step into their shoes and share their adrenaline-charged
emotions.

Based on John 20:1–10, the painting portrays the two running
in the direction of the empty tomb of Jesus (V. 4). The masterpiece captures the intensity of the two emotionally conflicted
disciples. Though at that juncture theirs wasn't a fully formed
faith, they were running in the right direction, and eventually
the resurrected Jesus revealed Himself to them (VV. 19–29). Their
search was not unlike that of Jesus seekers through the centuries. Although we may be removed from the experiences of an
empty tomb or a brilliant piece of art, we can clearly see the
good news. Scripture compels us to hope and seek and run in
the direction of Jesus and His love—even with doubts, questions
and uncertainties. Tomorrow, as we celebrate Easter, may we remember God's faithfulness: "You will seek me and find me when
you seek me with all your heart" (JEREMIAH 29:13). *ARTHUR JACKSON*

*If you don't know Jesus, what will you do to begin
running towards Him and His love? If you're a believer,
how will you share His love with others?*

Dear Jesus, lead me into Your loving arms today.

BIBLE IN A YEAR | 1 SAMUEL 10–12; LUKE 9:37–62

By his wounds we are healed.
[ISAIAH 53:5]

DEEPER HEALING

On Easter Sunday 2020, the famous Christ the Redeemer statue that overlooks Rio de Janeiro in Brazil was illuminated in a way that appeared to clothe Jesus in the attire of a doctor. This poignant portrayal of Christ was a tribute to the many frontline health-care workers battling the coronavirus pandemic. The imagery brings to life the common description of Jesus as our Great Physician (MARK 2:17).

Jesus healed many people of their physical afflictions during His earthly ministry: blind Bartimaeus (10:46–52), a leper (LUKE 5:12–16) and a paralytic (MATTHEW 9:1–8), to name a few. His care for the health of those following Him was also demonstrated in providing for their hunger by multiplying a simple meal to feed the masses (JOHN 6:1–13). Each of these miracles reveal both Jesus' mighty power and His genuine love for people.

His greatest act of healing, however, came through His death and resurrection, as foretold by the prophet Isaiah. It is "by [Jesus'] wounds we are healed" of our worst affliction: our separation from God as a result of our sins (ISAIAH 53:5). Though Jesus doesn't heal all our health challenges, we can trust the cure for our deepest need: the healing He brings to our relationship with God.

KIRSTEN HOLMBERG

How have you experienced the miraculous spiritual healing of God? How does your healed relationship through Jesus' sacrifice help you bear up under your physical ailments?

Jesus, thank You for Your sacrifice that brings healing to my spiritual sickness. Help me to trust You in my physical challenges.

BIBLE IN A YEAR | 1 SAMUEL 13–14; LUKE 10:1–24

The LORD said to Gideon, "You have too many men." [JUDGES 7:2]

STRENGTH IN WEAKNESS

When my son was nearly three, I needed an operation that would require a month or more of recovery. Prior to the procedure, I imagined myself in bed while stacks of dirty dishes accumulated in the sink. I wasn't sure how I'd take care of an active toddler and couldn't picture myself standing in front of the stove to cook our meals. I dreaded the impact my weakness would have on the rhythm of our lives.

God intentionally weakened Gideon's forces before his troops confronted the Midianites. Firstly, those who were afraid were allowed to leave—twenty-two thousand men went home (JUDGES 7:3). Then, of the ten thousand who remained, only those who scooped water into their hands to drink could stay. Just three hundred men were left, but this disadvantage prevented the Israelites from relying on themselves (VV. 5–6). They couldn't say, "My own strength has saved me" (V. 2).

Many of us experience times when we feel drained and powerless. When this happened to me, I realised how much I needed God. He encouraged me inwardly through His Spirit and outwardly through the helpfulness of friends and family. I had to let go of my independence for a while, but this taught me how to lean more fully on God. Because "[His] power is made perfect in weakness" (2 CORINTHIANS 12:9), we can have hope when we can't meet our needs on our own.

JENNIFER BENSON SCHULDT

How have you experienced God's power made perfect in your weakness? How could you help someone else who's experiencing weakness?

Dear God, help me to depend on You more and more each day.

BIBLE IN A YEAR | 1 SAMUEL 15-16; LUKE 10:25-42

Do the work of an evangelist.
[2 TIMOTHY 4:5]

SEIZE THE OPPORTUNITY

While waiting to begin university, twenty-year-old Shin Yi decided to commit three months of her break to serving in a youth mission organisation. It seemed like an odd time to do this, given the COVID-19 restrictions that prevented face-to-face meetings. But Shin Yi soon found a way. "We couldn't meet up with students on the streets, in shopping centres, or fast-food outlets like we usually did," she shared. "But we continued to keep in touch with the Christian students via Zoom to pray for one another and with the non-believers via phone calls."

Shin Yi did what the apostle Paul encouraged Timothy to do: "Do the work of an evangelist" (2 TIMOTHY 4:5). Paul warned that people would find teachers who would tell them what they *wanted* to hear and not what they *needed* to hear (VV. 3–4). Yet Timothy was called to take courage and "be prepared in season and out of season." He was to "correct, rebuke and encourage—with great patience and careful instruction" (V. 2).

Though not all of us are called to be evangelists or preachers, each one of us can play a part in sharing our faith with those around us. Unbelievers are perishing without Christ. Believers need strengthening and encouragement. With God's help, let's proclaim His good news whenever and wherever we can.

POH FANG CHIA

What discourages you from sharing your faith? How might remembering that Jesus is coming back help you to overcome your fear?

Dear Jesus, help me to seize every opportunity to share Your words with others that they may find hope and comfort in You.

BIBLE IN A YEAR | 1 SAMUEL 17–18; LUKE 11:1–28

Then Samuel said, "Speak, for your servant is listening." [1 SAMUEL 3:10]

GOD SPEAKING TO US

I received a phone call from an unknown number. Often, I let those calls go to voicemail, but this time I picked up. The random caller asked politely if I had just a minute for him to share a short Bible passage. He quoted Revelation 21:3–5 about how God "will wipe every tear from their eyes." He talked about Jesus, how he was our assurance and hope. I told him I already know Jesus as my personal Saviour. But the caller wasn't aiming to witness to me. Instead, he simply asked if he could pray with me. And he did, asking God to give me encouragement and strength.

That call reminded me of another 'call' in Scripture—God called out to the young boy Samuel in the middle of the night (1 SAMUEL 3:4–10). Three times Samuel heard the voice, thinking it was the elderly priest Eli. The final time, following Eli's instruction, Samuel realised that God was calling him: "Speak, for your servant is listening" (V. 10). Likewise, through our days and nights, God may be speaking to us. We need to 'pick up', which might mean spending more time in His presence and listening for His voice.

I then thought of 'the call' in another way. What if *we* sometimes are the messenger of God's words to someone else? We might feel we have no way of helping others. But as God guides us, we could phone a friend and ask, "Would it be okay if I just prayed with you today?" KENNETH PETERSEN

What message of encouragement did someone recently share with you? Who might be encouraged by a phone call from you?

Dear God, prompt me to think of others whom I can encourage with Your wisdom.

BIBLE IN A YEAR | 1 SAMUEL 19-21; LUKE 11:29-54

Sing the praises of the LORD, you his faithful people; praise his holy name. [PSALM 30:4]

TEARS OF PRAISE

Years ago, I cared for my mum as she was in hospice. I thanked God for the four months He allowed me to serve as her carer and asked Him to help me through the grieving process. I often struggled to praise God as I wrestled with my mixed emotions. But as my mum breathed her last breath and I wept uncontrollably, I whispered, "Hallelujah." I felt guilty for praising God in that devastating moment until, years later, I took a closer look at Psalm 30.

In David's song "for the dedication of the temple," he worshipped God for His faithfulness and mercy (VV. 1–3). He encouraged others to "praise his holy name" (V. 4). Then David explored how intimately God entwines hardship and hope (V. 5). He acknowledged times of grief and rejoicing, times of feeling secure and being dismayed (VV. 6–7). His cries for help remained laced with confidence in God (VV. 7–10). The echo of his praise wove through David's moments of wailing and dancing, grief and joy (V. 11). As if acknowledging the mystery and complexity of enduring affliction and anticipating God's faithfulness, David proclaimed his endless devotion to God (V. 12).

Like David, we can sing, "LORD my God, I will praise you forever" (V. 12). Whether we're happy or hurting, God can help us declare our trust in Him and lead us to worship Him with joyful shouts and tears of praise.   *XOCHITL DIXON*

How has God helped you trust Him with your mixed emotions? How can you praise Him while still processing hardship?

Dear God, please help me trust You and praise You as I process my emotions.

BIBLE IN A YEAR | 1 SAMUEL 22–24; LUKE 12:1–31

Let him do to me whatever seems good
to him. [2 SAMUEL 15:26]

UPHILL ALL THE WAY

Christina Rossetti, a poet and devotional writer, found that
nothing came easily for her. She suffered from depression
and various illnesses throughout her life and endured
three broken engagements. Eventually she died of cancer.

When David burst into Israel's national consciousness, it was
as a triumphant warrior. Yet throughout his life, David faced hardship. Late in his reign, his own son, along with his trusted advisor
and much of the country, turned against him (2 SAMUEL 15:1–12).
So David took the priests Abiathar and Zadok and the sacred ark
of God with him and fled Jerusalem (VV. 14, 24).

After Abiathar had offered sacrifices to God, David told the
priests, "Take the ark of God back into the city. If I find favour
in the LORD's eyes, he will bring me back and let me see it and
his dwelling place again" (V. 25). Despite the uncertainty, David
said, "If [God] says, 'I am not pleased with you,' . . . let him do
to me whatever seems good to him" (V. 26). He knew he could
trust God.

Christina Rossetti trusted God too, and her life ended in hope.
The road may indeed wind uphill all the way, but it leads to our
heavenly Father, who awaits us with open arms.   *TIM GUSTAFSON*

> *In what ways has life seemed uphill and winding to you?*
> *How will you trust God to lead you on the road you're*
> *travelling?*
>
> *Dear God, this life seems so hard sometimes. Yet I trust You*
> *to do what's right, for me and for everyone. Help me live in*
> *Your hope, anticipating the day I'll be with You.*

BIBLE IN A YEAR | 1 SAMUEL 25-26; LUKE 12:32-59

Be kind and compassionate to one another,
forgiving each other, just as in Christ God
forgave you. [EPHESIANS 4:32]

RECONCILING RELATIONSHIPS

My sister and I clashed frequently when we were younger,
but one time especially stands out in my memory. After
a bout of yelling back and forth where we'd both said
hurtful things, she said something that in the moment seemed
unforgivable. Witnessing the animosity growing between us,
my grandmother reminded us of our responsibility to love each
other: "God gave you one sister in life. You've got to show each
other a little grace," she said. When we asked God to fill us with
love and understanding, He helped us acknowledge how we'd
hurt each other and to forgive one another.

It can be so easy to hold on to bitterness and anger, but
God desires for us to experience the peace that can only come
when we ask Him to help us release feelings of resentment
(EPHESIANS 4:31). Instead of harbouring these feelings, we can
look to Christ's example of forgiveness that comes from a place
of love and grace, striving to be "kind and compassionate" and
to "[forgive] each other, just as in Christ God forgave [us]" (V. 32).
When we find it challenging to forgive, may we consider the
grace that He extends to us each day. No matter how many times
we fall short, His compassion never fails (LAMENTATIONS 3:22). God
can help us remove bitterness from our hearts, so we're free to
remain hopeful and receptive to His love.   *KIMYA LODER*

**When has someone hurt you? What did you learn from
that moment?**

*Heavenly Father, thank You for the people You've placed in
my life. Help me to have a loving and forgiving spirit.*

BIBLE IN A YEAR | 1 SAMUEL 27-29; LUKE 13:1-22

Greater love has no one than this: to
lay down one's life for one's friends.
[JOHN 15:13]

GREATER LOVE

Just days before Holy Week, when Christians around the world remember Jesus' sacrifice and celebrate His resurrection, a terrorist stormed into a supermarket in southwest France opening fire and killing two. After negotiation, the terrorist released all but one hostage, whom he turned into a human shield. Knowing the danger, police officer Arnaud Beltrame did the unthinkable: he volunteered to take the woman's place. The perpetrator released her, but in the ensuing scuffle Beltrame was injured and later died.

A minister who knew the police officer attributed his heroism to his faith in Jesus, pointing to His words in John 15:13: "Greater love has no one than this: to lay down one's life for one's friends." Those were the words Christ spoke to His disciples after their last meal together. He told His friends to "Love each other as I have loved you" (V. 12) and that the greatest love is to lay down one's life for another (V. 13). This is exactly what Jesus did the next day, when He went to the cross to save us from our sin—as only He could.

We may never be called to follow the heroism of Arnaud Beltrame. But as we remain in God's love, we can serve others sacrificially, laying down our own plans and desires as we seek to share the story of His great love.   *AMY BOUCHER PYE*

How do you react to stories such as that of Arnaud Beltrame? How can you serve someone sacrificially today?

Dear Jesus, You died to give me life everlasting. May I live with gratitude for this gift and share it with those you put in my path.

BIBLE IN A YEAR | 1 SAMUEL 30–31; LUKE 13:23–35

I will tell of the kindnesses of the LORD.
[ISAIAH 63:7]

REMEMBERING TO PRAISE

When our congregation built our first building, people wrote thankful reminders on the wall studs and concrete floors before the interior of the building was finished. Pull back the drywall from the studs and you'll find them there. Verse after verse from Scripture, written beside prayers of praise like "You are so good!" We left them there as a witness to future generations that regardless of our challenges, God had been kind and taken care of us.

We need to remember what God has done for us and tell others about it. Isaiah exemplified this when he wrote, "I will tell of the kindnesses of the LORD, the deeds for which he is to be praised, according to all the LORD has done for us" (ISAIAH 63:7). Later, the prophet also recounts God's compassion for His people throughout history, even telling how "in all their distress he too was distressed" (V. 9). But if you keep reading the chapter, you'll notice Israel is again in a time of trouble, and the prophet longs for God's intervention.

Remembering God's past kindnesses helps when times are hard. Challenging seasons come and go, but His faithful character never changes. As we turn to Him with grateful hearts in remembrance of all He's done, we discover afresh that He's always worthy of our praise. *JAMES BANKS*

What kindnesses has God shown you in the past? How does praising Him for them help you when you're going through challenging times?

Father, You're sovereign over all creation. I praise You because Your goodness doesn't change, and You're always with me.

BIBLE IN A YEAR | 2 SAMUEL 1-2; LUKE 14:1-24

These are written that you may believe that Jesus
is the Messiah, the Son of God. [JOHN 20:31]

TO BELIEVE

"Loch Ness Monster Caught on Camera" exclaimed the
article headline, reporting how the webcam of a "Monster Spotter" had picked up a "very large dark shape"
swimming across Loch Ness. It was big enough to be considered
the fifth official "sighting" of Nessie that year. But one person,
considering the low quality of the footage, commented, "I want
this to be Nessie, but I reckon it's natural phenomena."

I wonder if Thomas had his own "I want this, but I reckon"
moment when the disciples reported, "We have seen the Lord!"
(JOHN 20:25). Despite Jesus' empty tomb, Thomas needed evidence, saying emphatically: "I will not believe" (V. 25). Thomas
wasn't unreasonable in doubting Jesus' resurrection. After all,
his friends' story probably sounded just as fanciful to him as a
monster in a Scottish loch would to us. But then Jesus showed
up. Understanding Thomas' doubts, Jesus wanted to deepen his
faith in Him and to strengthen their relationship (V. 27).

We may have our own "I want this, but I reckon" questions
about Jesus' life, death and resurrection—or even of His love
for us. We can trust that just as Jesus turned up for Thomas,
He'll reveal Himself to us too. As we dwell in the Scriptures,
our faith will be strengthened so "that [we] may believe" (V. 31).
Then we will gain the confidence to respond: "My Lord and my
God" (V. 28).　　　　　　　　　　　　　　　　　　*CHRIS WALE*

*How do you feel about Jesus' life, death and resurrection? Who
could help you explore Scripture more deeply in these areas?*

*Lord God, thank You for knowing and understanding my
doubts and questions. Where my faith feels small and weak,
strengthen me with Your presence and the truth of Your Word.*

BIBLE IN A YEAR | 2 SAMUEL 3-5; LUKE 14:25-35

"For whom am I toiling," he asked, "and
why am I depriving myself of enjoyment?"
[ECCLESIASTES 4:8]

RENT-A-FRIEND?

For many around the world, life is getting lonelier. In some parts of the world, the number of people who have no friends has quadrupled since 1990. Certain European countries have up to 20 percent of their population feeling lonely. In Japan, some elderly folks have resorted to crime so they can have the companionship of inmates in jail.

Entrepreneurs have come up with a 'solution' to this loneliness epidemic—rent-a-friend. Hired by the hour, these people will meet you in a café to talk or accompany you to a party. One such 'friend' was asked who her clientele was. "Lonely, 30- to 40-year-old professionals," she said, "who work long hours and don't have time to make many friends."

Ecclesiastes 4 describes a person who is all alone, without "son nor brother". There's "no end" to this worker's toil, yet his success isn't fulfilling (V. 8). "For whom am I toiling . . . ?" he asks, waking up to his plight. Far better to invest in relationships, which will make his workload lighter and provide help in trouble (VV. 9–12). Because, ultimately, success without friendship is "meaningless" (V. 8).

Ecclesiastes tells us that a cord of three strands isn't quickly broken (V. 12). But neither is it quickly woven. Since true friends can't be rented, let's invest the time needed to form them, with God as our third strand, weaving us tightly together.

SHERIDAN VOYSEY

How are you investing time and effort into your friendships?
Who could you welcome into your friendship group now?

Father, help me to be a good and loyal friend to others.

BIBLE IN A YEAR | 2 SAMUEL 6–8; LUKE 15:1–10

Forgetting what is behind and straining
towards what is ahead, I press on.
[PHILIPPIANS 3:13–14]

PRESSING ON IN JESUS

O n a run in the forest, I tried to find a shortcut and went down an unfamiliar path. Wondering if I was lost, I asked a runner coming the other way if I was on the right track. "Yup," he replied confidently. Seeing my doubtful look, he quickly added: "Don't worry, I've tried all the wrong routes! But that's okay, it's all part of the run."

What an apt description of my spiritual journey! How many times have I strayed from God, given in to temptation, and been distracted by the things of life? Yet God has forgiven me each time and helped me to move on—knowing I will certainly stumble again. God knows our tendency to go down the wrong path. But He's always ready to forgive, again and again, if we confess our sins and allow His Spirit to transform us.

Paul too knew this was all part of the journey of faith. Fully aware of his sinful past and current weaknesses, he knew he had yet to obtain the Christlike perfection he desired (PHILIPPIANS 3:12). "But one thing I do," he added, "forgetting what is behind and straining towards what is ahead, I press on" (VV. 13–14). Stumbling is still part of our walk with God: even in our mistakes, He refines us. His grace enables us to press on, as forgiven children.   *LESLIE KOH*

> ***What mistakes can you confess to God today? How can His assurance of forgiveness help you to press on in your walk of faith?***
>
> *Thank You, God, for Your mercy. Help me to lead a life that pleases You, knowing that Your Spirit is working in me to transform me into Your Son's likeness.*

BIBLE IN A YEAR | 2 SAMUEL 9–11; LUKE 15:11–32

In his hand are the depths of the earth.
[PSALM 95:4]

DISCOVERING CREATION

Krubera-Voronja, in the Eurasian country of Georgia, is one of the deepest caves yet explored on planet Earth. A team of explorers have probed the dark and scary depths of its mostly vertical caverns to 2,197 metres—that's 7,208 feet into the earth! Similar caves, around four hundred of them, exist in other parts of the country and across the globe. More caverns are being discovered all the time and new depth records are being set.

The mysteries of creation continue to unfold, adding to our understanding of the universe we live in and causing us to wonder at the matchless creativity of God's handiwork on earth that we're called by God to care for (GENESIS 1:26–28). The psalmist invites us all to "sing for joy" and "shout aloud" to God because of His greatness (V. 1). Let's take a moment to consider God's incredible work of creation. All that it contains—whether we've yet discovered it or not—is cause for us to bow down in worship to Him (V. 6).

He doesn't just know the vast, physical places of His creation; He also knows the intimate depths of our hearts. And not unlike in the caverns of Georgia, we'll go through dark and perhaps scary seasons in life. Yet we know that God holds even those times in His powerful yet tender care. In the words of the psalmist, we're His people, the "flock under his care" (V. 7).

KIRSTEN HOLMBERG

How has God guided you through dark places? In what new place or way is He inviting you to trust Him now?

Creator God, help me to trust in Your care for me even in the darkest places!

BIBLE IN A YEAR | 2 SAMUEL 12–13; LUKE 16

You, Lord, are forgiving and good, abounding
in love to all who call to you. [PSALM 86:5]

THE POWER OF FORGIVENESS

A 2021 news reports told of seventeen missionaries that
had been kidnapped by a gang. The gang threatened
to kill the group (including children) if their ransom demands weren't met. Incredibly, all the missionaries were either
released or escaped to freedom. On reaching safety, they sent
a message to their captors: "Jesus taught us by word and by His
own example that the power of forgiving love is stronger than
the hate of violent force. Therefore, we extend forgiveness to
you."

Jesus made it clear that forgiveness is powerful. He said, "If
you forgive other people when they sin against you, your heavenly Father will also forgive you" (MATTHEW 6:14). Later, in answering Peter, Christ told how often we should forgive: "I tell you,
not seven times, but seventy-seven times" (18:22; SEE VV. 21–35).
And on the cross, He demonstrated godly forgiveness when He
prayed, "Father, forgive them, for they do not know what they
are doing" (LUKE 23:34).

Forgiveness at its fullest can be realised when both parties
move towards healing and reconciliation. And while it doesn't
remove the effects of harm done or the need to be discerning in
how to address painful or unhealthy relationships, it can lead to
restored ones—testifying to God's love and power. Let's look for
ways to extend forgiveness for His honour.   *DAVE BRANON*

> **When is forgiveness hardest? How can you trust the Holy
> Spirit to help you forgive?**
>
> *Jesus, help me to reach out to those who need me to
> forgive them as a testimony of Your power and goodness.*

BIBLE IN A YEAR | 2 SAMUEL 14–15; LUKE 17:1–19

He will wipe every tear from their
eyes. There will be no more death.
[REVELATION 21:4]

NO FEAR OF DEATH

On the last night of Isaac Watts' life, 24 November 1748, the person attending the pastor noted that he had taught his friends how to live and now he was teaching them how to die. Those sitting next to his bed listened intently. "If God has no more service for me to do," Watts explained, "through grace I am ready. . . . I trust all my sins are pardoned through the blood of Christ. . . . I have no fear of dying." This prolific author of hymns died shortly afterwards.

Those who love and believe in Jesus can share this absence of fear about death. We can trust the vision that John described in Revelation, that we will live for ever with Jesus, in the new heaven and the new earth (SEE REVELATION 21:1). There God promises to dwell with His people: "They will be his people, and God himself will be with them and be their God" (V. 3). No longer will we cry any tears, nor will we experience any pain: " 'He will wipe every tear from their eyes. There will be no more death' or mourning or crying or pain" (V. 4).

Dying is the great unknown, but we can trust our loving God and the promises He makes in His Word. We, like Isaac Watts, can affirm in faith, "I have no fear of dying." *AMY BOUCHER PYE*

How do you feel and think about dying? How can you find comfort and hope in God's promises in His Word?

Living God, thank You for Your promises that You'll welcome me into your kingdom. Give me peace and hope when I contemplate my own death.

I will rain down bread from heaven for you.
[EXODUS 16:4]

STRING TOO SHORT TO USE

Aunt Margaret's frugality was legendary. After she passed away, her nieces began the nostalgically bittersweet task of sorting her belongings. In a drawer, neatly arrayed inside a small plastic bag, they discovered an assortment of small pieces of string. The label read: "String too short to use."

What would motivate someone to keep and categorise something they knew to be of no use? Perhaps this person once knew extreme deprivation.

When the Israelites fled slavery in Egypt, they left behind a life of hardship. But they soon forgot God's miraculous hand in their exodus and started complaining about the lack of food.

God wanted them to trust Him. He provided manna for their desert diet, telling Moses, "The people are to go out each day and gather enough for that day" (EXODUS 16:4). God also instructed them to gather twice as much on the sixth day, because on the Sabbath no manna would fall (VV. 5, 25). Some of the Israelites listened. Some didn't, with predictable results (VV. 27–28).

In times of plenty and times of desperation, it's tempting to try to cling, to hoard, in a desperate attempt at control. There's no need to take everything into our own frantic hands. No need to save 'scraps of string'—or to hoard anything at all. Our faith is in God, who has promised, "Never will I leave you; never will I forsake you" (HEBREWS 13:5).　　　　*TIM GUSTAFSON*

In what ways do you sometimes take things into your own hands? How has God proven Himself to be faithful to you in the past?

Father, help me to take You at Your word and to trust You with everything.

BIBLE IN A YEAR | 2 SAMUEL 19–20; LUKE 18:1–23

Do not think about how to gratify the
desires of the flesh. [ROMANS 13:14]

LET IT GO

Augustine's autobiographical *Confessions* describes his long
and winding journey to Jesus. On one occasion, he was
riding to the palace to give a flattering speech for the emperor. He was fretting over his deceptive applause lines when he
noticed a drunken beggar "joking and laughing". He realised the
drunk already had whatever fleeting happiness his shifty career
might bring, and with much less effort. So Augustine stopped
striving for worldly success.

But he was still enslaved by lust. He knew he couldn't turn to
Jesus without turning *from* sin, and he still struggled with sexual
immorality. So he prayed, "Grant me chastity . . . but not yet."

Augustine stumbled along, torn between salvation and sin,
until finally he had enough. Inspired by others who had turned
to Jesus, he opened a Bible to Romans 13:13–14. "Let us behave
decently . . . not in carousing and drunkenness, not in sexual
immorality . . . . Rather, clothe yourselves with the Lord Jesus
Christ, and do not think about how to gratify the desires of the
flesh."

That did it. God used those inspired words to break Augustine's chains of lust and brought him "into the kingdom of the
Son . . . in whom we have redemption, the forgiveness of sins"
(COLOSSIANS 1:13–14). Augustine became a bishop who remained
tempted by fame and lust, but he now knew whom to see when
he sinned. He turned to Jesus. Have you?　　　　*MIKE WITTMER*

What's keeping you from giving your life to Jesus?
How might your life change if you let it go?

Dear Father, let nothing come between me and You.

BIBLE IN A YEAR | 2 SAMUEL 21–22; LUKE 18:24–43

The stone the builders rejected has become
the cornerstone. [PSALM 118:22]

STRONG AND GOOD

The young campus minister was troubled. But he looked conflicted when I dared to ask if he prays . . . for God's direction . . . for His help. To pray, as Paul urged, without ceasing. In reply, the young man confessed, "I'm not sure I believe anymore in prayer." He frowned. "Or believe that God is listening. Just look at the world." That young leader was 'building' a ministry in his own strength and, sadly, he was failing. Why? He was rejecting God.

Jesus, as the cornerstone of the church, has always been rejected—starting, in fact, with His own people (JOHN 1:11). Many still reject Him today, struggling to build their lives, work, even churches on lesser foundations—their own schemes, dreams and other unreliable ground. Yet, our good Saviour alone is our strength and defence (PSALM 118:14). Indeed, "the stone the builders rejected has become the cornerstone" (V. 22).

Set at the vital corner of our lives, He provides the only right alignment for anything His believers seek to accomplish for Him. To Him, therefore, we pray, "LORD, save us! LORD, grant us success!" (V. 25). The result? "Blessed is he who comes in the name of the LORD" (V. 26). May we give thanks to Him because He's strong and good.

PATRICIA RAYBON

**What dream or plans do you have as you build for God?
How can you put Christ at the cornerstone of your plan,
building it for Him?**

*I praise You, Jesus, for being the chief cornerstone. Only on
You can Your church and my life stand.*

BIBLE IN A YEAR | 2 SAMUEL 23–24; LUKE 19:1–27

So I say, walk by the Spirit, and you
will not gratify the desires of the flesh.
[GALATIANS 5:16]

WATERING THE WEEDS

This spring, weeds attacked our garden like something out of *Jurassic Park*. One got so big that when I tried to pull it out, I feared I might injure myself. Before I could find a spade to whack it down, I noticed that my daughter was actually pouring water on it. "Why are you watering the weeds?!" I exclaimed. "I want to see how big it will get!" she replied with an impish grin.

Weeds aren't something we *intentionally* nourish. But as I thought about it, I realised that sometimes we do water the 'weeds' in our spiritual lives, feeding desires that strangle our growth.

Paul writes about this in Galatians 5:13–26, where he contrasts living by the flesh with living by the Spirit. He says trying to follow the rules alone won't establish the kind of 'weed-free' life we long for. Instead, to avoid watering the weeds, he instructs us to "walk by the Spirit". He adds that being in regular step with God is what frees us from the impulse to "gratify the desires of the flesh" (V. 16).

It's a lifelong process to fully understand Paul's teaching. But I love the simplicity of his guidance: instead of growing something unwanted by nourishing our own self-focused desires, when we're cultivating our relationship with God, we grow fruit and reap the harvest of a godly life (VV. 22–25).   *ADAM R. HOLZ*

**What areas of your spiritual life need some 'weeding'?
How can you surrender to God and walk with Him?**

*Father, sometimes I water the weeds in my life. Help me to
instead experience being in step with You as You produce
spiritual fruit in my life.*

BIBLE IN A YEAR | 1 KINGS 1–2; LUKE 19:28–48

God has brought me laughter, and everyone
who hears about this will laugh with me.
[GENESIS 21:6]

LAUGHING OUT LOUD

Comedian John Branyan said, "We didn't think up laughter; that wasn't our idea. That was given to us by [God who] knew we were going to need it to get through life. [Because] He knew we were going to have hardship, He knew were going to have struggles, He knew . . . stuff was going to happen. . . . Laughter is a gift."

A quick look at the creatures God made can bring laughter, whether because of their oddities (such as duck-billed platypuses) or antics (such as playful otters). He made mammals that live in the ocean and long-legged birds that can't fly. God clearly has a sense of humour; and because we're created in His image, we too have the joy of laughter.

We first see the word *laughter* in the Bible in the story of Abraham and Sarah. God promised this elderly couple a child: "A son who is your own flesh and blood will be your heir" (GENESIS 15:4). And God had said, "Look up at the sky and count the stars . . . . So shall your offspring be" (V. 5). When Sarah finally gave birth at ninety, Abraham named their son Isaac, which means "laughter". As Sarah exclaimed, "God has brought me laughter, and everyone who hears about this will laugh with me" (21:6). It amazed her that she could nurse a child at her age! God transformed her sceptical laughter when she'd heard she'd give birth (18:12) into laughter of sheer joy.

Thank God for the gift of laughter!

ALYSON KIEDA

When has laughter been 'good medicine'? How can finding humour in your life help even in the most difficult times?

Dear God, thank You for giving me the gift of laughter.

BIBLE IN A YEAR | 1 KINGS 3-5; LUKE 20:1-26

The LORD is trustworthy in all he promises.
[PSALM 145:13]

ALWAYS TRUSTWORTHY

'm a worrier. Early mornings are the worst because I'm alone with my thoughts. So I taped this quote from Hudson Taylor on my bathroom mirror, where I can see it when I'm feeling vulnerable: "There is a living God. He has spoken in the Bible. He means what He says and will do all He has promised."

Taylor's words came from years of walking with God and remind us of who He is and all He can do through our times of illness, poverty, loneliness and grief. He didn't merely *know* that God is trustworthy–he'd *experienced* His trustworthiness. And because he'd trusted God's promises and obeyed Him, thousands of Chinese people gave their lives to Jesus.

Experiencing God and His ways helped David know that He's trustworthy. He wrote Psalm 145, a song of praise to the God he'd experienced to be good, compassionate and faithful to all His promises. When we trust and follow God, we realise (or understand better) that He is who He says He is and that He's faithful to His word (V. 13). And, like David, we respond by praising Him and telling others about Him (VV. 10–12).

When we face worrisome times, God can help us not to falter in our walk with Him, for He is trustworthy (HEBREWS 10:23).

KAREN HUANG

What have you been worried about lately, and which of God's promises can you hold on to? How does knowing that Hudson Taylor's and King David's faith wasn't in vain encourage you and give you hope?

Dear God, thank You for being trustworthy and keeping Your promises to me. Please help me to remember Your faithfulness as I trust and obey You each day.

BIBLE IN A YEAR | 1 KINGS 6–7; LUKE 20:27–47

Pray also for me, . . . so that I will fearlessly make
known the mystery of the gospel. [EPHESIANS 6:19]

FEARLESSLY TELLING

Scottish minister Robert Murray M'Cheyne (1813–43) loved
to preach God's Word from the pulpit. Yet he realised it
was one thing to speak the gospel to fellow Christians
who hung on his every word, but quite another to share it with
non-Christians who seemed disinterested or even aggressive.
Wrestling with God's call to evangelise, he realised he was putting too much value on the opinions of others. What did he do?
He prayed, knowing that freedom from worrying over the "es-
teem or contempt" of others "must be given from the Lord".

Fearing how others might react to our Christian witness appears to be one of the "devil's schemes" to make us ineffective
(EPHESIANS 6:11). That's why Paul asked his readers, "Pray also
for me . . . that I will fearlessly make known the mystery of the
gospel" (V. 19). Note that Paul wrote from prison, and that sharing the gospel wasn't just losing him friends, it was gaining him
powerful enemies who sought his death. Yet despite the pressure, he said: "Pray that I may declare it fearlessly, as I should"
(V. 20). Paul knew in the face of contempt that prayer was the key
to speaking boldly and joyfully about Jesus.

Does a fear of how others could react stop you from sharing
your faith? By prayer God will help us value His Word above the
opinions of others, giving us all we need to declare Him fearlessly.

CHRIS WALE

*How could you overcome the fears you have of how other
people will react to your faith? What do you think it looks
like to share your faith fearlessly?*

*Loving God, help me value Your opinion more than anyone
else's. Give me boldness to tell others about all that You
have done in my life.*

BIBLE IN A YEAR | 1 KINGS 8–9; LUKE 21:1-19

NO NEED TO ARGUE

I spent a year trying to persuade Li Jun that God existed. I told her that our beautiful world must have a Designer and that moral law requires a Lawgiver. She was unmoved. Later, as I was reading Romans chapter one, I noted that it says everyone knows God's "eternal power and divine nature," and that those who say they don't "are without excuse" (V. 20). The next time Li Jun raised the subject, those Scriptures came to mind.

"Professor Wittmer," she asked. "Why do you believe in God?"

I returned the question. "Tell me, Li Jun, why do you?"

"Oh!" she said. And suddenly, she realised that deep down, she really did believe in God. Several months later, Li Jun chose to believe in Jesus!

Of course, not everyone will respond this way. We need the Holy Spirit to stop our suppression of the truth and to open our hearts to Jesus (JOHN 16:7–11). But everyone intuitively knows that God exists, and that He's powerful and righteous (ROMANS 1:20, 32).

This knowledge frees us to avoid arguments. We don't have to prove something that people already know. The pressure's off! We're free to ask questions about their beliefs, buying another round of coffee to keep the conversation going. Perhaps our discussion will put a pebble in their shoe, and down the road they'll shake it out and receive Christ as Saviour. When we remember what people already know, we realise we don't need to debate them. We're free to be their friend.

Mike Wittmer, *Our Daily Bread* author

★ There are many tough questions people wrestle with as they consider if faith in Jesus is reasonable and real. This month, we're looking at the topic of apologetics—biblically defending our faith. The topic is addressed in the devotions for **May 1, 8** and **15**.

Always be prepared to give an answer
. . . for the hope that you have.
[1 PETER 3:15]

SEEDS OF FAITH

Last spring, the night before our lawn was to be aerated, a violent windstorm blew the seeds off our maple tree in one fell swoop. So when the aerating machine broke up the compacted soil by pulling small 'cores' out of the ground, it planted hundreds of maple seeds in my garden. Just two short weeks later, I had the beginnings of a maple forest growing up through my lawn!

As I (frustratedly) surveyed the misplaced foliage, I was struck by the prolific abundance of new life a single tree had spawned. Each of the miniature trees became a picture for me of the new life in Christ that I—as merely one person—can share with others. We each will have countless opportunities to "give the reason for the hope that [we] have" (1 PETER 3:15) in the course of our lives.

When we "suffer for what is right" with the hope of Jesus (V. 14), it's visible to those around us and might just become a point of curiosity to those who don't yet know God personally. If we're ready when they ask, then we may share the seed through which God brings forth new life. We don't have to share it with everyone all at once—in some kind of spiritual windstorm. Rather, we gently and respectfully drop the seed of faith into a heart ready to receive it.   *KIRSTEN HOLMBERG*

***Who in your life is asking about the reason for your
hope? What will you share with them?***

*Jesus, thank You for growing the seed of faith in my life.
Help me to share the reason for my hope—You—with
those who ask and may they grow in their love for You.*

BIBLE IN A YEAR | 1 KINGS 10-11; LUKE 21:20-38

Now this is eternal life: that they know you,
the only true God, and Jesus Christ, whom
you have sent. [JOHN 17:3]

LIFE EVERLASTING

"Don't be afraid of death, Winnie," said Angus Tuck, "be afraid of the unlived life." That quote from the book-turned-film *Tuck Everlasting* is made more interesting by the fact that it comes from a character who can't die. In the story, the Tuck family has become immortal. Young James Tuck, who falls in love with Winnie, begs her to seek immortality too so they can be together forever. But wise Angus understands that simply enduring forever doesn't bring fulfilment.

Our culture tells us that if we could be healthy, young and energetic forever, we would be truly happy. But that's not where our fulfilment is found. Before He went to the cross, Jesus prayed for His disciples and for future believers. He said, "Now this is eternal life: that they know you, the only true God, and Jesus Christ, whom you have sent" (JOHN 17:3). Our fulfilment in life comes from a relationship with God through faith in Jesus. He's our hope for the future and joy for this present day.

Jesus prayed that His disciples would take on the patterns of new life: that they would obey God (V. 6), believe that Jesus was sent by God the Father (V. 8) and be united as one (V. 11). As believers in Christ, we look forward to a future eternal life with Him. But during these days we live on earth, we can live the "rich and satisfying life" (10:10 NLT) that He promised—right here, right now.

KAREN PIMPO

**Where's your joy and contentment found in this life?
In what ways do you exhibit new life in Christ?**

*Jesus, help me take hold of the abundant life that
You've given to me.*

BIBLE IN A YEAR | 1 KINGS 12-13; LUKE 22:1-20

While we are in this tent, we groan and are
burdened. [2 CORINTHIANS 5:4]

TIRED TENTS

"The tent is tired!" Those were the words of my friend
Paul, who pastors a church in Nairobi, Kenya. Since
2015, the congregation has worshipped in a tent-like
structure. Now, Paul writes, "Our tent is worn out and it is leak-
ing when it rains."

My friend's words about their tent's structural weaknesses remind us of the apostle Paul's words regarding the frailty
of our human existence. "Outwardly we are wasting away
. . . . While we are in this tent, we groan and are burdened"
(2 CORINTHIANS 4:16; 5:4).

Though the awareness of our fragile human existence happens
relatively early in life, we become more conscious of it as we
age. Indeed, time picks our pockets. The vitality of youth surren-
ders reluctantly to the reality of ageing (SEE ECCLESIASTES 12:1–7).
Our bodies—our tents—get tired.

But tired tents need not equate to tired trust. Hope and heart
needn't fade as we age. "Therefore we do not lose heart," the
apostle says (2 CORINTHIANS 4:16). The One who has made our
bodies has made Himself at home there through His Spirit. And
when this body can no longer serve us, we'll have a dwelling not
subject to breaks and aches—we'll "have a building from God,
an eternal house in heaven" (5:1).   *ARTHUR JACKSON*

> **How does it make you feel that Christ resides in you by
> His Spirit (5:5)? When you find yourself "groaning", how
> does prayer help you?**

> *Father, thank You for Your continual presence. When I'm
> physically uncomfortable, help me to trust You even as I
> anticipate an eternal dwelling that will last forever.*

BIBLE IN A YEAR | 1 KINGS 14–15; LUKE 22:21–46

Jehoshaphat resolved to inquire of the LORD.
[2 CHRONICLES 20:3]

OPERATING WITH PRAYER

When my son needed orthopedic surgery, I was grateful for the doctor who performed the operation. The doctor, who was nearing retirement, assured us he'd helped thousands of people with the same problem. Even so, before the procedure, he prayed and asked God to provide a good outcome. And I'm so grateful He did.

Jehoshaphat, an experienced national leader, prayed too during a crisis. Three nations had united against him, and they were coming to attack his people. Although he had more than two decades of experience, he decided to ask God what to do. He prayed, "[We] will cry out to you in our distress, and you will hear us and save us" (2 CHRONICLES 20:9). He also asked for guidance, saying, "We do not know what to do, but our eyes are on you" (V. 12).

Jehoshaphat's humble approach to the challenge opened his heart to God's involvement, which came in the form of encouragement and divine intervention (VV. 15–17, 22). No matter how much experience we have in certain areas, praying for help develops a holy reliance on God. It reminds us that He knows more than we do, and He's ultimately in control. It puts us in a humble place—a place where He's pleased to respond and support us, no matter what the outcome may be. *JENNIFER BENSON SCHULDT*

How has prayer helped you? What current challenge in your life might benefit from prayer?

Dear God, thank You for listening and responding to prayer. I worship You as the all-knowing, all-powerful God. Please help me in each challenge I face today.

BIBLE IN A YEAR | 1 KINGS 16–18; LUKE 22:47–71

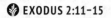

Moses was afraid and thought, "What I did must have become known." [EXODUS 2:14]

GRACE AND CHANGE

The crime was shocking, and the man who committed it was sentenced to life in prison. In the years that followed, the man—in solitary confinement—began a process of mental and spiritual healing. It led to repentance and a restored relationship with Jesus. These days he's been allowed limited interactions with other inmates. And, by God's grace, through his witness some fellow prisoners have received Christ as Saviour—finding forgiveness in Him.

Moses, though now recognised as a great man of faith, also committed a shocking crime. After he witnessed "an Egyptian beating a Hebrew," he looked "this way and that" and "killed the Egyptian" (EXODUS 2:11–12). Despite this sin, God in His grace wasn't done with His imperfect servant. Later, He chose Moses to free His people from their oppression (3:10). In Romans 5:14, we read, "Death reigned from the time of Adam to the time of Moses, even over those who did not sin by breaking a command." But in the following verses Paul states that "God's grace" makes it possible for us, regardless of our past sins, to be changed and made right with Him (VV. 15–16).

We might think that what we've done disqualifies us from knowing God's forgiveness and being used for His honour. But because of His grace, in Jesus we can be changed and set free to help others be changed for eternity.   *TOM FELTEN*

How has God and His grace changed you? What are the changes He's calling you to make these days?

Heavenly Father, thank You for Your life-changing grace.

BIBLE IN A YEAR | 1 KINGS 19–20; LUKE 23:1–25

Has no one returned to give praise to God
except this foreigner? [LUKE 17:18]

THANKFUL HEARTS

Hansle Parchment was in a predicament. He caught the bus
to the wrong place for his semi-final in the Tokyo Olympics and was left stranded with little hope of getting to
the stadium on time. But thankfully he met Trijana Stojkovic, a
volunteer helping out at the games. She gave him some money to take a taxi. Parchment made it to the semi-final on time
and eventually clinched the gold medal in the 110-metre hurdle.
Later, he went back to find Stojkovic and thanked her for her
kindness.

In Luke 17, we read of the Samaritan leper who came back to
thank Jesus for healing him (VV. 15–16). Jesus had entered a village
where He met ten lepers. All of them asked Jesus for healing,
and all of them experienced His grace and power. Ten were happy that they'd been healed, but only one returned to express his
gratitude. He "came back, praising God in a loud voice. He threw
himself at Jesus' feet and thanked him" (VV. 15–16).

Every day, we experience God's blessings in multiple ways.
It could be as dramatic as an answered prayer to an extended
time of suffering or receiving timely help from a stranger. Sometimes, His blessings can come in ordinary ways too, such as good
weather to accomplish an outdoor task. Like the Samaritan leper, let's remember to thank God for His kindness towards us.

POH FANG CHIA

***What can you thank God for today? How can you
cultivate a heart of gratitude?***

*Dear God, You've been so good to me. I give thanks to You
today for _____.*

He has sent me to bind up the broken-
hearted. [ISAIAH 61:1]

HUNT FOR INNER HEALING

Always a busy guy, Carson fished, rode dirt bikes and skate boarded. He loved everything outdoors. But he was in a motorcycle accident and became paralysed from the chest down. Soon depression sank in, and he didn't see much of a future. Then one day some of his friends got him to go fishing with them again. For a time he forgot about his injury as he enjoyed the beauty around him. This experience brought him inner healing and inspired a new purpose for his life—to provide the same experience for others like him through a non-profit organisation. He says his accident was "a blessing in disguise. . . . Now I'm able to give back, which I've always wanted to do. I'm happy." He's excited about providing a place for those with severe mobility disabilities and their carers to find inner healing.

The prophet Isaiah foretold the coming of One who would bring healing for brokenness (ISAIAH 61). He would "bind up the broken-hearted" and "comfort all who mourn" (VV. 1–2). After Jesus read this Scripture in His hometown synagogue, He said, "Today this scripture is fulfilled in your hearing" (LUKE 4:21). Jesus came to save us and make us whole.

Are you in need of inner healing? Turn to Jesus and He'll give you "a garment of praise instead of a spirit of despair" (ISAIAH 61:3). *ANNE CETAS*

> **In what ways do you need Jesus' healing? Who can you tell about Him and the salvation and wholeness He offers?**
>
> *Thank You, Jesus, for the healing You've brought to me and many others. I look forward to complete healing in heaven one day.*

BIBLE IN A YEAR | 2 KINGS 1–3; LUKE 24:1–35

[Having] carefully investigated everything from the beginning, I too decided to write an orderly account for you. [LUKE 1:3]

TRUTH SEEKERS

A woman once told me about a disagreement that was tearing her church apart. "What's the disagreement about?" I asked. "Whether the earth is flat," she said. A few months later, news broke of a Christian man who'd burst into a restaurant, armed, to rescue children supposedly being abused in its back room. There was no back room, and the man was arrested. In both cases, the people involved were acting on conspiracy theories they'd read on the internet.

Believers in Jesus are called to be good citizens (ROMANS 13:1-7), and good citizens don't spread misinformation. In Luke's day, numerous stories circulated about Jesus (LUKE 1:1), some of them were inaccurate. Instead of passing on everything he heard, Luke essentially became an investigative journalist, talking to eyewitnesses (V. 2), researching "everything from the beginning" (V. 3) and writing his findings into a gospel that contains names, quotes and historical facts based on people with first-hand knowledge, not unverified claims.

We can do the same. Since false information can split churches and put lives at risk, checking facts is an act of loving our neighbour (10:27). When a sensational story comes our way, we can verify its claims with qualified, accountable experts, being truth seekers—not error spreaders. Such an act brings credibility to the gospel. After all, we worship the One who's full of truth (JOHN 1:14).

SHERIDAN VOYSEY

Why do you think conspiracy theories spread so quickly? How can you be a truth seeker?

Father, help me discern truth from error as Your Spirit guides me.

BIBLE IN A YEAR | 2 KINGS 4-6; LUKE 24:36-53

[Mary] turned towards him and cried out . . .
"Rabboni!" [JOHN 20:16]

KNOWN BY GOD

After two brothers were separated by adoption, a DNA test
helped to reunite them almost twenty years later. When
Kieron texted Vincent, the man he believed was his
brother, Vincent thought, *Who is this stranger?* When Kieron
asked him what name he'd been given at birth, he immediately
answered, "Tyler." Then he knew they were brothers. He was
recognised by his name!

Consider how a name plays a key role in the Easter story. As
it unfolds, Mary Magdalene comes to Christ's tomb, and she
weeps when she finds His body missing. "Woman, why are you
crying?" Jesus asks (JOHN 20:15). She didn't recognise Him, however, until He spoke her name: "Mary" (V. 16).

Hearing Him say it, she "cried out in Aramaic, 'Rabboni!' (WHICH
MEANS 'TEACHER')" (V. 16). Her reaction expresses the joy believers
in Jesus feel on Easter morning, recognising that our risen Christ
conquered death for all, knowing each of us as His children. As
He told Mary, "I am ascending to my Father and your Father, to
my God and your God" (V. 17).

Two reunited brothers, bonded by name, vowed to take "this
relationship to the next level." At Easter, we praise Jesus for already taking the utmost step to rise in sacrificial love for those
He knows as His own. For you and me, indeed, He's alive!

PATRICIA RAYBON

> **How does it feel knowing that Jesus rose again and
> knows you by name? How can you know Him better?**
>
> *Your knowledge of me is humbling, dear Jesus.
> Thank You for the sacrificial gift of Your knowing love.*

BIBLE IN A YEAR | 2 KINGS 7–9; JOHN 1:1–28

You have struggled with God and with
humans and have overcome. [GENESIS 32:28]

STOLEN GODS

A carved wooden figure—a household god—had been stolen from a woman named Ekuwa, so she reported it to the authorities. Believing they had found the idol, law enforcement officials invited her to identify it. "Is this your god?" they asked. She said sadly, "No, my god is much larger and more beautiful than that."

People have long tried to give shape to their concept of deity, hoping for a handmade god to protect them. Perhaps that's why Jacob's wife Rachel "stole her father's household gods" as they fled from Laban (GENESIS 31:19). But God had His hand on Jacob, despite the idols hidden in his camp (V. 34).

Later, on that same journey, Jacob wrestled all night with "a man" (32:24). He must have understood this opponent was no mere human, because at daybreak Jacob insisted, "I will not let you go unless you bless me" (V. 26). The man renamed him Israel ("God fights") and then blessed him (VV. 28–29). Jacob called the spot Peniel ("face of God"), "because I saw God face to face, and yet my life was spared" (V. 30).

This God—the one true God—is infinitely larger and more beautiful than anything Ekuwa could have ever imagined. He can't be carved, stolen or hidden. Yet, as Jacob learned that night, we can approach Him! Jesus taught His disciples to call this God "our Father in heaven" (MATTHEW 6:9).   *TIM GUSTAFSON*

How would you describe God? How might your ideas of Him be too limited?

Heavenly Father, forgive me for seeing You as smaller than You really are. Help me embrace the reality of who You truly are.

BIBLE IN A YEAR | 2 KINGS 10–12; JOHN 1:29–51

Great is our Lord and mighty in power; his understanding has no limit. [PSALM 147:5]

GOD SEES, UNDERSTANDS AND CARES

Sometimes, living with chronic pain and fatigue leads to being isolated at home and feeling alone. I've often felt unseen by God and others. During an early morning prayer-walk with my service dog, I struggled with these feelings. I noticed a hot-air balloon in the distance. The people in its basket could enjoy a bird's-eye view of our quiet neighbourhood, but they couldn't really see me. As I continued walking past my neighbours' houses, I sighed. How many people behind those closed doors feel unseen and insignificant? As I finished my walk, I asked God to give me opportunities to let my neighbours know that I see them and care for them, and so does He.

God determined the exact number of stars that He spoke into existence. He identified each star with a name (PSALM 147:4), an intimate act that demonstrates His attention to the smallest details. His strength—insight, discernment and knowledge—have "no limit" in the past, present or future (V. 5).

God hears each desperate cry and sees each silent tear as clearly as He notices each sigh of contentment and belly laugh. He sees when we're stumbling and when we're standing in triumph. He understands our deepest fears, our innermost thoughts and our wildest dreams. He knows where we've been and where we're going. As God helps us see, hear and love our neighbours, we can trust Him to see, understand and care for us.

XOCHITL DIXON

How have your neighbours loved you?
How can you love others today?

God, please help me see, hear, and love others in practical ways.

BIBLE IN A YEAR | 2 KINGS 13-14; JOHN 2

We are citizens of heaven, where the Lord Jesus Christ lives. And we are eagerly waiting for him to return as our Saviour. [PHILIPPIANS 3:20]

CITIZENS OF HEAVEN

My kids hold two passports—one from the country where we live and one from the country of my birth. They're citizens of the United Kingdom and of the United States, but my husband and I remind them that their primary citizenship is of heaven.

The Apostle Paul spoke of this citizenship in his letter to the church at Philippi, which was made up of many Roman citizens who had settled in a Roman colony. Writing to those entitled to the benefits and privileges of the ruling power, he called them to a higher allegiance. He desired that they'd bring the practices of their heavenly citizenship to their earthly existence, that they'd not be ruled by their appetites or desires. Instead, he wanted them to reveal themselves as people transformed by their life in Christ.

Being citizens of heaven sets apart those who believe in Christ. My husband and I explained this to our kids when they wondered why we engage in nightly prayers or go to church regularly. As parents we desire that our children give their hearts fully to God, and that their heavenly passport will be their defining one.

Our longings for the Kingdom of God might make us feel like we don't fully belong at times. We can ask God to help us live with grace through these feelings of disconnect while spreading His love and truth.   *AMY BOUCHER PYE*

> ***Where do you place your allegiances? To a particular sports team? As a foodie? To the books you read? How does your heavenly citizenship trump all other ties?***
>
> *God of all the nations, help me to submit to Your lordship in every area of my life. I want to serve You fully.*

BIBLE IN A YEAR | 2 KINGS 15–16; JOHN 3:1–18

Be devoted to one another in love.
Honour one another above yourselves.
[ROMANS 12:10]

FOR LOVE'S SAKE

Running a marathon is about pushing yourself, physically and mentally. For one high school runner, however, competing in a cross-country race is all about pushing someone else. In every practice and race, fourteen-year-old Susan Bergeman pushes her older brother, Jeffrey, in his wheelchair. When Jeffrey was twenty-two months old, he went into cardiac arrest—leaving him with severe brain damage and cerebral palsy. Today, Susan sacrifices personal running goals so Jeffrey might compete with her. What love and sacrifice!

The apostle Paul had love and sacrifice in mind when he encouraged his readers to be "devoted to one another" (ROMANS 12:10). He knew that the believers in Rome were struggling with jealousy, anger and sharp disagreements (V. 18). So, he encouraged them to let divine love rule their hearts. This kind of love, rooted in Christ's love, would fight for the highest possible good of others. It would be sincere, and it would lead to generous sharing (V. 13). Those who love this way are eager to consider others more worthy of honour than themselves (V. 16).

As believers in Jesus, we're running a race of love while helping others finish the race too. Though it can be difficult, it brings honour to Jesus. So, for love's sake, let's rely on Him to empower us to love and serve others. *MARVIN WILLIAMS*

***What does it mean for you to love others as God loves them?
How does Jesus reveal that love is more than emotion?***

*God of love, for love's sake and Your glory, help me to
consider others before I consider myself.*

BIBLE IN A YEAR | 2 KINGS 17–18; JOHN 3:19–36

We dealt with each of you as a
father deals with his own children.
[1 THESSALONIANS 2:11]

LOVING LEADERSHIP

Aviral video of a mama bear trying to get her four energetic
little cubs across a busy road brought a knowing smile to
my face. It was delightfully relatable to watch her pick up
her cubs one-by-one and carry them across the road—only to
have the cubs wander back to the other side. After many seemingly frustrating attempts, the mama bear finally corralled all
four of her cubs, and they made it safely across the road.

The tireless work of parenting symbolised in the video matches imagery used by Paul to describe his care for the people in
the church of Thessalonica. Instead of emphasising his authority, the apostle compared his work among them to a mother
and father caring for young children (1 THESSALONIANS 2:7, 11). It
was deep love for the Thessalonians (V. 8) that motivated Paul's
ongoing efforts to encourage, comfort and urge them "to live
lives worthy of God" (V. 12). This impassioned call to godly living
was borne out of his loving desire to see them honour God in all
areas of their lives.

Paul's example can serve as a guide for us in all our leadership opportunities—especially when the responsibilities make
us weary. Empowered by God's Spirit, we can gently and persistently love those under our care as we encourage and guide
them towards Jesus.   *LISA M. SAMRA*

**How have you experienced leadership motivated by love?
How might you encourage those under your care?**

*Heavenly Father, help me to extend to others the loving
care You graciously show to me.*

BIBLE IN A YEAR | 2 KINGS 19–21; JOHN 4:1-30

Lift up your eyes and look to the heavens:
who created all these? He who brings out
the starry host one by one. [ISAIAH 40:26]

EXPLORING THE STARS

In 2021, a multi-nation effort led to the launch of the James Webb Space Telescope—deployed nearly a million miles from earth to better investigate the universe. This marvel will peer into deep space and examine the stars and other celestial wonders.

This is indeed a fascinating astronomical piece of technology, and if everything works, it will provide us with amazing photos and information. But its mission isn't new. In fact, the prophet Isaiah described searching the stars when he said, "Lift up your eyes and look to the heavens: who created all these? He who brings out the starry host one by one" (ISAIAH 40:26). "Night after night" they speak of our Creator who hurled this imperceptibly immense universe into existence (PSALM 19:2)—and with it the countless luminous bodies that silently grace our night sky (V. 3).

And it's God Himself who decided how many of the shining objects there are: "He determines the number of the stars and calls them each by name" (PSALM 147:4). When mankind sends complicated, fascinating probes to explore the universe, we can enjoy with spellbound wonder the discoveries they make, because each observation points back to the One who made the solar system and everything beyond it. Yes, the "heavens declare the glory of God" (19:1)—stars and all.   *DAVE BRANON*

> **How do the stars and the entire universe speak of God
> and His creative ways? What thoughts and emotions
> strike you as you think about His power?**

*Heavenly Father, thank You for creating such an amazing
universe for me to enjoy.*

BIBLE IN A YEAR | 2 KINGS 22-23; JOHN 4:31-54

To all who did receive him . . . [Jesus]
gave the right to become children of God.
[JOHN 1:12]

WHO AM I?

In 1859, Joshua Abraham Norton declared himself Emperor of the USA. Norton had made—and lost—his fortune, so he wanted a new identity: America's first emperor. When a newspaper printed 'Emperor' Norton's announcement, most readers laughed. Norton made pronouncements aimed at correcting society's ills, printed his own currency and even wrote letters to Queen Victoria asking her to marry him and unite their kingdoms. He wore royal military uniforms designed by local tailors. One observer said Norton looked "every inch a king". But of course, he wasn't. We don't get to make up who we are.

Many of us spend years searching for who we are and wondering what value we possess. We flail, trying to name or define ourselves, when only God can truly tell us the truth about who we are. And, thankfully, He calls us His sons and daughters when we receive salvation in His Son, Jesus. "To all who did receive him," John writes, "he gave the right to become children of God" (JOHN 1:12). And this identity is purely a gift. We are His beloved "children born not of natural descent, nor of human decision . . . but born of God" (V. 13).

God gives us our name and our identity in Christ. We can stop striving and comparing ourselves to others, because He tells us who we are.   *WINN COLLIER*

How do you know you're chosen by God? How does being His child help you understand your true identity?

God, I know that I'm Yours. Help me feel confidence in knowing that I'm born of You—a child of the King.

BIBLE IN A YEAR | 2 KINGS 24-25; JOHN 5:1-24

Do not fear, for I have redeemed you; I have summoned you by name; you are mine.
[ISAIAH 43:1]

GOD REMEMBERS NAMES

The Sunday after I'd started working as a youth leader at a church and had met several of the young people, I spoke to a teen seated next to her mum. As I greeted the shy girl with a smile, I said her name and asked how she was doing. She lifted her head and her beautiful brown eyes widened. She too smiled and said in a small voice: "You remembered my name." By simply calling that young girl by name—a girl who may have felt insignificant in a church filled with adults—I began a relationship of trust. She felt seen and valued.

In Isaiah 43, God is using the prophet Isaiah to convey a similar message to the Israelites: they were seen and valued. Even through captivity and time in the wilderness, God saw them and knew them "by name" (V. 1). They were not strangers; they belonged to Him. Even though they may have felt abandoned, they were "precious," and His "love" was with them (V. 4). And along with the reminder that God knew them by name, He shared all that He would do for them, especially during trying times. When they went through trials, He would be with them (V. 2). They didn't need to be afraid or worried since God remembered their names.

God knows each of His children's names—and that's good news, especially as we pass through the deep, difficult waters in life.   *KATARA PATTON*

What trials are you facing these days? How can focusing on the fact that God knows you by name help you walk through trying times with confidence?

Thank You for knowing me by name, dear God.

BIBLE IN A YEAR | 1 CHRONICLES 1-3; JOHN 5:25-47

He will take great delight in you.
[ZEPHANIAH 3:17]

GRANDMOTHER RESEARCH

Researchers at one university used MRI scans to study the brains of grandmothers. They measured empathetic responses to images that included their own grandchild, their own adult child and one anonymous child. The study showed that grandmothers have a higher empathy towards their own grandchild than even their own adult child. This is attributed to what they call the "cute factor"—their own grandchild being more "adorable" than the adult.

Before we say, "Well, duh!" we might consider the words of James Rilling, who conducted the study: "If their grandchild is smiling, [the grandmother is] feeling the child's joy. And if their grandchild is crying, they're feeling the child's pain and distress."

One prophet paints an 'MRI image' of God's feelings as He looks upon His people: "He will take great delight in you; in his love he will . . . rejoice over you with singing" (ZEPHANIAH 3:17). Some translate this to say, "You will make His heart full of joy, and He will sing loudly." Like an empathetic grandmother, God feels our pain: "In all their distress he too was distressed" (ISAIAH 63:9), and He feels our joy: "The LORD takes delight in his people" (PSALM 149:4).

When we feel discouraged, it's good to remember that God has real feelings for us. He's not a cold, distant God, but One who loves and delights in us. It's time to draw close to Him, feel His smile—and listen to His singing.　　　*KENNETH PETERSEN*

How have you felt the pleasure of God?
How does this make you feel?

Dear God, help me to feel Your smile upon me.

BIBLE IN A YEAR | 1 CHRONICLES 4–6; JOHN 6:1–21

He turned his ear to me.
[PSALM 116:2]

YOU ARE HEARD

In the book *Physics,* Charles Riborg Mann and George Ransom Twiss ask: "When a tree falls in a lonely forest, and no animal is nearby to hear it, does it make a sound?" Over the years, this question has prompted philosophical and scientific discussions about sound, perception and existence. A definitive answer, however, has yet to emerge.

One night, while feeling lonely and sad about a problem I hadn't shared with anyone, I recalled this question. *When no one hears my cry for help,* I thought, *does God hear?*

Facing the threat of death and overcome by distress, the writer of Psalm 116 may have felt abandoned. So he called out to God—knowing He was listening and would help him. "He heard my voice," the psalmist wrote, "he heard my cry for mercy. . . . [He] turned his ear to me" (VV. 1–2). When no one knows our pain, God knows. When no one hears our cries, God hears.

Knowing that God will show us His love and protection (VV. 5–6), we can be at rest in difficult times (V. 7). The Hebrew word translated "rest" (*manoakh*) describes a place of quiet and safety. We can be at peace, strengthened by the assurance of God's presence and help.

The question posed by Mann and Twiss led to numerous answers. But the answer to the question, *Does God hear?* is simply yes. *KAREN HUANG*

What do you do when you're feeling alone or abandoned? What will you ask God, who hears your every cry and cares for you?

Father, thank You for always hearing the cries of my heart. Your help and presence are my rest.

BIBLE IN A YEAR | 1 CHRONICLES 7-9; JOHN 6:22-44

Pray to your Father.
[MATTHEW 6:6]

KEEP IN TOUCH

Madeleine made it a habit to call her mother once a week. As her mother moved into her later years, she called more frequently, "just to keep in touch". In the same way, Madeleine liked her children to call and maintain that connection. Sometimes it was a lengthy conversation filled with significant questions and answers. Other times a quick call to 'check in' was sufficient. She later wrote, "It is good for the children to keep in touch. It is good for all of us children to keep in touch with our Father."

Most of us are familiar with the Lord's Prayer in Matthew 6:9–13. But the verses that precede it are just as important, for they set the tone for what follows. Our prayers aren't to be showy, "to be seen by others" (V. 5). And while there's no limit on how long our prayers need to be, "many words" (V. 7) doesn't automatically equate to quality prayer. The emphasis seems to be on maintaining regular contact with our Father who knows our need "before [we] ask him" (V. 8). Jesus stresses how good it is for us to keep in touch with our Father. Then instructs us: "This, then, is how you should pray" (V. 9).

Prayer is a good, vital choice for it keeps us in touch with the God and Father of us all.   *JOHN BLASE*

> **How can you better stay in touch with others? How have**
> **you experienced keeping in touch with the Father?**
>
> *Father, thank You for knowing my needs before I even*
> *speak them.*

Without the shedding of blood there is no
forgiveness. [HEBREWS 9:22]

NO HEALING WITHOUT BLOOD

"There's no healing without blood."
I didn't hear this short, compelling sermon from my
pastor, but from my physiotherapist. When I asked
why he wanted to use ultrasound on my injured shoulder, he explained that a combination of massage, exercise and ultrasound
would force blood into the area. Without a flow of blood, he
explained, healing would be impossible.

The Bible agrees: there's no healing without blood. In the Old
Testament, the blood of animals was used to pay for sin, so that
God's people would be clean before Him. "How much more,
then, will the blood of Christ, who through the eternal Spirit
offered himself unblemished to God, cleanse our consciences
from acts that lead to death!" (HEBREWS 9:14).

A clean conscience is something which we all long to experience. But because we still sin, we still wrestle with feelings
of guilt, forgetting that there is an answer beyond just trying
harder. My efforts cannot cover even one sin—but Jesus' blood
cleanses even the worst one. What was true on the first day of
our salvation is still true today: healing only comes through the
flow of Christ's blood, shed upon the cross for us.

"Without the shedding of blood there is no forgiveness" (V. 22).
Praise Jesus! In Him, we are forgiven; cleansed—healed. Jesus
has done this "once for all" (10:10). The flow of blood still cov-
ers and restores; healing and hope can be found in Him alone.

DEBBI FRALICK

**Is your instinct to 'do better' when you feel guilty? How does Jesus'
"once-for-all" sacrifice bring you comfort and reassurance today?**

*Jesus, forgive me for trying to cover my own sin. Thank You
for doing everything to clean and heal me by Your blood.*

BIBLE IN A YEAR | 1 CHRONICLES 13-15; JOHN 7:1-27

Sovereign LORD, my strong deliverer, you shield
my head in the day of battle. [PSALM 140:7]

HIDDEN DANGER

"**D**addy!" The piercing cry made the hairs on the back
of my neck stand on end. Toby, my five-year-old, had
been sitting quietly watching me work. I spun round
to see his arms flailing. The angry buzzing told me all I needed to
know: wasps. Everywhere.

Wrapping my body around his, I ran to the house. After applying ointment and checking for major reactions, we counted
the stings—four ugly red blobs. We'd had no idea there was a
wasps' nest at the end of our garden.

King David feared hidden dangers too: "The arrogant have
hidden a snare for me; they have spread out the cords of their
net" (PSALM 140:5). He couldn't anticipate every secret scheme by
his enemies to destroy his rule and reputation.

Perhaps you know this fear too—people in your home or
workplace wanting to trip you up in your faith because you follow Jesus. Or maybe you are conscious of the daily hidden dangers of illness, accidents and loss.

Yet our hope is the same as David's: "Sovereign LORD, my strong
deliverer, you shield my head in the day of battle" (V. 7). No danger
is hidden from Him. God is never unprepared for battle. He uses
the plans of those who wish us harm for His own purposes, and
He carries us protectively through the storm of life's 'stings'.

We don't know what dangers lurk today, but we cling to One
who does.   *CHRIS WALE*

**What hidden dangers are worrying you at the moment? How
can you entrust them to the Lord and rest in His deliverance?**

*Heavenly Father, I am so thankful that You are always with
me. No dangers or problems can sneak up on You; in Your
presence I find refuge, strength and peace.*

BIBLE IN A YEAR | 1 CHRONICLES 16–18; JOHN 7:28–53

Wake up, sleeper, rise from the dead, and
Christ will shine on you. [EPHESIANS 5:14]

NOT A DREAM

I t's like living in a dream you can't wake up from. People who
struggle with what's sometimes called "derealisation" or
"depersonalisation" often feel like nothing around them is
quite real. While those who chronically have this feeling can be
diagnosed with a disorder, it's believed to be a common mental
health struggle, especially during stressful times. But sometimes
the feeling persists even when life is seemingly good. It's as if
our minds can't trust that good things are really happening.

Scripture describes a similar struggle of God's people at times
to experience His power and deliverance as something real, not
just a dream. In Acts 12, when an angel delivers Peter from prison—and possible execution (VV. 2, 4)—the apostle is described as
being in a daze, not sure it was really happening (VV. 9–10). When
the angel left him outside the jail, Peter finally "came to his senses" and realised it had all been real (V. 11 NLT).

In both bad times and good, it can be hard sometimes to fully
believe or experience that God is really at work in our lives. But
we can trust that as we wait on Him, His resurrection power
will one day become undeniably, wonderfully real. God's light
will rouse us from our sleep into the reality of life with Him
(EPHESIANS 5:14).   *MONICA LA ROSE*

> **Why is it sometimes hard for you to feel God's power and
> love? How can you experience His love more tangibly?**
>
> *Dear God, thank You that in good times and bad, whether I
> can feel it or not, You're real, creating new life and hope.*

Without [God], who can eat or find
enjoyment? [ECCLESIASTES 2:25]

BLESSED ROUTINE

Watching the morning crowd pour onto the train, I felt
the Monday blues kick in. From the sleepy, grumpy faces of those in the jam-packed train, I could tell no one
looked forward to going to work. Frowns broke out as some jostled for space and more tried to squeeze in. *Here we go again,
another mundane day of work.*

Then, it struck me that just a year before, the trains would
have been empty because the COVID-19 lockdowns had thrown
our daily routines into disarray. We couldn't even leave the
house, and some actually missed going to the office. But now
we were almost back to normal, and many were going back to
work—as usual. 'Routine', I realised, was good news, and 'boring' was a blessing!

King Solomon came to a similar conclusion after reflecting
on the seeming pointlessness of daily toil (ECCLESIASTES 2:17–23).
At times, it appeared endless, "meaningless", and unrewarding
(V. 21). But then he realised that simply being able to eat, drink
and work each day was a blessing from God (V. 24).

When we're deprived of routine, we can see that these simple actions are a luxury. Let's thank God that we can eat and
drink and find satisfaction in all our toil, for this is His gift (3:13).

LESLIE KOH

> *What simple blessings can you thank God for today?
> What can you do for someone who's in need or is unable
> to enjoy life's simple routines?*
>
> *Dear God, thank You for my 'usual' routines, no matter
> how boring they may seem at times. Help me to be
> grateful for Your every blessing in life.*

BIBLE IN A YEAR | 1 CHRONICLES 22–24; JOHN 8:28–59

Whatever you do, whether in word or deed, do it all
in the name of the Lord Jesus. [COLOSSIANS 3:17]

ALL FOR JESUS

When Jeff was fourteen, his mum took him to see a famous singer. Earlier in his career the musician had got
caught up in a self-destructive lifestyle while on music
tours. But that was before he and his wife were introduced to
Jesus. Their lives were radically changed when they became believers in Christ.

On the night of the concert, the singer began to entertain
the enthusiastic crowd. But after performing a few of his well-
known songs, one guy yelled out from the audience, "Hey, sing
one for Jesus!" Without any hesitation, he responded, "I just
sang four songs for Jesus."

It's been a few decades since then, but Jeff still remembers that
moment when he realised that *everything* we do should be for Jesus—even things that some might consider to be 'non-religious'.

We're sometimes tempted to divvy up the things we do in
life. Read the Bible. Share our story of coming to faith. Sing a
hymn. *Sacred stuff.* Mow the lawn. Go for a run. Sing a pop song.
Secular stuff.

Colossians 3:16 reminds us that the message of Christ indwells us in activities like teaching, singing and being thankful,
but verse 17 goes even further. It emphasises that as God's children, "whatever [we] do, whether in word or deed, [we] do it all
in the name of the Lord Jesus."

We do it all for Him.   *CINDY HESS KASPER*

> ***How can you do all things in the name of Jesus? How might
> you allow God to use your actions and words for His glory?***
>
> *Loving God, help me to surrender every one of my activities
> and words to You.*

BIBLE IN A YEAR | 1 CHRONICLES 25–27; JOHN 9:1–23

Look! I see four men walking around in the fire, unbound and unharmed, and the fourth looks like a son of the gods. [DANIEL 3:25]

JESUS IS THE ANSWER

The tale is told that after yet another stop on Albert Einstein's lecture tour, his chauffeur mentioned that he'd heard enough of the speech that he could give it. Einstein suggested they switch places at the next college, as no one there had seen his picture. The chauffer agreed and delivered a fine lecture. Then came the question-and-answer period. To one aggressive inquirer, the chauffer replied, "I can see you're a brilliant professor, but I'm surprised you would ask a question so simple that even my chauffeur could answer it." Then his 'chauffeur'—Albert Einstein himself—did answer it! So ends the fun but fictional story.

Daniel's courageous three friends were truly on the hot seat. King Nebuchadnezzar threatened to throw them into a blazing furnace if they didn't worship his idol. He asked, "What god will be able to rescue you from my hand?" (DANIEL 3:15). The friends still refused to bow, so the king heated the furnace seven times hotter and had them tossed in.

They didn't go alone. An "angel" (V. 28), perhaps Jesus Himself, joined them in the fire, keeping them from harm and providing an undeniable answer to the king's question (VV. 24–25). Nebuchadnezzar praised the "God of Shadrach, Meshach and Abednego" and conceded that "no other god can save in this way" (VV. 28–29).

At times, we may feel in over our heads. But Jesus stands with those who serve Him. He'll carry us. 		*MIKE WITTMER*

What problem are you unable to solve? How might Jesus relieve the pressure that you feel to fix your challenge?

Jesus, You're the answer when there's no answer.

BIBLE IN A YEAR | 1 CHRONICLES 28–29; JOHN 9:24–41

Who dares despise the day of small things?
[ZECHARIAH 4:10]

SMALL BUT GREAT

Will I make the Olympics? The young swimmer worried her speed was too slow. But when a maths professor studied her swim techniques, he saw how to improve her time by six seconds—a substantial difference at that level of competition. Attaching sensors to the swimmer's back, he didn't come up with major changes to improve her time. Instead, he identified tiny corrective actions that, if applied, could make the swimmer more efficient in the water, making the winning difference.

Small corrective actions in spiritual matters can make a big difference for us too. The prophet Zechariah taught a similar principle to a remnant of discouraged Jews struggling, along with their builder Zerubbabel, to rebuild God's temple after their exile. But "not by might nor by power, but by my Spirit," the Lord told Zerubbabel (ZECHARIAH 4:6).

As Zechariah declared, "Who dares despise the day of small things?" (V. 10). The exiles had worried that the temple wouldn't match the one built during King Solomon's reign. But just as the swimmer made the Olympics—winning a medal after surrendering to small corrections—Zerubbabel's band of builders learned that even a small, right effort made with God's help can bring victorious joy if our small acts glorify Him. In God, small becomes great.   *PATRICIA RAYBON*

Where have big, splashy actions led you to spiritual frustration? What small changes have enhanced your spiritual life?

Point me to small, good actions, dear God, that make a big difference in me for You.

BIBLE IN A YEAR | 2 CHRONICLES 1-3; JOHN 10:1-23

All of them were filled with the Holy Spirit
and began to speak in other tongues as the
Spirit enabled them. [ACTS 2:4]

WHAT ONLY THE SPIRIT CAN DO

During the discussion of a book on the Holy Spirit written by a ninety-four-year-old German theologian named Jürgen Moltmann, an interviewer asked him: "How do you activate the Holy Spirit? Can you take a pill? Do the pharmaceutical companies [deliver the Spirit]?" Moltmann's bushy eyebrows shot up. Shaking his head, he grinned, answering in accented English. "What can I do? Don't do anything. Wait on the Spirit, and the Spirit will come."

Moltmann highlighted our mistaken belief that our energy and expertise make things happen. Acts reveals that God makes things happen. At the start of the church, it had nothing to do with human strategy or impressive leadership. Rather, the Spirit arrived "like the blowing of a violent wind" into a room of frightened, helpless and bewildered disciples (ACTS 2:2). Next, the Spirit shattered all ethnic superiorities by gathering people who were at odds into one new community. The disciples were as shocked as anyone to see what God was doing within them. They didn't make anything happen; "the Spirit enabled them" (V. 4).

The church—and our shared work in the world—isn't defined by what we can do. We're entirely dependent on what only the Spirit can do. This allows us to be both bold and restful. On this, the day we celebrate Pentecost, may we wait for the Spirit and respond.   *WINN COLLIER*

How are you tempted to rely on your own efforts or tenacity? Where do you need to wait for what the Spirit can do?

God, I've exhausted myself by believing that I must make things happen. Holy Spirit, come and help me.

BIBLE IN A YEAR | 2 CHRONICLES 4-6; JOHN 10:24-42

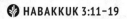

I will rejoice in the LORD, I will be joyful in
God my Saviour. [HABAKKUK 3:18]

HOPE THAT HOLDS

"I know Daddy's coming home because he sent me flowers." Those were my seven-year-old sister's words to our mother when Dad was missing in action during wartime. Before Dad left for his mission, he pre-ordered flowers for my sister's birthday, and they arrived while he was missing. But she was right: Dad did come home—after a harrowing combat situation. And decades later, she still keeps the vase that held the flowers as a reminder to always hold on to hope.

Sometimes holding on to hope isn't easy in a broken, sinful world. Daddies don't always come home, and children's wishes sometimes go unfulfilled. But God gives hope in the most difficult circumstances. In another time of war, the prophet Habakkuk predicted the Babylonian invasion of Judah (HABAKKUK 1:6; SEE 2 KINGS 24) but still affirmed that God is always good (HABAKKUK 1:12–13). Remembering God's kindness to His people in the past, Habakkuk proclaimed: "Though the fig tree does not bud and there are no grapes on the vines, though the olive crop fails and the fields produce no food, though there are no sheep in the pen and no cattle in the stalls, yet I will rejoice in the LORD, I will be joyful in God my Saviour" (3:17–18).

Some commentators believe Habakkuk's name means "to cling". We can cling to God as our ultimate hope and joy even in trials because He holds on to us and will never let go.

JAMES BANKS

***How does rejoicing in God help you in difficult times?
What can you do to praise Him today?***

*Father, thank You that come what may, my future is bright
with You!*

BIBLE IN A YEAR | 2 CHRONICLES 7–9; JOHN 11:1–29

I will make breath enter you, and you will
come to life. [EZEKIEL 37:5]

THE GOD WHO RESTORES

O n 4 November, 1966, a disastrous flood swept through
Florence, Italy, submerging Giorgio Vasari's renowned
work of art *The Last Supper* under a pool of mud, water and heating oil for more than twelve hours. With its paint
softened and its wooden frame significantly damaged, many
believed that the piece was beyond repair. However, after a te-
dious fifty-year conservation effort, experts and volunteers were
able to overcome monumental obstacles and restore the valuable painting.

When the Babylonians conquered Israel, the people felt hopeless—surrounded by death and destruction and in need of restoration (SEE LAMENTATIONS 1). During this period of turmoil, God
took the prophet Ezekiel to a valley and gave him a vision where
he was surrounded by dry bones. "Can these bones live?" God
asked. Ezekiel responded, "LORD, you alone know" (EZEKIEL 37:3).
God then told him to prophesy over the bones so they might
live again. "As I was prophesying," Ezekiel recounted, "there was
a noise, a rattling sound, and the bones came together" (V. 7).
Through this vision, God revealed to Ezekiel that Israel's restoration could only come through Him.

When we feel as if things in life have been broken and are beyond repair, God assures us He can rebuild our shattered pieces.
He'll give us new breath and new life.　　　　　*KIMYA LODER*

***What's broken in your life? How might you rely on God to
bring restoration?***

*Dear God, parts of my life seem like they'll never be
restored. I've tried to fix them on my own, but my only
hope of restoration is found in You.*

BIBLE IN A YEAR | 2 CHRONICLES 10-12; JOHN 11:30-57

No one could distinguish the sound of the
shouts of joy from the sound of weeping.
[EZRA 3:13]

SORROW AND JOY

A ngela's family reeled with sorrow as they experienced three
bereavements in just four weeks. After the one involving
the sudden death of her nephew, Angela and her two
sisters gathered around the kitchen table for three days, only
leaving to buy an urn, get takeout and attend the funeral. As
they wept over his death, they also rejoiced over the ultrasound
photos of the new life growing within their youngest sister.

In time, Angela found comfort and hope from the Old Testament book of Ezra. It describes God's people returning to Jerusalem after the Babylonians destroyed the temple and deported
them from their beloved city (SEE EZRA 1). As Ezra watched the
temple being rebuilt, he heard joyful praises to God (3:10–11). But
he also listened to the weeping of those who remembered life
before exile (V. 12).

One verse especially consoled Angela: "No one could distinguish the sound of the shouts of joy from the sound of weeping,
because the people made so much noise" (V. 13). She realised
that even if she was drenched in deep sorrow, joy could still appear.

We too might grieve the death of a loved one or mourn a
different loss. If so, we can express our cries of pain along with
our moments of rejoicing to God, knowing that He hears us and
gathers us in His arms.   *AMY BOUCHER PYE*

**Why do you think you can experience both joy and sorrow at
the same time? How can you cultivate joy today?**

*Loving God, in this world we experience pain and suffering.
Spark joy in me as I look to You for hope and peace.*

BIBLE IN A YEAR | 2 CHRONICLES 13-14; JOHN 12:1-26

GROWING IN CHRIST

O nce we've trusted Christ as our Saviour, how do we grow in our relationship with Him?

Jesus is called the "Good Shepherd" because He leads and watches over those who follow Him. He said: "My sheep listen to my voice; I know them, and they follow me" (JOHN 10:27). But how do we hear the Shepherd? Our sensitivity to His voice depends on communication in four areas.

God Talks to Us. As we read the Bible, He speaks to us through His own words and self-revelation (2 TIMOTHY 3:16).

We Talk to God. As we receive understanding from Him, we respond to Him with the affections and needs of our hearts (JOHN 15:7).

We Talk with Our New Family. As we connect with others who share our faith in Christ, we experience mutual encouragement and motivation to love as we ourselves have been loved (HEBREWS 10:24–25).

We Talk with Others about Christ. Christ desires for us to be His representatives to those who haven't yet believed (MATTHEW 4:19). One of the best ways to do this is to show honest concern for them. If they see our changed life and see that we're genuinely interested in them, they're more likely to be curious about the difference they see in us. No two believers have an identical relationship with the Saviour, but a genuine believer will have a desire to listen to God, to respond to Him, to fellowship with other believers, and to witness to those who don't yet know Jesus. As you begin your journey as a believer in Christ, let God creatively guide your path to a growing relationship with Him.

Dennis Fisher, *Our Daily Bread* author

★ What does it mean to experience spiritual growth in Jesus? As believers in Him, we're called to pursue maturity of faith, repentance and more. The topic is addressed in the devotions for **June 1, 8, 15** and **22**.

The one who calls you is faithful,
and he will do it. [1 THESSALONIANS 5:24]

IN GOD'S HANDS

Turning eighteen ushered in a new era in my daughter's life: legally an adult, she now had the right to vote in future elections and would soon embark on life after finishing college. This shift had instilled in me a sense of urgency—I would have precious little time with her under my roof to impart to her the wisdom she'd need to face the world on her own: how to manage finances, stay alert to world issues and make sound decisions.

My sense of duty to equip my daughter to handle her life was understandable. After all, I loved her and desired for her to flourish. But I realised that while I had an important role, it wasn't solely—or even primarily—my job. In Paul's words to the Thessalonians—a group of people he considered his children in the faith because he'd taught them about Jesus—he urged them to help one another (1 THESSALONIANS 5:14–15), but ultimately he trusted their growth to God. He acknowledged that God would "sanctify [them] through and through" (V. 23).

Paul trusted God to do what he couldn't: prepare them—"spirit, soul and body"—for the eventual return of Jesus (V. 23). Though his letters to the Thessalonians contained instructions, his trust in God for their wellbeing and preparedness teaches us that growth in the lives of those we care for is ultimately in God's hands (1 CORINTHIANS 3:6).   *KIRSTEN HOLMBERG*

How have you observed God helping you to grow in Him?
Whose growth do you need to entrust to Him?

Father, thank You for being the initiator and finisher of my spiritual growth. Please help me to trust You for that good work.

BIBLE IN A YEAR | 2 CHRONICLES 15-16; JOHN 12:27-50

He will judge between the nations.
[ISAIAH 2:4]

UNITING NATIONS

The longest international border in the world is shared by America and Canada, covering an incredible 5,525 miles of land and water. Workers regularly cut down ten feet of trees on both sides of the boundary to make the border line unmistakable. This lengthy ribbon of cleared land, called "the Slash", is dotted by more than eight thousand stone markers so visitors always know where the dividing line falls.

The physical deforestation of "the Slash" represents a separation of government and of cultures. As believers in Jesus, we look forward to a time when God will reverse that and unite all nations across the world under His rule. The prophet Isaiah spoke of a future where His temple will be firmly established and exalted (ISAIAH 2:2). People from all nations will gather to learn God's ways and "walk in his paths" (V. 3). No longer will we rely on human efforts that fail to maintain peace. As our true King, God will judge between nations and settle all disputes (V. 4).

Can you imagine a world without division and conflict? That's what God promises to bring! Regardless of the disunity around us, we can "walk in the light of the LORD" (V. 5) and choose to give Him our allegiance now. We know that God rules over all, and He will someday unite His people under one banner. *KAREN PIMPO*

What disunity in the world is heavy on your heart today? How does looking forward to God's eternal kingdom give you strength?

Dear God, I acknowledge Your sovereignty over every power in the world today! You reign above it all.

BIBLE IN A YEAR | 2 CHRONICLES 17–18; JOHN 13:1–20

Where can I go from your Spirit? Where can
I flee from your presence? [PSALM 139:7]

WITHIN GOD'S REACH

After an officer searched me, I stepped into the prison, signed the visitor's log, and sat in the crowded lobby. I prayed silently, watching adults fidgeting and sighing while young children complained about the wait. Over an hour later, an armed guard called a list of names including mine. He led my group into a room and motioned us to our assigned chairs. When my stepson sat in the chair on the other side of the thick glass window and picked up the telephone receiver, the depth of my helplessness overwhelmed me. But as I wept, God assured me that my stepson was still within His reach.

In Psalm 139, David says to God, "You know me. . . ; you are familiar with all my ways" (VV. 1–3). His proclamation of an all-knowing God leads to a celebration of His intimate care and protection (V. 5). Overwhelmed by the vastness of God's knowledge and the depth of His personal touch, David asks two rhetorical questions: "Where can I go from your Spirit? Where can I flee from your presence?" (V. 7).

When we or our loved ones are stuck in situations that leave us feeling hopeless and helpless, God's hand remains strong and steady. Even when we believe we've strayed too far for His loving redemption, we're always within His reach.　　*XOCHITL DIXON*

How has knowing the vastness of God's extensive reach affected your faith? How has He comforted you during a time when you felt hopeless and helpless?

Loving Father, help me to remember that You're always willing and able to reach me and my loved ones.

BIBLE IN A YEAR | 2 CHRONICLES 19-20; JOHN 13:21-38

Whoever does not take up their cross
and follow me is not worthy of me.
[MATTHEW 10:38]

COURAGE TO STAND FOR JESUS

n AD 155, the early church father Polycarp was threatened with death by fire for his faith in Christ. He replied, "For eighty and six years I have been his servant, and he has done me no wrong. And how can I now blaspheme my king who saved me?" Polycarp's response can be an inspiration for us when we face extreme trial because of our faith in Jesus, our King.

Just hours before Jesus' death, Peter boldly pledged His allegiance to Christ: "I will lay down my life for you" (JOHN 13:37). Jesus, who knew Peter better than Peter knew himself, replied, "Very truly I tell you, before the rooster crows, you will disown me three times!" (V. 38). However, after Jesus' resurrection, the same one who'd denied Him began to serve Him courageously and would eventually glorify Him through his own death (SEE 21:16–19).

Are you a Polycarp or a Peter? Most of us, if we're honest, are more of a Peter with a 'courage outage'—a failure to speak or act honourably as a believer in Jesus. Such occasions—whether in a classroom, boardroom or breakroom—needn't indelibly define us. When those failures occur, we must prayerfully dust ourselves off and turn to Jesus, the One who died for us and lives for us. He'll help us to be faithful to Him and courageously live for Him daily in difficult places.　　*ARTHUR JACKSON*

***When do you need extra doses of courage to stand for
Jesus? What do you find helpful in your witness for Him?***

*Heavenly Father, forgive me when I shrink back in fear and
betray You by my words or actions. I need Your strength to
live boldly as a believer in Jesus.*

BIBLE IN A YEAR | 2 CHRONICLES 21–22; JOHN 14

There is a time for everything, and a season
for every activity under the heavens.
[ECCLESIASTES 3:1]

SEASONS

I recently came across a helpful word: *wintering*. Just as winter
is a time of slowing down in much of the natural world, author
Katherine May uses this word to describe our need to rest
and recuperate during life's 'cold' seasons. I found the analogy
helpful after losing my father to cancer, which sapped me of energy for months. Resentful of this forced slowing down, I fought
against my winter, praying summer's life would return. But I had
much to learn.

Ecclesiastes famously says there's "a season for every activity
under the heavens"—a time to plant and to harvest, to weep
and to laugh, to mourn and to dance (3:1-4). I had read these
words for years but only started to understand them in my wintering season. For though we have little control over them, each
season is finite and will pass when its work is done. And while
we can't always fathom what it is, God is doing something significant in us through them (V. 11). My time of mourning wasn't
over. When it was, dancing would return. Just as plants and animals don't fight winter, I needed to rest and let it do its renewing work.

"Lord," a friend prayed, "would You do Your good work in
Sheridan during this difficult season." It was a better prayer than
mine. For in God's hands, seasons are purposeful things. Let's
submit to His renewing work in each one.   *SHERIDAN VOYSEY*

When have you wanted a season to end before its time?
What do you think God wants to do in you this season?

Father God, thank You for using every season for Your glory
and my good.

BIBLE IN A YEAR | 2 CHRONICLES 23-24; JOHN 15

Elijah climbed to the top of Carmel, bent down to the ground and put his face between his knees. [1 KINGS 18:42]

POWERFUL PRAYERS

The gold medal was nearly his. Home favourite Matthew Hudson-Smith hurtled towards the finish line. Yet then, out of nowhere, a blur zoomed past. Zambian sprinter Muzala Samukonga suddenly found a furious burst of speed—from well behind the race leader—to snatch victory in Birmingham's 2022 Commonwealth 400m sprint.

The crowd's amazement quickly turned to shock and concern, however. Samukonga collapsed, vomiting and shaking violently. Dangerously exhausted, he was wheeled away for medical care.

The prophet Elijah knew that feeling too. He had just claimed a huge victory against false prophets who were leading Israel astray. "LORD, answer me, so these people will know that you, LORD, are God," he prayed (1 KINGS 18:37), and fire rained down from heaven.

But then, as he asked God to end the severe drought, he couldn't have looked less like a champion. He "bent down to the ground and put his face between his knees" (V. 42). Wearied and weak, Elijah huddled up like a small child. Yet Scripture describes this prayer as "powerful and effective" (SEE JAMES 5:16–18).

Have you ever felt like Elijah, trying to pray when life's race has drained you? Powerful prayers rise when we are weakest. For powerful prayers are not prayed by powerful people, but by weak people to their all-powerful God. In weakness, we entrust our needs to the One who can rain both fire and water from the sky (VV. 38, 45). God never lacks power.　　*CHRIS WALE*

What weakness, exhaustion and need can you bring to God today? How does it encourage you to know that it is He, not you, who makes your prayers powerful?

Heavenly Father, I come before You just as I am: weak, worn out and in desperate need of Your loving care. Please work powerfully in my life today.

BIBLE IN A YEAR | 2 CHRONICLES 25–27; JOHN 16

If your brother or sister sins, go and point
out their fault, just between the two of you.
[MATTHEW 18:15]

A LOVING WARNING

In 2010, a tsunami struck the Indonesian island of Sumatra, killing more than four hundred people. But the deaths could have been prevented or minimised had the tsunami warning system been working properly. The tsunami detection networks (buoys) had become detached and drifted away.

Jesus said His disciples had a responsibility to warn fellow disciples of things that could harm them spiritually—including unrepentant sin. He outlined a process in which a believer who's been sinned against by another can humbly, privately and prayerfully "point out" the sin to the offending believer (MATTHEW 18:15). If the person repents, then the conflict can be resolved and the relationship restored. If the believer refuses to repent, then "one or two others" can help resolve the conflict (V. 16). If the sinning person still doesn't repent, then the issue is to be brought before "the church" (V. 17). If the offender still won't repent, the individual is to be removed from assembly fellowship, but he or she can certainly still be prayed for and shown Christ's love.

As believers in Jesus, let's pray for the wisdom and courage we need to care enough to lovingly warn one another of the dangers of unrepentant sin. Then, together, we can seek the joys of being restored to our heavenly Father and other believers. Jesus will be "there . . . with [us]" as we do (V. 20).   *MARVIN WILLIAMS*

**How can you humbly and lovingly confront someone regarding
a sin issue? What are the dangers of unrepentant sin?**

*Dear God, help me to love others enough to lovingly warn
them when I see them falling into sin.*

BIBLE IN A YEAR | 2 CHRONICLES 28–29; JOHN 17

We know that suffering produces perseverance;
perseverance, character; and character, hope.
[ROMANS 5:3–4]

STRENGTHENED THROUGH TRIALS

The memories flooded back when I rustled through some envelopes and glimpsed a sticker that said, "I've had an eye test." In my mind I saw my four-year-old son proudly wearing the sticker after enduring stinging eyedrops. Because of weak eye muscles, he had to wear a patch for hours each day over his strong eye—thereby forcing the weaker eye to develop. He also needed surgery. He met these challenges one by one, looking to us as his parents for comfort and depending on God with child-like faith. Through these challenges he developed resilience.

People who endure trials and suffering are often changed by the experience. But the apostle Paul went further and said to "glory in our sufferings" because through them we develop perseverance. With perseverance comes character; and with character, hope (ROMANS 5:3–4). Paul certainly knew trials—not only shipwrecks but imprisonment for his faith. Yet he wrote to the believers in Rome that "hope does not put us to shame, because God's love has been poured out into our hearts through the Holy Spirit" (V. 5). The apostle recognised that God's Spirit keeps our hope in Jesus alive when we put our trust in Him.

Whatever hardships you face, know that God will pour out His grace and mercy on you. He loves you.　　　*AMY BOUCHER PYE*

> *How have trials and challenges actually helped you trust God more? How could you commit yourself to His care in what you currently face?*

Ever-loving God, You promise that You'll never leave me. Help me to hold on to Your promises even when I'm struggling.

BIBLE IN A YEAR | 2 CHRONICLES 30–31; JOHN 18:1–18

The LORD watches over you—the LORD is
your shade at your right hand. [PSALM 121:5]

OUR PLACE OF SAFETY

Retired teacher Debbie Stephens Browder is on a mission to convince as many people as possible to plant trees. The reason? Heat. Soaring summer temperatures are causing more deaths each year. In response, she says, "I'm starting with trees." The canopy of heat protection that trees provide is one significant way to protect communities. "It's life or death. It's not just about beautifying the community."

The fact that shade isn't just refreshing but potentially life-saving would have been well known to the psalmist who wrote Psalm 121; in the Middle East, the risk of sunstroke is constant. This reality adds depth to the psalm's vivid description of God as our surest place of safety, the One in whose care "the sun will not harm [us] by day, nor the moon by night" (V. 6).

This verse can't mean that believers in Jesus are somehow immune to pain or loss in this life (or that heat isn't dangerous!). After all, Christ tells us, "In this world you will have trouble" (JOHN 16:33). But this metaphor of God as our shade does vividly reassure us that, whatever comes our way, our lives are held in His watchful care (PSALM 121:7–8). There we can find rest through trusting Him, knowing that nothing can separate us from His love (JOHN 10:28; ROMANS 8:39).   *MONICA LA ROSE*

*How have you experienced life-saving shade in God's
care? How does remembering you're always held in His
care give you courage?*

*Loving God, thank You for being my place of shade and
safety. Help me to find rest and courage as I grow in
trusting You.*

BIBLE IN A YEAR | 2 CHRONICLES 32-33; JOHN 18:19-40

In all your ways submit to him, and he will
make your paths straight. [PROVERBS 3:6]

LEAP OF FAITH

As I prepared to ride a zip line from the highest point of a
rainforest on the Caribbean Island of St. Lucia, fear welled
up inside me. Seconds before I jumped from the platform,
thoughts of everything that could go wrong filled my mind. But
with all the courage I could muster (and few options for turning back), I released. Dropping from the pinnacle of the forest,
I whizzed through the lush green trees, wind flowing through
my hair and my worries slowly fading. As I moved through the
air allowing gravity to carry me, my view of the next platform
became clearer and, with a gentle stop, I knew I'd arrived safely.

My time on the zip line became a picture for me of the times
God has us undertake new, challenging endeavours. Scripture
teaches us to put our trust in God and "lean not on [our] own
understanding" (PROVERBS 3:5) when we feel doubt and uncertainty. When our minds are filled with fear and doubt, our paths
can be unclear and distorted. But once we've made the decision
to step out in faith by submitting our way to God, "he will make
[our] paths straight" (V. 6). We become more confident taking
leaps of faith by learning who God is through spending time in
prayer and the Scriptures.

We can find freedom and tranquillity even in life's challenges
as we hang on to God and allow Him to guide us through the
changes in our lives.   *KIMYA LODER*

*What changes or challenges in your life require you
to put total trust in God? What's preventing you from
taking that leap of faith?*

*Dear Father, please give me the wisdom and strength I
need to trust You with my life.*

BIBLE IN A YEAR | 2 CHRONICLES 34-36; JOHN 19:1-22

He has given us new birth into a living hope.
[1 PETER 1:3]

GOD'S GARDEN

A reminder of the beauty and brevity of life grows outside my front door. Last spring, my wife planted moonflower vines, so named because of their large and round white blooms that resemble a full moon. Each flower opens for one night and then withers in the bright sun the following morning, never to bloom again. But the plant is prolific, and every evening presents a fresh parade of flowers. We love watching it as we come and go each day, wondering what new beauty will greet us when we return.

These fragile flowers call to mind a vital truth from Scripture. The apostle Peter, recalling the words of the prophet Isaiah, wrote, "You have been born again, not of perishable seed, but of imperishable, through the living and enduring word of God. For, 'All people are like grass, and all their glory is like the flowers of the field; the grass withers and the flowers fall' " (1 PETER 1:23–24). But he assures us that God keeps His promises forever (V. 25)!

Like flowers in a garden, our lives on earth are short when compared with eternity. But God has spoken beauty into our brevity. Through the good news of Jesus, we make a fresh beginning with God and trust His promise of unlimited life in His loving presence. When earth's sun and moon are but a memory, we will praise Him still.   *JAMES BANKS*

> **What do you most look forward to about eternity with God? Which of His promises are your favourites?**
>
> *Beautiful Saviour, I praise You for the gift of my salvation. Your love lasts forever, and I love You for it.*

BIBLE IN A YEAR | EZRA 1–2; JOHN 19:23–42

You are free . . . but you must not eat from
the tree of the knowledge of good and evil.
[GENESIS 2:16–17]

FREEING OBEDIENCE

The look on the young teen's face reflected angst and shame. Heading into the 2022 Winter Olympics, her success as a figure skater was unparalleled—a string of championships had made her a near certainty to win a gold medal. But then a test result revealed a banned substance in her system. With the immense weight of expectations and condemnation pressing down on her, she fell multiple times during her free-skate programme and didn't stand on the victors' platform—no medal. She'd displayed artistic freedom and creativity on the ice prior to the scandal, but now an accusation of a broken rule bound her to crushed dreams.

From the early days of humanity, God has revealed the importance of obedience as we exercise our free will. Disobedience led to devastating effects for Adam, Eve and all of us as sin brought brokenness and death to our world (GENESIS 3:6–19). It didn't have to be that way. God had told the two, "You are free to eat from any tree" but one (2:16–17). Thinking their "eyes [would] be opened, and [they would] be like God," they ate of the banned "tree of the knowledge of good and evil" (3:5; 2:17). Sin, shame and death followed.

God graciously provides freedom and so many good things for us to enjoy (JOHN 10:10). In love, He also calls us to obey Him for our good. May He help us choose obedience and find life full of joy and free of shame. *TOM FELTEN*

How does the world view freedom? Why is it ultimately freeing to obey God and His ways?

Father, thank You for the true freedom and life found in choosing obedience to You.

BIBLE IN A YEAR | EZRA 3–5; JOHN 20

How deserted lies the city, once so
full of people! [LAMENTATIONS 1:1]

IT'S EMPTY NOW

My brothers and our families spent the day moving our parents' belongings from our childhood home. Late in the afternoon, we went back for one last pickup and, knowing this would be our final time in our family home, posed for a picture in the back garden. I was fighting tears when my mum turned to me and said, "It's all empty now." That pushed me over the edge. The house that holds fifty-four years of memories is empty now. I try not to think of it.

The ache in my heart resonates with Jeremiah's first words of Lamentations: "How deserted lies the city, once so full of people!" (1:1). An important difference is that Jerusalem was empty "because of her many sins" (v. 5). God exiled His people to Babylon because they rebelled against Him and refused to repent (v. 18). My parents weren't moving because of sin, at least not directly. But ever since Adam's sin in the garden of Eden, each person's health has declined over their lifetime. As we age, it's not unusual for us to downsize into homes that are easier to maintain.

I'm thankful for the memories that made our modest home special. Pain is the price of love. I know the next goodbye won't be to my parents' home but to my parents themselves. And I cry. I cry out to Jesus to come, put an end to goodbyes and restore all things. My hope is in Him. 　　　　　　　　　*MIKE WITTMER*

> ***What place holds fond memories for you? Thank God for
> the people who loved you there. How might you make
> new memories today?***
>
> *Father, thank You for giving me a home in Your forever family.*

BIBLE IN A YEAR | EZRA 6–8; JOHN 21

We do not belong to those who shrink back
. . . but to those who have faith and are
saved. [HEBREWS 10:39]

TEXTS, TROUBLES AND TRIUMPHS

Jimmy hadn't allowed the reality of social unrest, danger and discomfort to keep him from travelling to one of the poorest countries in the world to encourage ministry couples. The steady stream of text messages to our team back home revealed the challenges he encountered. "Okay, boys, activate the prayer line. We've gone ten miles in the last two hours. . . . Car has overheated a dozen times." Transportation setbacks meant that he arrived just before midnight to preach to those who'd waited for five hours. Later we received a text with a different tone. "Amazing, sweet time of fellowship. . . . About a dozen people came forward for prayer. It was a powerful night!"

Faithfully serving God can be challenging. The exemplars of faith listed in Hebrews 11 would agree. Compelled by their faith in God, ordinary men and women faced uncomfortable and unfathomable circumstances. "Some faced jeers and flogging, and even chains and imprisonment" (V. 36). Their faith compelled them to take risks and rely on God for the outcome. The same is true for us. Living out our faith may not take us to risky places far away, but it may well take us across the street or across the campus or to an empty seat in a lunchroom or boardroom. Risky? Perhaps. But the rewards, now or later, will be well worth the risks as God helps us.   *ARTHUR JACKSON*

How can you take a risk and follow Jesus even though it might be uncomfortable? What keeps you 'playing it safe'?

Dear Father, please give me strength and courage to let go of my life and entrust it to You.

BIBLE IN A YEAR | EZRA 9–10; ACTS 1

He who began a good work in you will carry
it on to completion until the day of Christ
Jesus. [PHILIPPIANS 1:6]

PUTTING THE PIECES TOGETHER

While our family quarantined due to the global pandemic, we took on an ambitious project—an eighteen-thousand-piece puzzle! Even though we worked on it almost daily, often we felt like we weren't making much progress. Five months after we began, we finally celebrated adding the final piece to the nine-by-six-foot puzzle that covered our dining room floor.

Sometimes my life feels a bit like a giant puzzle—many pieces in place, but a whole lot more still lying in a jumble on the floor. While I know that God is at work transforming me to be more and more like Jesus, sometimes it can be hard to see much progress.

I take great comfort in Paul's encouragement in his letter to the Philippians when he said he prayed for them with joy because of the good work they were doing (1:3-4). But his confidence came not from their abilities but from God, believing that "he who began a good work . . . [would] carry it on to completion" (V. 6).

God has promised to finish His work in us. Like a puzzle, there may be sections that still need our attention, and there are times when we don't seem to make much progress. But we can have confidence that our faithful God is still putting the pieces together.   *LISA M. SAMRA*

Where do you see God currently working in your life? What are some of the beautiful areas of your life He's pieced together?

Heavenly Father, please give me eyes of faith to see how You're at work in my life.

BIBLE IN A YEAR | NEHEMIAH 1–3; ACTS 2:1–21

I will not forget you!
[ISAIAH 49:15]

GOD'S UNFAILING MEMORY

Aman owned more than £340 million in bitcoin, but he couldn't access a penny of it. He lost the password for the device storing his funds, and disaster loomed: after ten password attempts, the device would self-destruct. A fortune lost forever. For a decade, the man had agonised, desperately trying to recall the password to his life-altering investment. He tried eight passwords and failed eight times. In 2021, he lamented that he had just two more chances before it all went up in smoke.

We're a forgetful people. Sometimes we forget small things (where we placed our keys), and sometimes we forget massive things (a password that unlocks millions). Thankfully, God isn't like us. He never forgets the things or people that are dear to Him. In times of distress, Israel feared that God had forgotten them. "The LORD has forsaken me, the Lord has forgotten me" (ISAIAH 49:14). Isaiah assured them, however, that their God *always* remembers. "Can a mother forget the baby at her breast?" the prophet asks. Of course, a mother will not forget her suckling child. Still, even if a mother were to commit such an absurdity, we know God will never forget us (V. 15).

"See," God says, "I have engraved you on the palms of my hands" (V. 16). God has etched our names into His own being. Let's remember that He can't forget us—the ones He loves.

WINN COLLIER

When have you forgotten something important?
How does God's strong memory assure you?

Dear God, I'm grateful Your memory is resilient and
trustworthy.

BIBLE IN A YEAR | NEHEMIAH 4–6; ACTS 2:22–47

Speak, for your servant is listening.
[1 SAMUEL 3:10]

KEEP ON LISTENING

Grandpa appeared at the bedroom door to look in on the two little girls. "I've told you twice already," he said to my young daughter and her cousin, tucked up together in a double bed for their overnight sleepover. "You need to be quiet and go to sleep."

"But she keeps on talking," my daughter protested.

Her cousin shot back, "That's because she keeps on listening."

The young boy Samuel kept on listening too. He'd been learning to serve God in the tabernacle but hadn't encountered Him personally (V. 7). Not until the night he heard a voice calling his name. Samuel assumed it was his ageing mentor, Eli. But after three visits from the boy, Eli realised Samuel was hearing God and advised him what to do. So the next time Samuel heard the voice, he said, "Speak, for your servant is listening" (V. 10). Although the message was unpleasant to hear, Samuel obediently passed it on. In fact, he kept on listening to God, bringing His guidance and judgements to Israel, right into his old age.

When we long to hear God, Samuel's words of welcome and obedience help focus our attention. They prompt us to still our thoughts and to listen as we start praying or reading Scripture. They can also help us to pause and pay attention to God through our day. Be encouraged that God will speak to you too.

ANNE LE TISSIER

How do good listeners you know inspire your own attentive listening to God? If you struggle to hear God's voice, whom could you approach to help you nurture greater discernment?

Father, You have so much You want to say to me through prayer, Your word, circumstances and relationships. Please keep on speaking as I learn to listen and respond.

BIBLE IN A YEAR | NEHEMIAH 7-9; ACTS 3

I kneel before the Father, from whom every
family in heaven and on earth derives its
name. [EPHESIANS 3:14–15]

FIXING GO-KARTS

The garage of my childhood home holds many memories. On Saturday mornings, my dad would roll our car down the driveway so we had room to work—with my favourite project being a broken go-kart we'd found. On that garage floor, we gave it new wheels, attached a sporty, plastic windshield, and—with Dad on the street looking out for traffic—I would race down the driveway with such excitement! Looking back, I see more was going on in that garage than simply fixing go-karts. Instead, a young boy was being shaped by his dad—and getting a glimpse of God in the process.

Human beings have been patterned on God's own nature (GENESIS 1:27–28). Human parenting has its origin in Him too, for He is "the Father, from whom every family in heaven and on earth derives its name" (EPHESIANS 3:14–15). Just as parents imitate God's life-giving abilities by bringing children into the world, when they nurture and protect their kids, they express qualities not sourced in themselves but in Father God. He's the model all parenting is based on.

My father wasn't perfect. Like every father and mother, his parenting sometimes failed to imitate heaven's. But when it so often did imitate God, it gave me a glimpse of His own nurture and protection—right there, as we fixed go-karts on the garage floor.   SHERIDAN VOYSEY

***How do you see good parenting reflecting God's nature?
How can you reflect His nurture and protection to others today?***

*Father God, help me nurture and protect our children and
others today, revealing Your good qualities to them.*

BIBLE IN A YEAR | NEHEMIAH 10-11; ACTS 4:1-22

They will never follow a stranger; . . . because
they do not recognise a stranger's voice.
[JOHN 10:5]

LOVING BEING HIS

When I found her, she was hungry, grubby and meowing
desperately for attention. A litter tray, some food and
a large vet's bill later, Elma came with me to her new
home.

At first, she would go to anyone and climb up on their lap. But
now that she's bonded with me, she refuses to leave my side.
She loves being my cat—sleeping next to me and following me
everywhere. She is much more confident, but much more wary
of strangers.

When Jesus found us, we too were in a state of dire need. Sin
and shame made us feel grubby and desperate for loving restoration. Likening us to sheep, and calling Himself the "Good Shepherd", Jesus taught, "whoever enters through me will be saved.
They will come in and go out, and find pasture" (JOHN 10:9). He
saves us, cleans us, provides for us and leads us.

When we hear other voices in the world inviting us to try a
different way of life—to 'move on' from Jesus—may we react
like my Elma. "[My sheep] will never follow a stranger; in fact,
they will run away from him because they do not recognise a
stranger's voice" (V. 5).

Jesus, the Good Shepherd, has rescued us. And we love being
His sheep, like Elma loves being my cat. He delights to give us
"life to the full" (V. 10).   *DEBBI FRALICK*

What do you love most about belonging to Jesus?
How would you describe the fullness of life He gives you?

*Jesus, thank You for finding me, saving me, restoring me
and making me Your own. I love being Yours.*

BIBLE IN A YEAR | NEHEMIAH 12-13; ACTS 4:23-37

Religion that God our Father accepts . . .
is this: to look after orphans and widows in
their distress. [JAMES 1:27]

TRUE RELIGION

During one summer break in my university years, a classmate died unexpectedly. I'd seen him just a few days prior and he looked fine. My classmates and I were young and in what we thought was the prime of our lives.

But what I remember most about my classmate's death was witnessing my friends live out what the apostle James calls "genuine religion" (JAMES 1:27 NLT). Several of the men became like brothers to the sister of the deceased. They attended her wedding and travelled to her baby shower years after her brother's death. One even gifted her a phone to contact him whenever she needed to call.

True religion, according to James, is "to look after orphans and widows in their distress" (V. 27). While my friend's sister wasn't an orphan in the literal sense, she no longer had her brother. Her new 'brothers' filled in the gap.

And that's what all of us who want to practise true and pure life in Jesus can do—"do what [Scripture] says" (V. 22), including caring for those in need (2:14–17). Our faith in Him prompts us to look after the vulnerable as we keep ourselves from the negative influences of the world as He helps us. After all, it's the true religion God accepts.   *KATARA PATTON*

> **How have you seen true religion played out? How can
> you display genuine faith to others?**
>
> *Heavenly Father, open my eyes to see where I can help the
> most vulnerable as You lead me.*

How good and pleasant it is when God's
people live together in unity! [PSALM 133:1]

STEP BY STEP

Adozen teams, each including three people standing shoulder to shoulder, prepared for the four-legged race. Each outside person bound to the person in the middle by colourful rags at their ankles and knees, every trio locked their eyes on the finish line. When the whistle blew, the teams lunged forward. Most of them fell and struggled to regain their footing. A few groups chose to hop instead of walk. Some gave up. But one team delayed their start, confirmed their plan, and communicated as they moved forward. They stumbled along the way but pressed on and soon passed all the teams. Their willingness to cooperate, step by step, enabled them to cross the finish line together.

Living for God within the community of believers in Jesus often feels as frustrating as trying to move forward during a four-legged race. We often stumble when interacting with people who hold different opinions from us.

Peter speaks of prayer, hospitality and using our gifts to align ourselves in unity for life ahead. He urges believers in Jesus to "love each other deeply" (1 PETER 4:8), to be hospitable without complaining and to "serve others, as faithful stewards of God's grace in its various forms" (V. 10). When we ask God to help us communicate and cooperate, we can lead the race in showing the world how to celebrate differences and live together in unity.

XOCHITL DIXON

**When have you struggled to work with someone who
was different from you? How has God helped you?**

*Mighty God, please help me communicate and cooperate
with others as I learn to love like You.*

BIBLE IN A YEAR | ESTHER 3-5; ACTS 5:22-42

Faith comes from hearing the message, and the message is heard through the word about Christ. [ROMANS 10:17]

FAITH COMES FROM HEARING

When Pastor Bob suffered an injury that affected his voice, he entered fifteen years of crisis and depression. What, he wondered, does a pastor do who can't talk? He struggled with this question, pouring out his grief and confusion to God. He reflected, "I only knew one thing to do—to go after the Word of God." As he spent time reading the Bible, his love for God grew: "I've devoted my life to absorbing and immersing myself in the Scripture because faith comes from hearing and hearing by the word of God."

We find the phrase "faith comes from hearing" in the apostle Paul's letter to the Romans. Paul longed for all of his fellow Jewish people to believe in Christ and be saved (ROMANS 10:9). How would they believe? Through the faith that "comes from hearing the message . . . through the word about Christ" (V. 17).

Pastor Bob seeks to receive and believe in Christ's message, especially as he reads the Bible. He can only speak for an hour a day and has constant pain when he does so, but he continues to find peace and contentment from God through his immersion in Scripture. So too we can trust that Jesus will reveal Himself to us in our struggles. He will increase our faith as we hear His message, whatever challenges we face. *AMY BOUCHER PYE*

How could immersing yourself in Scripture strengthen your faith? How have you found contentment even when life is challenging?

Loving God, You give me hope even when I feel stuck and in pain. Shape me into the person You want me to be.

BIBLE IN A YEAR | ESTHER 6-8; ACTS 6

When the Israelites saw the mighty hand
of the LORD . . . [they] put their trust in him.
[EXODUS 14:31]

GOD'S MIGHTY POWER

The seemingly impossible happened when hurricane-force winds changed the flow of a mighty river. In August 2021, Hurricane Ida came ashore on the US coast, and the astonishing result was a 'negative flow' along the Mississippi River, meaning water actually flowed *upriver* for several hours.

Experts estimate that over its life cycle a hurricane can expend energy equivalent to ten thousand nuclear bombs! Such incredible power to change the course of flowing water helps me understand the Israelites' response to a far more significant 'negative flow' recorded in Exodus.

While fleeing the Egyptians who'd enslaved them for centuries, the Israelites came to the edge of the Red Sea. In front of them was a wide body of water and behind them was the heavily armoured Egyptian army. In that seemingly impossible situation, "the LORD drove the sea back with a strong east wind and turned it into dry land . . . and the Israelites went through the sea" (EXODUS 14:21–22). Rescued in that incredible display of power, "the people feared the LORD" (V. 31).

Responding with awe is natural after experiencing the immensity of God's power. But it didn't end there; the Israelites also "put their trust" in Him (V. 31).

As we experience God's power in creation, we too can stand in awe of His might and place our trust in Him.   *LISA M. SAMRA*

> **When have you experienced a display of God's power in
> creation? How did that lead to a greater trust in Him?**
>
> *Creator God, please help me to trust You more when I see
> awesome displays of Your power.*

BIBLE IN A YEAR | ESTHER 9–10; ACTS 7:1–21

Gather the pieces that are left over.
Let nothing be wasted. [JOHN 6:12]

HE MAKES US NEW

As a travelling executive, Shawn Seipler wrestled with an odd question. What happens to leftover soap in hotel rooms? Thrown out as rubbish for landfills, millions of soap bars could instead find new life, Seipler believed. So he launched Clean the World, a recycling venture that has helped more than eight thousand hotels, cruise lines and resorts turn millions of pounds of discarded soap into sterilised, newly moulded soap bars. Sent to people in need in more than one hundred countries, the recycled soap helps prevent countless hygiene-related illnesses and deaths.

As Seipler said, "I know it sounds funny, but that little bar of soap on the counter in your hotel room can literally save a life."

The gathering up of something used or dirty to give it new life is also one of the most loving traits of our Saviour, Jesus. In that manner, after He fed a crowd of five thousand with five small barley loaves and two small fish, He still said to His disciples, "Gather the pieces that are left over. Let nothing be wasted" (JOHN 6:12).

In our lives, when we feel washed out, God sees us not as wasted lives but as His miracles. Never throwaways in His sight, we have divine potential for new kingdom work. "Therefore, if anyone is in Christ, the new creation has come: the old has gone, the new is here!" (2 CORINTHIANS 5:17). What makes us new? Christ within us.   *PATRICIA RAYBON*

When have you felt like you possessed little value?
How has Jesus given you new life?

When I feel worthless, dear Father, help me see
my new life in You.

BIBLE IN A YEAR | JOB 1-2; ACTS 7:22-43

We have been made holy through the sacrifice
of the body of Jesus Christ once for all.
[HEBREWS 10:10]

ON HIS HEAD

Back in 1779, Charles Simeon's interests were horses, games
and fashion. But an upcoming communion service at his Cam-
bridge college would lead to him considering God's Word.

He discovered in the Old Testament that God's people had
placed their hands on sacrificial animals' heads to transfer the
guilt of their sin (SEE LEVITICUS 4:15; 16:21). The Holy Spirit showed
him the connection between this action and Christ's sacrifice.
"May I transfer all my guilt to another?" he wondered. "Has God
provided an offering for me, that I may lay my sins on his head?"
That day he laid his sins "upon the sacred head of Jesus".

The writer of Hebrews wants us to make this connection
too. The sacrificial system was "only a shadow" of the salvation
Christ would bring (HEBREWS 10:1). In reality, "It is impossible for
the blood of bulls and goats to take away sins" (V. 4). But Jesus
was born in a body prepared to bear the weight of our sin and
guilt (VV. 5–7). "And by that will, we have been made holy through
the sacrifice of the body of Jesus Christ once for all" (V. 10).

Real freedom from sin is found in laying every shameful
thought, word and deed on the bowed head of Jesus hanging
upon the cross. He did what no animal or human can do: He
"offered for all time one sacrifice for sins" (V. 12).　　*CHRIS WALE*

> ***How do you respond to the image of Christ bowing His
> head on the cross for you to lay your sin upon Him? Will
> you offer Him humble thanks and praise today?***
>
> *Jesus, I humble myself before You in trembling awe. How
> incredible that You are not only my King, but my sacrifice
> for sin too.*

BIBLE IN A YEAR | JOB 3-4; ACTS 7:44-60

Where your treasure is, there your heart
will be also. [MATTHEW 6:21]

EASY MONEY

I n the late 1700s, a young man discovered a mysterious depression on Nova Scotia's Oak Island. Guessing that pirates
had buried treasure there, he and a couple of companions
started digging. They never found any treasure, but the rumour
took on a life of its own. Over the centuries, others continued
digging at the site—expending a great amount of time and expense. The hole is now more than one hundred feet (thirty metres) deep.

Such obsessions betray the emptiness in the human heart. A
story in the Bible shows how one man's behaviour revealed just
such a void in his heart. Gehazi had long been a reliable servant
of the great prophet Elisha. But when Elisha declined the lavish
gifts of a military commander whom God had healed of leprosy,
Gehazi concocted a story to get some of the loot (2 KINGS 5:22).
When Gehazi returned home, he lied to the prophet (V. 25). But
Elisha knew. He asked him, "Was not my spirit with you when the
man got down from his chariot to meet you?" (V. 26). In the end,
Gehazi got what he wanted, but lost what was important (V. 27).

Jesus taught us not to pursue this world's treasures and to
instead "store up . . . treasures in heaven" (MATTHEW 6:20).

Beware of any shortcuts to your heart's desires. Following Jesus is the way to fill the emptiness with something real.
TIM GUSTAFSON

**What do you long for the most? What pursuits and
obsessions have left you feeling empty?**

*Dear God, I give my desires over to You. Please help me
crave the treasures that You value.*

BIBLE IN A YEAR | JOB 5-7; ACTS 8:1-25

Give [your enemy] food to eat. . . . In doing
this, you will heap burning coals on his head.
[PROVERBS 25:21–22]

HEAPING COALS ON ENEMIES

Dan endured daily beatings from the same prison guard. He felt compelled by Jesus to love this man, so one morning, before the beating was about to begin, Dan said, "Sir, if I'm going to see you every day for the rest of my life, let's become friends." The guard said, "No sir. We can never be friends." Dan insisted and reached out his hand.

The guard froze. He began to shake, then grabbed Dan's hand and wouldn't let go. Tears streamed down his face. He said, "Dan, my name is Rosoc. I would love to be your friend." The guard didn't beat Dan that day, or ever again.

Scripture tells us, "If your enemy is hungry, give him food to eat; if he is thirsty, give him water to drink. In doing this, you will heap burning coals on his head, and the LORD will reward you" (PROVERBS 25:21–22). The "coals" imagery may reflect an Egyptian ritual in which a guilty person showed his repentance by carrying a bowl of hot coals on his head. Similarly, our kindness may cause our enemies to become red in the face from embarrassment, which may lead them to repentance.

Who is your enemy? Who do you dislike? Dan discovered that the kindness of Christ was strong enough to change any heart—his enemy's and his own. We can show the same kindness too.

MIKE WITTMER

***What kind act might you do today for an enemy?
How might you pray specifically for them?***

*Dear Jesus, I praise You that Your kindness leads me to
repentance and inspires me to be kind to my enemies.*

BIBLE IN A YEAR | JOB 8–10; ACTS 8:26–40

You are with me.
[PSALM 23:4]

WHEN YOU'RE LONELY

At 7 p.m., Hui-Liang was in his kitchen, eating rice and leftover fish balls. The Chua family in the flat next door was having dinner too, and their laughter and conversation cut through the silence of Hui-Liang's unit, where he had lived alone since his wife died. He'd learned to live with loneliness; over the years, its stabbing pain had become a dull ache. But tonight, the sight of the one bowl and pair of chopsticks on his table pierced him deeply.

Before he went to bed that night, Hui-Liang read Psalm 23, his favourite psalm. The words that mattered most to him are only four syllables: "You are with me" (V. 4). More than the shepherd's practical acts of care towards the sheep, it was his steadfast presence and loving gaze over every detail of the life of the sheep (VV. 2–5) that gave Hui-Liang peace.

Just knowing that someone is there, that someone is with us, brings great comfort in those lonely moments. God promises His children that His love will always be with us (PSALM 103:17), and that He'll never leave us (HEBREWS 13:5). When we feel alone and unseen—whether in a quiet kitchen, on the bus going home from work, or even in a crowded supermarket—we can know that the Shepherd's gaze is always on us. We can say, "You are with me."

KAREN HUANG

> ***When do you usually feel lonely?***
> ***How does Psalm 23 encourage you?***
>
> *Loving God, thank You for always being with me.*

Many tax collectors and sinners were
eating with him. [MARK 2:15]

THE GOSPEL IN UNEXPECTED PLACES

Recently, I found myself in a place I'd seen in movies and on TV more times than I could count: Hollywood, California. There, in the foothills of Los Angeles, those enormous white letters marched proudly across that famous hillside as I viewed them from my hotel window.

Then I noticed something else: down to the left was a prominent cross. I'd never seen *that* in a movie. And the moment I left my hotel room, some students from a local church began to share Jesus with me.

We might sometimes think of Hollywood as only the epicentre of worldliness, in utter contrast with God's kingdom. Yet clearly Christ was at work there, catching me by surprise with His presence.

The Pharisees were consistently surprised by where Jesus turned up. He didn't hang out with the people they expected. Instead, Mark 2:13–17 tells us He spent time with "tax collectors and sinners" (V. 15), people whose lives practically screamed, "Unclean!" Yet there Jesus was, among those who needed Him most (VV. 16–17).

More than two thousand years later, Jesus continues to plant His message of hope and salvation in unexpected places, among the most unexpected of people. And He's called and equipped us to be a part of that mission.   *ADAM R. HOLZ*

> **When have you noticed God at work in a place that
> surprised you? What adjustments might you make to be
> open to the Spirit leading you into unexpected places?**
>
> *Heavenly Father, thank You for showing up even in places
> where I'm tempted to believe You're absent. Thank You for
> calling me to be a part of Your mission.*

BIBLE IN A YEAR | JOB 14–16; ACTS 9:22–43

The Lord is not slow . . . He is patient
with you, not wanting anyone to perish.
[2 PETER 3:9]

PARTING WORDS

As he neared the end of his life, John M. Perkins had a message for the people he would leave behind. Perkins, known for advocating racial reconciliation, said, "Repentance is the only way back to God. Unless you repent, you will all perish."

These words mirror the language of Jesus and many other people in the Bible. Christ said, "Unless you repent, you too will all perish" (LUKE 13:3). The apostle Peter said, "Repent, then, and turn to God, so that your sins may be wiped out" (ACTS 3:19).

Much earlier in Scripture, we read the words of yet another person who desired that his people would turn to God. In his farewell address "to all Israel" (1 SAMUEL 12:1), the prophet, priest and judge Samuel said, "Do not be afraid. You have done . . . evil; yet do not turn away from the LORD, but serve the LORD with all your heart" (V. 20). This was his message of repentance—to turn from evil and follow God wholeheartedly.

We all sin and miss the mark of His standard. So we need to repent, which means to turn away from sin and turn to Jesus, who forgives us and empowers us to follow Him. Let's heed the words of two men, John Perkins and Samuel, who recognised how God can use the power of repentance to change us into people He can use for His honour.   *DAVE BRANON*

Why is it vital to turn from sin and ask Christ for forgiveness?
What does it mean for you to follow God with all your heart?

Dear God, guide me to true repentance. Please help me
to recognise my sin and put my total trust in the saving
power of Jesus.

BIBLE IN A YEAR | JOB 17–19; ACTS 10:1–23

LED BY THE SPIRIT

The teaching about the Holy Spirit, the third person of the Trinity, is at the core of the Christian faith. Included in this teaching is the Spirit's leading in our lives, for He guides us in our everyday living.

Romans 8 refers to the Spirit multiple times. Verse 14 says, "Those who are led by the Spirit of God are the children of God." This is in the section that speaks of the believer in Jesus' battle against our sinful human nature, "the flesh" (SEE VV. 12–13). The Spirit's leading is invisible, internal and informed by Scripture (the "sword of the Spirit"; see Ephesians 6:17).

Believers in Jesus aren't without God's help as they seek to honour Him in their earthly living. The dynamics and privileges of family membership continue in Romans 8:15: "The Spirit you received does not make you slaves . . . ; rather, the Spirit you received brought about your adoption to sonship. And by him we cry, 'Abba, Father.' "

Far from being the privilege of an elite group, the Spirit's leading is the heritage of every child of God. Practically speaking, what does His leading look like? It looks like a shepherd lovingly leading his sheep as expressed in Psalm 23:3: "He guides me along right paths for his name's sake." The Spirit of God leads us along "right paths". As we spend time in prayer and the Scriptures, we learn how to live by His leading and walk in step with Him. Then our light shines, and He gets the glory.

Arthur Jackson, *Our Daily Bread* author

★ What does it mean to follow the Holy Spirit's leading? How do we keep in step with the Spirit? The topic is addressed in the devotions for **July 1, 8, 15** and **22**.

Do not quench the Spirit.
[1 THESSALONIANS 5:19]

CONNECTED TO THE POWER SOURCE

Despite knowing that the electricity wasn't working in our house after a strong storm (an inconveniently common occurrence in my part of the world), I instinctively flipped on the light switch when I entered the room. Of course, nothing happened. I was still enveloped in darkness.

That experience—expecting light even when I knew the connection to the power source was broken—vividly reminded me of a spiritual truth. Too often we expect power even as we fail to rely on the Spirit.

In 1 Thessalonians, Paul wrote of the way God caused the gospel message to come "not simply with words but also with power, with the Holy Spirit and deep conviction" (1:5). And when we accept God's forgiveness, believers too have immediate access to the power of His Spirit in our lives. That power cultivates in us characteristics such as love, joy, peace and patience (GALATIANS 5:22–23) and it empowers us with gifts to serve the church, including teaching, helping and guiding (1 CORINTHIANS 12:28).

Paul warned his readers that it's possible to "quench the spirit" (1 THESSALONIANS 5:19). We might restrict the power of the Spirit by ignoring God's presence or rejecting His conviction (JOHN 16:8). But we don't have to live disconnected from Him. God's power is always available to His children.   *LISA M. SAMRA*

**When have you felt like the Spirit's power was limited?
How have you experienced the power of God's Spirit?**

*Almighty God, help me experience the power of Your Spirit
in my life.*

BIBLE IN A YEAR | JOB 20–21; ACTS 10:24–48

But I trust in you, LORD; . . . My times are in
your hands. [PSALM 31:14–15]

SECURE IN GOD'S HANDS

It was the last thing Monica expected after thirty-three years of
marriage: her husband announced he was leaving. This threatened her home, her income, her future pension and, not least,
the companionship of the man she loved. His rejection sowed
feelings of deep inadequacy. Devastated, she feared the loss of
friends, and her new identity as a divorcee filled her with shame.

For hours Monica sat with God as her world caved in, overwhelmed by grief and stress. But God's Word still held true: He
still had a plan for her. She was not in her husband's hands: her
changing times were in God's hands. She could trust Him for help,
comfort and provision, just like David had done in Psalm 31.

David felt hunted, rejected and isolated by the threats against
him (PSALM 31:4,11–13). In "soul and body" he was utterly drained
by his distress (VV. 9–10). But his hope was in God: his "refuge" of
righteousness, deliverance and guidance (VV. 1–3). David could
trust in God, despite his circumstances, because he believed his
times were in God's hands (VV. 14–15).

"How abundant are the good things that [God] has stored up"
for us (V. 19). As we wait for the fulfilment, we can take refuge "in
the shelter of [His] presence" (V. 20). And as we affirm who God
is, we are strengthened and encouraged for whatever we may
face (VV. 21–24).　　　　　　　　　　　　　　*ANNE LE TISSIER*

> **Which of Monica and David's fears or emotions do you
> most identify with? How does the knowledge that God
> sees, cares and promises to provide help you receive His
> peace, strength and reassurance?**
>
> *Father, I choose to believe Your promises as a reality to
> grasp hold of. Thank You for reassuring me that my life is in
> no other hands but Yours.*

BIBLE IN A YEAR | JOB 22–24; ACTS 11

"He himself bore our sins" in his body on the cross, so that we might die to sins and live for righteousness. [1 PETER 2:24]

THE GREATEST OF ALL TIME

Many football fans eat, breathe and sleep their sport. But one prominent football manager doesn't count football as the key thing in his life. That place he gives to a person: Jesus Christ.

Jürgen Klopp claims that Jesus is the most important person the world has ever known. Why? Because when Jesus "took all of our sins" and was nailed to the cross, that was the "most decisive thing that ever happened . . . because it changed everything".

In affirming this, the German football manager echoes Peter, the disciple who had betrayed Jesus, but whom Jesus restored. In one of his letters, Peter highlights the importance of Christ dying for us: He bore our sins on the cross "so that we might die to sins and live for righteousness" (1 PETER 2:24). His wounds bring us healing (V. 24). And when we stray like wandering sheep, we can return "to the Shepherd and Overseer" of our souls (V. 25). Peter shared the good news of Jesus widely, wanting others to enjoy the restoration he himself had experienced.

As Klopp says, Jesus dying for the sins of others was the greatest act ever. It's also one that gives him a huge comfort. We might love or loathe football, but we too can find hope, healing and salvation when we join this manager in following the GOAT—the greatest of all time—Jesus. *AMY BOUCHER PYE*

> ***What difference does it make to believe in, and follow, Jesus? How can Christians influence others through their love of Jesus?***
>
> *Saving Jesus, thank You for dying on the cross, so that I can be free from the burden of my wrongdoing. Help me to share Your love today.*

BIBLE IN A YEAR | JOB 25-27; ACTS 12

God blesses those who patiently endure testing and temptation. [JAMES 1:12 NLT]

UNCHANGING GOD

An iconic photo shows the tread of a boot against a grey background. It's astronaut Buzz Aldrin's footprint, which he left on the moon in 1969. Scientists say that footprint is probably still there, unchanged after all these years. Without wind or water, nothing on the moon gets eroded, so what happens on the lunar landscape stays there.

It's even more awesome to reflect on the constant presence of God Himself. James writes, "Every good and perfect gift is from above, coming down from the Father of the heavenly lights, who does not change like shifting shadows" (JAMES 1:17). The apostle puts this in the context of our own struggles: "When troubles of any kind come your way, consider it an opportunity for great joy" (V. 2 NLT). Why? Because we're loved by a great and unchanging God!

In times of trouble, we need to remember God's constant provision. Perhaps we might recall the words of the great hymn "Great Is Thy Faithfulness": "There is no shadow of turning with thee; / thou changest not, thy compassions, they fail not; / as thou hast been thou forever wilt be." Yes, our God has left His permanent footprint on our world. He will always be there for us. Great is His faithfulness. *KENNETH PETERSEN*

What kind of troubles are you facing today?
How does understanding God's unchanging presence
help you in your struggles?

God, I'm discouraged because of these hardships of late.
I worry about how things will turn out. Yet I know You're
here and will provide. Help me to rest in that assurance.

BIBLE IN A YEAR | JOB 28–29; ACTS 13:1–25

Do not conform to the pattern of this world, but
be transformed by the renewing of your mind.
[ROMANS 12:2]

MIMIC JESUS

A master of disguise lives in the waters of Indonesia and in the Great Barrier Reef. The mimic octopus, like other octopuses, can change its skin pigment to blend in with its surroundings. This intelligent creature also changes its shape, movement pattern and behaviour when threatened to mimic such creatures as the venomous lionfish and even deadly sea snakes.

Unlike the mimic octopus, believers in Jesus are meant to stand out in the world that surrounds us. We may feel threatened by those who disagree with us and become tempted to blend in so we won't be recognised as followers of Christ. The apostle Paul, however, urges us to offer our bodies as a "living sacrifice, holy and pleasing to God" (ROMANS 12:1), representing Jesus in every aspect of our lives.

Friends or family members may try to pressure us to conform to the "pattern of this world" (V. 2). But we can show who we serve by aligning our lives with what we say we believe as God's children. When we obey the Scriptures and reflect His loving character, our lives can demonstrate that the rewards of obedience are always greater than any loss. How will you mimic Jesus today?   *XOCHITL DIXON*

**When have you been tempted to become an unrecognisable
believer in Jesus? When have you become alienated from
family members or friends because you chose to represent
Jesus through your words and actions?**

*Loving Jesus, please give me courage and confidence to
reflect You to others.*

BIBLE IN A YEAR | JOB 30–31; ACTS 13:26–52

While we were still sinners, Christ died for us.
[ROMANS 5:8]

HOPE BEYOND CONSEQUENCES

Have you ever done something in anger you later regretted? When my son was wrestling with drug addiction, I said some harsh things in reaction to his choices. My anger only discouraged him more. But eventually he encountered believers who spoke life and hope to him, and in time he was set free.

Even someone as exemplary in faith as Moses did something he later regretted. When the people of Israel were in the desert and water was scarce, they complained bitterly. So God gave Moses and Aaron specific instructions: "Speak to that rock before their eyes and it will pour out its water" (NUMBERS 20:8). But Moses reacted in anger, giving himself and Aaron credit for the miracle instead of God: "Listen, you rebels, must we bring you water out of this rock?" (V. 10). Then he disobeyed God directly and "raised his arm and struck the rock twice with his staff" (V. 11).

Even though water flowed, there were tragic consequences. Neither Moses nor Aaron was allowed to enter the land God promised His people. But He was still merciful, allowing Moses to see it from afar (27:12–13).

As with Moses, God still mercifully meets us in the desert of our disobedience to Him. Through Jesus' death and resurrection, He kindly offers us forgiveness and hope. No matter where we've been or what we've done, if we turn to Him, He'll lead us into life.　　　　　*JAMES BANKS*

> **What undeserved kindnesses has God shown you?**
> **How can you share His kindness with someone today?**
>
> *Thank You, loving Father, that despite difficult*
> *consequences, You give me eternal hope.*

BIBLE IN A YEAR | JOB 32–33; ACTS 14

Moses said to them, "It is the bread the LORD
has given you to eat." [EXODUS 16:15]

CHOCOLATE SNOWFLAKES

Residents of Olten, Switzerland, were surprised by a shower of chocolate shavings covering the entire town. The ventilation system at a nearby chocolate factory had malfunctioned, sending cocoa into the air and dusting the area with confectionary goodness. The chocolate coating sounds like a dream come true for chocoholics!

While chocolate doesn't adequately provide for one's nutritional needs, God supplied the Israelites with heavenly showers that did. As they travelled through the desert, they began to grumble about the variety of food they'd left behind in Egypt. In response, God said He would "rain down bread from heaven" to sustain them (EXODUS 16:4). When the morning dew dried up each day, a thin flake of food remained. Approximately two million Israelites were instructed to gather as much as they needed that day. For forty years of their desert wanderings, they were nourished by God's supernatural provision in manna.

We know little about manna except that it was "white like coriander seed and tasted like wafers made with honey" (V. 31). Though manna may not sound as appealing as a steady diet of chocolate, the sweetness of God's provision for His people is clear. Manna points us to Jesus who described Himself as the "bread of life" (JOHN 6:48) that sustains us daily and assures us of life eternal (V. 51).   *KIRSTEN HOLMBERG*

*How has God provided for you? How does Jesus being the
"bread of life" encourage you to trust Him?*

*Father God, thank You for providing for my deepest need in
Jesus and sustaining me every day.*

BIBLE IN A YEAR | JOB 34–35; ACTS 15:1–21

They were unschooled, ordinary men, . . . and they
took note that these men had been with Jesus.
[ACTS 4:13]

FREE IN THE SPIRIT

Neither Orville nor Wilbur Wright had a pilot's licence. Neither had gone to college. They were bicycle mechanics with a dream and the courage to try to fly. On 17 December, 1903, they took turns piloting their *Wright Flyer* on four separate flights. The longest lasted only a minute, but it changed our world forever.

Neither Peter nor John had a preaching licence. Neither had gone to Bible college. They were fishermen who, filled with the Spirit of Jesus, courageously proclaimed the good news: "Salvation is found in no one else, for there is no other name under heaven given to mankind by which we must be saved" (ACTS 4:12).

The Wright brothers' neighbours didn't immediately appreciate their accomplishment. Their local newspaper didn't believe their story, and said that even if true, the flights were too brief to be significant. It took several more years of flying and refining their planes before the public recognised what they had truly done.

The religious leaders didn't like Peter and John, and they ordered them to stop telling others about Jesus. Peter said, *No way.* "We cannot help speaking about what we have seen and heard" (V. 20).

You may not be on the approved list. Perhaps you're scorned by those who are. No matter. If you have the Spirit of Jesus, you're free to live boldly for Him!

MIKE WITTMER

> ***What task or person causes you to feel inadequate? How
> might you rely on the indwelling presence of the Holy
> Spirit to step into that challenge today?***
>
> *Jesus, I'm Yours. Use me in whatever way You want.*

BIBLE IN A YEAR | JOB 36–37; ACTS 15:22–41

Loose the chains of injustice and untie the
cords of the yoke . . . set the oppressed free.
[ISAIAH 58:6]

A CRY FOR HELP

David Willis had been upstairs in Waterstones Bookshop
when he came downstairs and found the lights were
turned off and the doors locked. He was trapped inside
the shop! Not knowing what else to do, he turned to Twitter
and tweeted: "Hi @Waterstones. I've been locked inside of your
Trafalgar Square bookstore for 2 hours now. Please let me out."
Not too long after his tweet, he was rescued.

It's good to have a way to get help when we're in trouble. Isaiah said there's Someone who will answer our cries when we're
trapped in a problem of our own making. The prophet wrote
that God had charged His people with practising their religious
devotion irresponsibly. They were going through the motions
of religion but masking their oppression of the poor with empty and self-serving rituals (ISAIAH 58:1–7). This didn't win divine
favour. God hid His eyes from them and didn't answer their
prayers (1:15). He told them to repent and display outward acts
of caring for others (58:6–7). If they did that, He told them, "You
will call, and the LORD will answer; you will cry for help, and he
will say: Here am I. 'If you do away with the yoke of oppression,
with the pointing finger and malicious talk' " (V. 9).

Let's get close to those in need, saying to them: "I am here."
For God hears our cries for help and says to us, "I am here."

MARVIN WILLIAMS

***What behaviour or attitude could prevent you from experiencing
answered prayer? Of what do you need to repent?***

*Dear God, thank You for hearing my prayers. Please help
me to be there for others.*

BIBLE IN A YEAR | JOB 38–40; ACTS 16:1–21

Whoever lives by the truth comes into
the light. [JOHN 3:21]

FROM DARKNESS TO LIGHT

Nothing could pull Aakash out of his dark depression. Severely injured in a car accident, he was taken to a missionary hospital in Southwest Asia. Eight operations repaired his broken bones, but he couldn't eat. Depression set in. His family depended on him to provide, which he couldn't do, so his world grew darker.

One day a visitor read to Aakash from the gospel of John in his language and prayed for him. Touched by the hope of God's free gift of forgiveness and salvation through Jesus, he placed his faith in Him. His depression soon left. When he returned home, he was afraid at first to mention his newfound faith. Finally, though, he told his family about Jesus—and six of them trusted Him as well!

John's gospel is a beacon of light in a world of darkness. In it we read that "whoever believes in [Jesus] shall not perish but have eternal life" (3:16). We discover that "whoever hears [Jesus'] word and believes [God] has eternal life" (5:24). And we hear Jesus say, "I am the bread of life. Whoever comes to me will never go hungry" (6:35). Indeed, "whoever lives by the truth comes into the light" (3:21).

The troubles we face may be great, but Jesus is greater. He came to give us "life . . . to the full" (10:10). Like Aakash, may you place your faith in Jesus—the hope of the world and the light for all humanity.   *DAVE BRANON*

How do the world's problems threaten to overwhelm you?
How does the message and presence of Jesus encourage you?

Dear heavenly Father, thank You for the hope found in Your Son.

BIBLE IN A YEAR | JOB 41–42; ACTS 16:22–40

Every house is built by someone, but God is the builder of everything. [HEBREWS 3:4]

WHO DESERVES THE PRAISE?

From the spiral staircase to the expansive bedroom, from the hardwood floors to the plush carpeting, from the huge laundry room to the well-organised office, the estate agent showed a potential home to the young couple. At every corner they turned, they raved about its beauty: "This house is amazing!" Then the agent responded with something they thought a bit unusual yet true: "I'll pass along your compliment to the builder. The one who built the house deserves the praise; not the house itself or the one who shows it off."

The agent's words echo the writer of Hebrews: "The builder of a house has greater honour than the house itself" (3:3). The writer was comparing the faithfulness of Jesus, the Son of God, with the prophet Moses (VV. 1–6). Though Moses was privileged to speak to God face-to-face and to see His form (NUMBERS 12:8), he was still only "a servant" in the house of God (HEBREWS 3:5). Christ as the Creator (1:2, 10) deserves honour as the divine "builder of everything" and as the Son "over God's house" (3:4, 6). God's house is His people.

When we serve God faithfully, it's Jesus the divine builder who deserves the honour. Any praise we, God's house, receive ultimately belongs to Him.   *ANNE CETAS*

> **What has God built into you? What are unique ways you can give honour to Jesus if you're complimented?**
>
> *Jesus, You deserve all my praise. May my life and words give You that praise on this day.*

BIBLE IN A YEAR | PSALMS 1–3; ACTS 17:1-15

Wash me, and I will be whiter than snow.
[PSALM 51:7]

WASH ME!

"**W**ash me!" Though those words weren't written on my vehicle, they could have been. So, off to the car wash I went, and so did other drivers who wanted relief from the grimy leftovers from salted roads following a recent snowfall. The lines were long, and the service was slow. But it was worth the wait. I left with a clean vehicle and, for compensation for service delay, the car wash was free of charge!

Getting cleaned at someone else's expense—that's the gospel of Jesus Christ. God, through the death and resurrection of Jesus, has provided forgiveness for our sins. Who among us hasn't felt the need to 'bathe' when the 'dirt and grime' of life have clung to us? When we're stained by selfish thoughts or actions that harm ourselves or others and rob us of peace with God? Psalm 51 is the cry of David when temptation had triumphed in his life. When confronted by a spiritual mentor about his sin (SEE 2 SAMUEL 12), he prayed a "Wash me!" prayer: "Cleanse me with hyssop, and I will be clean; wash me, and I will be whiter than snow" (V. 7).

Feeling dirty and guilty? Make your way to Jesus and remember these words: "If we confess our sins, he is faithful and just and will forgive us our sins and purify us from all unrighteousness" (1 JOHN 1:9).　　　　　　　　*ARTHUR JACKSON*

**What does it mean for you to cry out to God, "Wash me"?
What's keeping you from asking for His free forgiveness
and cleansing through Jesus now?**

God of heaven, You see every stain in my life that needs to be dealt with. Wash me, forgive me and help me to honour You.

BIBLE IN A YEAR | PSALMS 4-6; ACTS 17:16-34

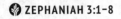

They were still eager to act corruptly in all they did. [ZEPHANIAH 3:7]

PERSONAL RESPONSIBILITY

My friend's eyes revealed what I was feeling—*fear!* We two teens had behaved poorly and were now cowering before the camp director. The man, who knew our dads well, shared lovingly but pointedly that our fathers would be greatly disappointed. We wanted to crawl under the table— feeling the weight of personal responsibility for our offence.

God gave Zephaniah a message for the people of Judah that contained potent words about personal responsibility for sin (ZEPHANIAH 1:1, 6–7). After describing the judgements He would bring against Judah's foes (CH. 2), He turned His eyes on His guilty, squirming people (CH. 3). "What sorrow awaits rebellious, polluted Jerusalem," God proclaimed (3:1 NLT). "They [are] still eager to act corruptly" (V. 7).

He'd seen the cold hearts of His people—their spiritual apathy, social injustice and ugly greed—and He was bringing loving discipline. And it didn't matter if the individuals were "leaders", "judges" or "prophets" (VV. 3–4 NLT)—everyone was guilty before Him.

The apostle Paul wrote the following to believers in Jesus who persisted in sin, "You are storing up terrible punishment for yourself. . . . [God] will judge everyone according to what they have done" (ROMANS 2:5–6 NLT). So, in Jesus' power, let's live in a way that honours our holy, loving Father and leads to no remorse.

TOM FELTEN

Why should you take personal responsibility for your sin?
How do your wrong choices bring shame to God?

Heavenly Father, please help me pursue good choices for You.

BIBLE IN A YEAR | PSALMS 7–9; ACTS 18

The purposes of a person's heart are
deep waters. [PROVERBS 20:5]

DEEP WATERS

When Bill Pinkney sailed solo around the world in 1992—
taking the hard route around the perilous Great Southern Capes—he did it for a higher purpose. His voyage
was to inspire and educate children. That included students at
his former school. His goal? To show how far they could go by
studying hard and making a commitment—the word he chose
in naming his boat. When Bill takes schoolkids on the water in
Commitment, he says, "They've got that tiller in their hand and
they learn about control, self-control, they learn about team-
work . . . all the basics that one needs in life to be successful."

Pinkney's words paint a portrait of Solomon's wisdom. "The
purposes of a person's heart are deep waters, but one who has
insight draws them out" (PROVERBS 20:5). He invited others to examine their life goals. Otherwise, "it is a trap," said Solomon,
"to dedicate something rashly and only later to consider one's
vows" (V. 25).

In contrast, William Pinkney had a clear purpose that eventually inspired thirty thousand students to learn from his journey.
"The kids were watching," he said. With similar purpose, let's
set our course by the deep counsel of God's instructions to us.

PATRICIA RAYBON

In your life, what is the *why* for your work or ministry?
What legacy do you hope to leave by what you
accomplish?

Inspire me, faithful God, to commit to working with a
purpose that glorifies You.

BIBLE IN A YEAR | PSALMS 10–12; ACTS 19:1–20

Whatever you do, whether in word or deed,
do it all in the name of the Lord Jesus.
[COLOSSIANS 3:17]

EMPOWERED FOR THE EVERYDAY

Every Moment Holy is a beautiful book of prayers for a variety of activities, including ordinary ones like preparing a meal or doing the laundry. Necessary tasks that can feel repetitive or mundane. The book reminded me of the words of author G. K. Chesterton, who wrote, "You say grace before meals. All right. But I say grace before sketching, painting, swimming, fencing, boxing, walking, playing, dancing and grace before I dip the pen in the ink."

Such encouragement lifts my perspective on the activities of my day. Sometimes I'm inclined to divide my activities into ones that appear to have spiritual value, like reading devotions before a meal, and other activities I think have little spiritual value, such as doing the dishes after the meal. Paul erased that divide in a letter to the people of Colossae who had chosen to live for Jesus. He encouraged them with these words: "Whatever you do, whether in word or deed, do it all in the name of the Lord Jesus" (3:17). Doing things in Jesus' name means both honouring Him as we do them and having the assurance that His Spirit helps strengthen us to accomplish them.

"Whatever you do." All the ordinary activities of our lives, every moment, can be empowered by God's Spirit and done in a way that honours Jesus.   *LISA M. SAMRA*

> **How might you reconsider your perspective on everyday activities? How can you rely on God's Spirit for the tasks of your day?**
>
> *Jesus, empower me by Your Spirit to honour You today in all I do.*

BIBLE IN A YEAR | PSALMS 13–15; ACTS 19:21–41

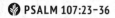

They cried out to the LORD in their trouble,
and he brought them out of their distress.
[PSALM 107:28]

PRAYER AND TRANSFORMATION

In 1982, pastor Christian Führer began Monday prayer meetings at Leipzig's St. Nicholas Church. For years, a handful gathered to ask God for peace amid global violence and the oppressive East German regime. Though communist authorities watched churches closely, they were unconcerned until attendance swelled and spilled over to mass meetings outside the church gates. On 9 October, 1989, seventy thousand demonstrators met and peacefully protested. Six thousand East German police stood ready to respond to any provocation. The crowd remained peaceful, however, and historians consider this day a watershed moment. A month later, the Berlin Wall fell. The massive transformation all started with a prayer meeting.

As we turn to God and begin relying on His wisdom and strength, things often begin to shift and reshape. Like Israel, when we cry "out to the LORD in [our] trouble," we discover the God who alone is capable of profoundly transforming even our most dire predicaments and answering our most vexing questions (PSALM 107:28). God stills "the storm to a whisper" and turns "the desert into pools of water" (VV. 29, 35). The One to whom we pray brings hope out of despair and beauty out of ruin.

But it's God who (in His time—not ours) enacts transformation. Prayer is how we participate in the transforming work He's doing.   *WINN COLLIER*

**When have you seen God do something transformative?
What's the connection between His actions and our prayers?**

*God, I need Your transforming work. Please change what
only You can change.*

BIBLE IN A YEAR | PSALMS 16-17; ACTS 20:1-16

I am reminded of your sincere faith which first lived in your grandmother Lois and in your mother Eunice. [2 TIMOTHY 1:5]

WHAT'S MY PURPOSE?

❝ I felt so useless," Harold said. "Widowed and retired, kids busy with their own families, spending quiet afternoons watching shadows on the wall." He'd often tell his daughter, "I'm old and have lived a full life. I have no purpose anymore. God can take me any time."

One afternoon, however, a conversation changed Harold's mind. "My neighbour had some problems with his kids, so I prayed for him," Harold said. "Later, I shared the gospel with him. That's how I realised I *still* have a purpose! As long as there are people who haven't heard of Jesus, I must tell them about the Saviour."

When Harold responded to an everyday, ordinary encounter by sharing his faith, his neighbour's life was changed. In 2 Timothy 1, the apostle Paul mentions two women who'd likewise been used by God to change another person's life: the life of Paul's young co-worker, Timothy. Lois, Timothy's grandmother, and Eunice, his mother, had a "sincere faith" which they'd passed on to him (V. 5). Through everyday events in an ordinary household, young Timothy learned a genuine faith that was to shape his growth into a faithful disciple of Jesus and, eventually, his ministry as leader of the church at Ephesus.

No matter what our age, background or circumstances, we have a purpose—to tell others about Jesus.   *KAREN HUANG*

> **Whom can you encourage to believe in Jesus? What opportunities to share the gospel can you pray for?**
>
> *Dear Jesus, open my eyes and heart to people around me who need to hear of Your love. Please give me the opportunity to share the gospel with them.*

BIBLE IN A YEAR | PSALMS 18–19; ACTS 20:17–38

In his distress he sought the favour of the
LORD his God and humbled himself greatly.
[2 CHRONICLES 33:12]

DOING SOMETHING RIGHT

The letter from "Jason", an inmate, surprised my wife and me. We raise puppies to become service dogs to assist people with disabilities. One such puppy had graduated to the next training phase, which was run by prisoners who have been taught how to train the dogs. Jason's letter to us expressed sorrow for his past, but then he said, "Snickers is the seventeenth dog I've trained, and she is the best one. When I see her looking up at me, I feel like I'm finally doing something right."

Jason isn't the only one with regrets. We all have them. Manasseh, king of Judah, had plenty. Some of his atrocities are outlined in 2 Chronicles 33: building sexually explicit altars to pagan gods (V. 3), practising witchcraft and sacrificing his own children (V. 6). He led the entire nation down this sordid path (V. 9).

"The LORD spoke to Manasseh and his people, but they paid no attention" (V. 10). Eventually, God got his attention. The Assyrians invaded, "put a hook in his nose . . . and took him to Babylon" (V. 11). Next, Manasseh finally did something right. "He sought the favour of the LORD his God and humbled himself greatly" (V. 12). God heard him and restored him as king. Manasseh replaced the pagan practices with worship of the one true God (VV. 15–16).

Do your regrets threaten to consume you? It's not too late. God hears our humble prayer of repentance.　　*TIM GUSTAFSON*

***What regrets do you have? How might you honour God
by letting Him redeem them and use you to serve Him?***

*Thank You, Father, that You're always ready to hear my
honest prayers.*

BIBLE IN A YEAR | PSALMS 20-22; ACTS 21:1-17

Whoever conceals their sins does not
prosper, but the one who confesses
and renounces them finds mercy.
[PROVERBS 28:13]

SLOW-WALKING SIN OUT THE DOOR

Our dog Winston *knows* he's not supposed to chew them.
So he's adopted a sly strategy. We call it *slow-walking*. If
Winston spies a discarded, unguarded shoe, he'll casually
meander in that direction, grab it and just keep walking. *Slowly.*
Nothing to see here. Right out the door if no one notices. "Uh,
Mum, Winston just slow-walked your shoe out the door."

It's apparent that sometimes we think we can 'slow-walk' our
sin past God. We're tempted to think that He won't notice. It's
no big deal, we rationalise—whatever 'it' is. But, like Winston,
we know better. We know those choices don't please God.

Like Adam and Eve in the garden, we may try to hide due
to the shame of our sin (GENESIS 3:10) or pretend like it didn't
happen. But Scripture invites us to do something very different:
to run to God's mercy and forgiveness. Proverbs 28:13 tells us,
"Whoever conceals their sins does not prosper, but the one who
confesses and renounces them finds mercy."

We don't have to try to slow-walk our sin and hope no one notices. When we tell the truth about our choices—to ourselves,
to God, to a trusted friend—we can find freedom from the guilt
and shame of carrying secret sin (1 JOHN 1:9).   *ADAM R. HOLZ*

> *Are there any ways you're sometimes tempted to 'slow-walk'*
> *your sin? What barriers keep you from confession?*

> *Father, thank You that my sin doesn't have the last word.*
> *Help me to remember, as I tell You and others the truth,*
> *that I can be confident of Your mercy and forgiveness.*

BIBLE IN A YEAR | PSALMS 23–25; ACTS 21:18–40

[Jesus] took the humble position of a slave and was born as a human being. [PHILIPPIANS 2:7 NLT]

PUTTING ON HUMILITY

The CEO of a frozen treats franchise went undercover on a television series called *Undercover Boss,* donning a shop assistant's uniform. Working at one of the franchise's shops, her wig and makeup disguised her identity as she became the 'new' employee. Her goal was to see how things were really working from the inside and on the ground. Based on her observations, she was able to solve some of the issues the shop was facing.

Jesus took on a "humble position" (PHILIPPIANS 2:7 NLT) to solve our issues. He became human—walking the earth, teaching us about God and ultimately dying on a cross for our sins (V. 8). This sacrifice exposed Christ's humility as He obediently gave His life as our sin offering. He walked the earth as a man and experienced what we experience—from ground level.

As believers in Jesus, we're called to have the "same attitude" as our Saviour especially in our relationships with other believers (V. 5 NLT). God helps us to clothe ourselves in humility (V. 3) and adopt the mindset of Christ (V. 5). He prompts us to live as servants ready to meet others' needs and willing to lend a helping hand. As God leads us to humbly love others, we're in a better position to serve them and to compassionately seek solutions to the issues they face.

KATARA PATTON

> **How can you lovingly address the needs and issues others are facing? What does it mean for you to live out the humility of Jesus?**

> *Holy God, thank You for the sacrifice of Jesus for me.*
> *Please give me the mindset of Christ as I humbly serve my brothers and sisters.*

BIBLE IN A YEAR | PSALMS 26–28; ACTS 22

After the fire came a gentle whisper.
[1 KINGS 19:12]

ROOM FOR SILENCE

I f you like peace and quiet, there's a room that you'll love. It absorbs 99.99 percent of all sound! The world-famous anechoic (echo-free) chamber of the Orfield Laboratories has been called the "quietest place on earth". People who want to experience this soundless space are required to sit down to avoid getting disoriented by the lack of noise, and no one has ever been able to spend more than forty-five minutes in the room.

Few of us need that much silence. Yet we do sometimes long for a little quiet in a loud and busy world. Even the news we watch and the social media we ingest bring a kind of clamorous 'noise' that competes for our attention. So much of it is infused with words and images that stir up negative emotions. Immersing ourselves in it can easily drown out the voice of God.

When the prophet Elijah went to meet God on the mountain of Horeb, he didn't find Him in the loud, destructive wind or in the earthquake or in the fire (1 KINGS 19:11–12). It wasn't until Elijah heard a "gentle whisper" that he covered his face and ventured out of the cave to meet with "the LORD God Almighty" (VV. 12–14).

Your spirit may well be craving quiet but—even more so—it may be yearning to hear the voice of God. Find room for silence in your life so you'll never miss God's "gentle whisper" (V. 12).

CINDY HESS KASPER

What are some ways God communes with His children?
Why is it vital to regularly communicate with Him?

Loving Father, quiet my heart and mind so I'm ready to
meet with You today.

BIBLE IN A YEAR | PSALMS 29–30; ACTS 23:1–15

Be not drunk with wine, wherein is
excess; but be filled with the Spirit.
[EPHESIANS 5:18 KJV]

DRENCHED BY THE SPIRIT

Author Scot McKnight shares how when he was in high
school, he had what he calls a "Spirit-drenched experience". While at a camp, the speaker challenged him to
enthrone Christ in his life by surrendering to the Spirit. Later,
he sat under a tree and prayed, "Father, forgive me of my sins.
And Holy Spirit, come inside and fill me." Something mighty happened, he said. "From that moment my life has been completely
different. Not perfect, but different." He suddenly had the desire
to read the Bible, pray, meet with other believers in Jesus and
serve God.

Before the risen Jesus ascended to heaven, He told His
friends: "Do not leave Jerusalem, but wait for the gift my Father
promised" (ACTS 1:4). They would "receive power" to become His
"witnesses in Jerusalem, and in all Judea and Samaria, and to
the ends of the earth" (V. 8). God gives the Holy Spirit to indwell
everyone who believes in Jesus. This first happened at Pentecost
(SEE ACTS 2); today it occurs whenever someone trusts in Christ.

God's Spirit also continues to fill those who believe in Jesus.
We too, with the help of the Spirit, bear the fruit of changed
character and desires (GALATIANS 5:22–23). Let's praise and thank
God for comforting us, convicting us, partnering with us and loving us.   *AMY BOUCHER PYE*

> *How can you see the difference that the Holy Spirit has
> made in you? How can you welcome God's Spirit to work
> in and through you more?*

> *Loving God, thank You for the gift of Your Spirit.
> Help me to love You and others more today.*

BIBLE IN A YEAR | PSALMS 31-32; ACTS 23:16-35

I always thank my God as I remember you in my prayers. [PHILEMON 1:4]

REMEMBER IN PRAYER

Malcolm Cloutt was named a 2021 Maundy Money honouree by Queen Elizabeth II—an annual service award. Cloutt, who was one hundred years old at the time of the recognition, was honoured for having given out one thousand Bibles during his lifetime. Cloutt has kept a record of everyone who's received a Bible and has prayed for them regularly.

Cloutt's faithfulness in prayer is a powerful example of the kind of love we find throughout Paul's writings in the New Testament. Paul often assured the recipients of his letters that he was regularly praying for them. To his friend Philemon, he wrote, "I always thank my God as I remember you in my prayers" (PHILEMON 1:4). In his letter to Timothy, Paul wrote, "Night and day I constantly remember you in my prayers" (2 TIMOTHY 1:3). To the church in Rome, Paul emphasised that he remembered them in prayer "constantly" and "at all times" (ROMANS 1:9–10).

While we might not have a thousand people to pray for like Malcolm, intentional prayer for those we know is powerful because God responds to our prayers. When prompted and empowered by His Spirit to pray for a specific individual, I've found a simple prayer calendar can be a useful tool. Dividing names into a daily or weekly calendar helps me be faithful to pray. What a beautiful demonstration of love when we remember others in prayer. *LISA M. SAMRA*

What has helped you be faithful in prayer? How have you been blessed by someone's prayers for you?

Father, help me to be faithful in prayer, knowing You always hear me.

BIBLE IN A YEAR | PSALMS 33–34; ACTS 24

Do not grieve like the rest of mankind, who have no hope. [1 THESSALONIANS 4:13]

HOPE IN GRIEF

Louise was a lively, playful girl who brought smiles to all she met. At the age of five, she tragically succumbed to a rare disease. Her sudden passing was a shock to her parents, Day Day and Peter, and to all of us who worked with them. We grieved along with them.

Yet, Day Day and Peter have found the strength to keep going. When I asked Day Day how they were coping, she said they drew strength from focusing on where Louise was—in Jesus' loving arms. "We rejoice for our daughter whose time is up to go into eternal life," she said. "By God's grace and strength, we can navigate through the grief and continue to do what He has entrusted us to do."

Day Day's comfort is found in her confidence in the heart of God who revealed Himself in Jesus. Biblical hope is much more than mere optimism; it's an absolute certainty based on God's promise, which He will never break. In our sadness, we can cling to this powerful truth, as Paul encouraged those grieving over departed friends: "We believe that Jesus died and rose again, and so we believe that God will bring with Jesus those who have fallen asleep in him" (1 THESSALONIANS 4:14). May this certain hope give us strength and comfort today—even in our grief.

LESLIE KOH

> **How can you draw strength from God's promises to those who follow Him? How can you comfort someone grieving over a loved one or friend?**

> *Father, thank You for Your hope and comfort today. Strengthen me today so I can encourage others too.*

BIBLE IN A YEAR | PSALMS 35–36; ACTS 25

The LORD God is a sun and shield; . . . no good thing does he withhold from those whose way of life is blameless. [PSALM 84:11]

OUR SUN AND SHIELD

Her life was slipping away. He sat quietly and simply read to her from the comforting truth of God's Word. Then the Lord gently spoke to his heart through the promise: "No good thing does he withhold from those whose way of life is blameless" (PSALM 84:11).

Reflecting later on that painful yet precious moment, George Müller (1805–1898)—understanding he was "blameless" by faith—said to himself, "If it is really good for me, my darling wife will be raised up again, sick as she is. God will restore her again. But if she is not restored again, then it would not be a good thing for me. And so my heart was at rest. I was satisfied with God."

We've all experienced loss, whether the passing of loved ones or the changing of the seasons. Sometimes such moments make us question God's goodness. Yet the psalmist reminds us that "the LORD God is a sun and shield" (V. 11). As our sun, He brings life and growth to the good things He gives us; as our shield, He protects and guards us when we face heartache in this world of sad goodbyes.

Through tears, Müller put his faith in the Lord to define what would be truly good during that heart-breaking season of his life.

No good thing will be withheld from us today either; for "blessed is the one who trusts in [God]" to be their sun and their shield (V. 12).　　　　　　　　　　　　　　　*CHRIS WALE*

When has God's goodness satisfied you in difficult seasons? How can you seek the blessings He has for you in your current situation?

Lord God, You are my sun and my shield. I trust that You will provide what is truly good for me today.

BIBLE IN A YEAR | PSALMS 37–39; ACTS 26

The end of all things is near. Therefore be
alert and of sober mind so that you may pray.
[1 PETER 4:7]

CASTAWAY FAITH

In June 1965, six Tongan teenagers sailed from their island home in search of adventure. But when a storm broke their mast and rudder the first night, they drifted for days without food or water before reaching the uninhabited island of 'Ata. It would be fifteen months before they were found.

The boys worked together on 'Ata to survive, setting up a small food garden, hollowing out tree trunks to store rainwater, even building a makeshift gym. When one boy broke his leg from a cliff fall, the others set it using sticks and leaves. Arguments were managed with mandatory reconciliation, and each day began and ended with singing and prayer. When the boys emerged from their ordeal healthy, their families were amazed—their funerals had already been held.

Being a believer in Jesus in the first century could be an isolating experience. Persecuted for your faith and often stranded from family, one could feel adrift. The apostle Peter's encouragement to such castaways was to stay disciplined and prayerful (1 PETER 4:7), to look after each other (V. 8) and use whatever abilities one has to get the work done (VV. 10–11). In time, God would bring them through their ordeal "strong, firm and steadfast" (5:10).

In times of trial, 'castaway faith' is needed. We pray and work in solidarity, and God brings us through.   *SHERIDAN VOYSEY*

> **In times of ordeal, are you more likely to ask for help or
> try and face the problem alone? What 'castaway' do you
> know who needs encouragement?**

> *Dear God, give me 'castaway faith' to face times of
> difficulty well.*

BIBLE IN A YEAR | PSALMS 40–42; ACTS 27:1-26

For it is by grace you have been
saved, through faith . . . not by works.
[EPHESIANS 2:8–9]

EXTRA GRACE REQUIRED

While we decorated for a special event at church, the woman in charge griped about my inexperience. After she walked away, another woman approached me. "Don't worry about her. She's what we call an E.G.R.—Extra Grace Required."

I laughed. Soon I started using that label every time I had a conflict with someone. Years later, I sat in that same church sanctuary listening to that E.G.R.'s obituary. The pastor shared how the woman had served God behind the scenes and given generously to others. I asked God to forgive me for judging and gossiping about her and anyone else I'd labelled as an E.G.R. in the past. After all, I needed extra grace as much as any other believer in Jesus.

In Ephesians 2, the apostle Paul states that all believers were "by nature deserving of wrath" (v. 3). But God gave us the gift of salvation, a gift which we did nothing to deserve, a gift we'd never be able to earn "so that no one can boast" (v. 9). No one.

As we submit to God moment by moment during this lifelong journey, the Holy Spirit will work to change our character so we can reflect the character of Christ. Every believer requires extra grace. But we can be grateful that God's grace is sufficient (2 CORINTHIANS 12:9).　　　　　　　　　*XOCHITL DIXON*

*When have you judged others for requiring extra grace?
In what area of your life do you require grace today?*

*Father God, please help me extend grace to others as
freely and generously as You've lavished Your abounding
grace on me.*

BIBLE IN A YEAR | PSALMS 43–45; ACTS 27:27–44

Then the LORD said to Moses, "Now you will see what I will do to Pharaoh." [EXODUS 6:1]

THE LONG GAME

When Tun's country suffered a coup, the military began terrorising believers in Jesus and killing their farm animals. Having lost their livelihood, Tun's family scattered to various countries. For nine years, Tun existed in a refugee camp far from his family. He knew God was with him, but during the separation, two family members died. Tun grew despondent.

Long ago, another people group faced brutal oppression. So God appointed Moses to lead those people—the Israelites—out of Egypt. Moses reluctantly agreed. But when he approached Pharaoh, the Egyptian ruler only intensified the oppression (EXODUS 5:6–9). "I do not know the LORD and I will not let Israel go," he said (V. 2). The people complained to Moses, who complained to God (VV. 20–23).

In the end, God freed the Israelites and they got the freedom they wanted—but in God's way and timing. He plays a long game, teaching us about His character and preparing us for something greater.

Tun made good use of his years in a refugee camp, earning a master's degree from a New Delhi Bible college. Now he's a pastor to his own people—refugees like him who have found a new home. "My story as a refugee forms the crucible for leading as a servant," he says. In his testimony, Tun cites Moses' song in Exodus 15:2: "The LORD is my strength and my defence." And today, He's ours as well.   *TIM GUSTAFSON*

> ***What questions do you have for God?***
> ***How will you trust Him to keep His word?***
>
> *Heavenly Father, I can always rely on You. Forgive me*
> *when I lose sight of that truth.*

BIBLE IN A YEAR | PSALMS 46–48; ACTS 28

I am the vine; you are the branches. If you remain in me and I in you, you will bear much fruit. [JOHN 15:5]

SIMPLY BE

"**Y**our mum came round today, but it was strange—she wouldn't tell me what she wanted."

Russell's brow furrowed, "Didn't you invite her in?" I hadn't done. In my home culture, people don't just pop round. Her visit had flummoxed me, but, clearly, I had badly misunderstood the situation. An explanatory phone call and a British culture lesson later, I realised how foolish I had been. I'd assumed my mother-in-law wanted something from me when she simply wanted to *be with me*. I was so busy trying to work out her expectations that I missed the opportunity simply to enjoy her presence.

It's something I find myself doing with God too. We so easily get caught up in the things we need to do as His people that sometimes we forget the most important thing: just *being with Jesus*, enjoying His presence.

Jesus reminds us, "I am the vine; you are the branches. If you remain in me and I in you, you will bear much fruit" (JOHN 15:5). No branch can produce fruit by itself, no matter how hard it tries. Instead, Jesus' command is to "remain"—or "stay connected"—in the vine.

Bearing fruit—serving Jesus—doesn't require a frenzy of self-effort that leaves Him waiting at the door. But as we abide in Him, He promises, "You will bear much fruit". Let's take time to enjoy His presence today—and He will grow His fruit in us. *DEBBI FRALICK*

What stops you making time to rest in Jesus' presence? When have you experienced His fruit growing in Your life simply because you've spent more time with Him?

Jesus, thank You for inviting me to be close to You right now. There's nowhere else I'd rather be.

Those parts of the body that seem
to be weaker are indispensable.
[1 CORINTHIANS 12:22]

LOWER DECK PEOPLE

A friend of mine works on a hospital ship called *Africa Mercy,*
which takes free healthcare to developing countries. The
staff daily serve hundreds of patients whose ailments
would otherwise go untreated.

TV crews who periodically board the ship, point their cameras
on its amazing medical staff, who fix cleft palates and reset club
feet. Sometimes they go below deck to interview other crew
members, but the work Mick does typically goes unnoticed.

Mick, an engineer, admits being surprised about where he'd
been assigned to work—in the ship's sewage plant. With up to
forty thousand litres of waste produced each day, managing this
toxic material is serious business. Without Mick tending its pipes
and pumps, *Africa Mercy*'s life-giving operations would stop.

It's easy to applaud those on the 'top deck' of Christian ministry while overlooking those in the galleys below. When the Corinthians elevated those with extraordinary gifts above others,
Paul reminded them that every believer has a role in Christ's
work (1 CORINTHIANS 12:7–20), and every gift is important, whether it's miraculous healing or helping others (VV. 27–31). In fact,
the less prominent the role, the greater honour it deserves
(VV. 22–24).

Are you a 'lower deck' person? Then lift your head high. Your work
is honoured by God and indispensable to us all.   SHERIDAN VOYSEY

What happens when you compare your gifts with others?
Which 'lower deck' person can you affirm the efforts of today?

I'm important to You, God. Thank You for noticing me
whether others do or not.

BIBLE IN A YEAR | PSALMS 51–53; ROMANS 2

Hear, Israel, the decrees and laws I declare in your hearing today. Learn them and be sure to follow them. [DEUTERONOMY 5:1]

STAYING ON TRACK WITH GOD

Years ago, a train carrying 218 people derailed in north-western Spain, killing 79 people and hospitalising 66 more. The driver couldn't explain the accident, but the video footage could and did. The train was going far too fast before it hit a deadly curve. The allowable speed limit had been created to protect everyone on board the train. Despite being a thirty-year veteran of Spain's national rail company, however, the driver had for whatever reason ignored the speed boundary and many people lost their lives.

In Deuteronomy 5, Moses reviewed God's original covenant boundaries for His people. Moses encouraged a new generation to regard God's instruction as their own covenant with Him (V. 3), and then he restated the Ten Commandments (VV. 7–21). By repeating the commandments and drawing lessons from the previous generation's disobedience, Moses invited the Israelites to be reverent, humble and mindful of God's faithfulness. God had made a way for His people so they wouldn't wreck their lives or the lives of others. If they ignored His wisdom, they would do so at their own peril.

Today, as God leads us, let's make all of Scripture our delight, counsellor and the guardrail for our lives. And as the Spirit guides us, we can keep on track within His wise protection and devote our lives wholeheartedly to Him. *MARVIN WILLIAMS*

When do God's boundaries seem strict, rather than liberating? How do His boundaries show His love for you?

Dear God, help me to show my love for You through my obedience to You.

BIBLE IN A YEAR | PSALMS 54–56; ROMANS 3

FELLOW CITIZENS

I've been hearing conversations lately by church leaders realising the need for the church to regain a central focus on the cross and resurrection of Christ—the story of God's cosmic defeat of the principalities and powers of death and evil—for truly sustaining hope. Sadly, some faith communities have lost this emphasis in exchange for a primarily individualistic emphasis of a personal experience of forgiveness merged with positive advice for a happy life.

But during the pandemic, many church leaders began to realise that—for those grieving the loss of loved ones or loss of a livable income, or those weighed down by the suffering they saw all around them—messages focused on individual happiness were ringing hollow.

We need hope that truly reckons with the full weight of sin and death's wounding of our world—hope that's deeper than death.

The gospel is the story of God's redemption of a wounded cosmos through the cross and resurrection of Jesus—an event that's changed the fabric of reality. One that, in God's grace, we've been invited to share with the world.

Only when we fully reckon with the *bad* news—the depth of sin and death's stranglehold over creation—can we grasp the wonder of the *good* news, that "creation itself will be liberated from its bondage to decay and brought into the freedom and glory of the children of God" (ROMANS 8:21).

Even as we lament honestly the "groaning" of creation (V. 22), we can experience the good news that *Jesus is alive!* Working through communities of people filled with the Spirit and with hope. Carrying us from death into glorious resurrection life.

Monica La Rose, *Our Daily Bread* author

★ How does the unfolding story found in the Bible help believers in Jesus understand their mission for Him? As believers, we're called to participate in God's grand mission in the world. This topic is addressed in the devotions for **September 1, 8** and **22**.

Jesus . . . said, "Let the little children come to me."
[LUKE 18:16]

FAITH OF A CHILD

As our adopted granny lay in her hospital bed after suffering several strokes, her doctors were unsure of the amount of brain damage she had endured. They needed to wait until she was a bit better to test her brain function. She spoke very few words and even fewer were understandable. But when the eighty-six-year-old woman—who had babysat my daughter for twelve years—saw me, she opened her parched mouth and asked: "How is Kayla?" The first words she spoke to me were about my child whom she had loved so freely and fully.

Jesus loved children too and put them in the forefront even though His disciples disapproved. Some parents would seek out Christ and present their children to Him. He chose to bless the children as He "[placed] his hands on them" (LUKE 18:15). But not everyone was happy that He was blessing little ones. The disciples scolded the parents and asked them to stop bothering Jesus. But He intervened and said, "Let the little children come to me" (V. 16). He called them an example of how we should receive God's kingdom—with simple dependence, trust and sincerity.

Young children rarely have a hidden agenda. What you see is what you get. As our heavenly Father helps us regain child-like trust, may our faith and dependence on Him be as open as a child's.   *KATARA PATTON*

How can you imitate a child's sincerity in your relationship with God? How do you bless children in your family and community?

Father, help me to be as open and sincere as a child as I receive Your kingdom.

BIBLE IN A YEAR | PSALMS 57–59; ROMANS 4

You are great and do marvellous deeds;
you alone are God. [PSALM 86:10]

MARVELLOUS DEEDS

A few years before his death in 2022, Andrew van der Bijl (also known as Brother Andrew) looked back on his extraordinary missionary life. He reflected on the many dangers of smuggling Bibles into countries where Christianity was illegal. Then, with breath-taking humility, he said, "I am just an ordinary guy. What I did, anyone can do."

We may not instinctively feel like we could do the daring things that Brother Andrew did. Yet his assessment of himself matches the psalmist's: "No deed can compare with yours. . . . For you are great and do marvellous deeds; you alone are God" (PSALM 86:10). Brother Andrew was not the source of his marvellous deeds; God was.

If the most marvellous deeds come from the Lord, then all of us can be channels of His love and wisdom—even if we don't feel like we have much to offer. And we don't need to go overseas or into danger to experience this. The psalmist continues, "Teach me your way, LORD, that I may rely on your faithfulness; give me an undivided heart" (V. 11). Our role is wholeheartedly to draw close to the Source of all marvellous deeds, allowing Him to lead and work through us.

It is okay to feel ordinary, just like Brother Andrew did. We don't have to muster up our own strength to do marvellous deeds; God will work through us as we draw near and learn to rely on His faithfulness.

CHRIS WALE

How do the examples of Brother Andrew and other Christians to whom you look up inspire you? How can you seek to become more of a channel for God's marvellous deeds?

Dear God, I praise You for Your marvellous deeds throughout the world. Please help me to live by Your strength and faithfulness, so that You may work mightily through me as well.

BIBLE IN A YEAR | PSALMS 60–62; ROMANS 5

Confess your sins to each other and pray for each other so that you may be healed. [JAMES 5:16]

AUTHENTIC AND VULNERABLE

"**H**ey, Poh Fang!" A church friend texted. "For this week's small group meeting, let's get everyone to do what James 5:16 says. Let's create a safe environment of trust and confidentiality, so we can share an area of struggle in our life and pray for each other."

For a moment, I wasn't sure how to reply. While our small group members have known each other for years, we'd never really openly shared all our hurts and struggles with one another. After all, it's scary to be vulnerable.

But the truth is, we're all sinners and we all struggle. We all need Jesus. Authentic conversations about God's amazing grace and our dependency on Christ have a way of encouraging us to keep trusting in Him. With Jesus, we can stop pretending to have trouble-free lives.

So I replied, "Yes! Let's do that!" Initially, it was awkward. But as one person opened up and shared, another soon followed. Though a few kept silent, there was understanding. No one was pressured. We ended the time by doing what the second part of James 5:16 says, "Pray for each other."

That day I experienced the beauty of fellowship with believers in Jesus. Because of our common faith in Christ, we can be vulnerable with each other and depend on Him and others to help us in our weaknesses and struggles. *POH FANG CHIA*

While we must be discerning, what can you do to encourage more authentic sharing in your church community? Who can you share your struggles with?

Father, thank You for placing me in Your family so I might find support as I grow to become more and more like Christ.

BIBLE IN A YEAR | PSALMS 63-65; ROMANS 6

Spread the corner of your garment over me,
since you are a guardian-redeemer of our family.
[RUTH 3:9]

PEOPLE OF REFUGE

Phil and Sandy, moved by stories of refugee children, opened their hearts and home to two of them. After they picked them up at the airport, they nervously drove home in silence. *Were they ready for this?* They didn't share the same culture, language or religion, but they'd become people of refuge for these precious children.

Boaz was moved by the story of Ruth. He'd heard how she left her people to support Naomi. When Ruth came to glean in his field, Boaz prayed this blessing over her, "May the LORD repay you for what you have done. May you be richly rewarded by the LORD, the God of Israel, under whose *wings* you have come to take refuge" (RUTH 2:12).

Ruth reminded Boaz of his blessing when she interrupted his sleep one night. Awakened by movement at his feet, Boaz asked, "Who are you?" Ruth replied, "I am your servant Ruth. Spread the *corner of your garment* over me, since you are a guardian-redeemer of our family" (3:9).

The Hebrew word for *corner of garment* and *wings* is the same. Boaz gave Ruth refuge by marrying her, and their great-grandson David echoed their story in his praise to the God of Israel: "How priceless is your unfailing love, O God!" he wrote. "People take refuge in the shadow of your wings" (PSALM 36:7).   *MIKE WITTMER*

When has someone given you refuge and how did it make you feel? How might you—in big or small ways—provide refuge for others?

Father, I take refuge in You. Use me to extend Your refuge to others.

BIBLE IN A YEAR | PSALMS 66–67; ROMANS 7

Mary has chosen what is better.
[LUKE 10:42]

PRIORITY OF GOD'S PRESENCE

I n 2009, a research team at one university studied more than two hundred students in an experiment that included switching between tasks and memory exercises. Surprisingly, the study found that students who viewed themselves as good multi-taskers, because they were in the habit of doing several things at once, did worse than those who preferred to perform one task at a time. Multi-tasking made it more difficult to focus their thoughts and filter irrelevant information. Maintaining focus when our minds are distracted can be a challenge.

When Jesus visited Mary and Martha's home, Martha was busy working and "distracted by all the preparations" (LUKE 10:40). Her sister Mary chose to sit and listen to Jesus teach, gaining wisdom and peace that would never be taken away from her (VV. 39–42). When Martha asked Jesus to encourage Mary to help her, He responded, "You are worried and upset about many things, but few things are needed—or indeed only one" (VV. 41–42).

God desires our attention. But, like Martha, we're often distracted by tasks and problems. We neglect God's presence even though He alone can provide the wisdom and hope we need. When we make spending time with Him through prayer and meditating on Scripture a priority, He'll give us the guidance and strength we need to address the challenges we face. *KIMYA LODER*

> *What has taken your focus away from God?*
> *How might shifting it back to Him bring you clarity?*

Dear Father, sometimes I try to juggle so many things.
Please help me to remove those distractions and draw
closer to You.

BIBLE IN A YEAR │ PSALMS 68–69; ROMANS 8:1–21

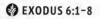

I will free you from being slaves to them.
[EXODUS 6:6]

RELEASE FROM SLAVERY

"**Y**ou are like Moses, leading us out from slavery!" Jamila exclaimed. As a bonded brick-kiln worker in Pakistan, she and her family suffered because of the exorbitant amount they owed the kiln owner. They used much of their earnings just to pay off the interest. But when they received a gift from a non-profit agency that released them from their debt, they felt tremendous relief. In thanking the agency's representative for their freedom, Jamila, a believer in Jesus, pointed to the example of God's release of Moses and the Israelites from slavery.

The Israelites had been oppressed by the Egyptians for hundreds of years, labouring under harsh conditions. They cried out to God, asking for help (EXODUS 2:23). But their workload increased, because the new pharaoh ordered them not only to make bricks but also to gather the straw for these bricks (5:6–8). When the Israelites continued to cry out against the oppression, God reiterated His promise to be their God (6:7). No longer would they be slaves, because He would redeem them with "an outstretched arm" (V. 6).

Under God's direction, Moses led the Israelites out of Egypt (SEE CH.14). Today God still delivers us through the outstretched arms of His Son, Jesus, on the cross. We're set free from a far greater enslavement to the sin that once controlled us. We're no longer slaves, but free!　　　　　*AMY BOUCHER PYE*

> *How has God brought you freedom? How could you encourage others who are enslaved in some way?*
>
> *Dear God, thank You for sending Your Son to give me freedom from my sin.*

BIBLE IN A YEAR | PSALMS 70–71; ROMANS 8:22–39

Let your light shine before others, that they
may see your good deeds and glorify your
Father in heaven. [MATTHEW 5:16]

THE LAMPLIGHTER

Dusk gave way to darkness across Victorian London. The horse-drawn cab carrying Charles Spurgeon clattered towards the bottom of the hill. A single light appeared up ahead. Then another. And another. Ascending, one by one, to the summit. A lamplighter, invisible in the gloom, was igniting the wicks of the streetlamps.

Public preacher, author and activist for the poor, Spurgeon was a well-known figure. Yet he was deeply stirred by the influence of the humble, unknown lamplighter. "I do wish," he wrote, "that my life may be spent igniting one soul after another with the sacred flame of eternal life." Significantly, he added, he himself should remain, as far as possible, unseen.

It is natural to want to be noticed for the things that we do. Yet the unseen lamplighter's influence beautifully illustrates what it means to live as "the light of the world" (V. 14). When we're prepared to turn the focus away from ourselves, others "will see [our] good deeds and glorify [our] Father in heaven" (V. 16). What a privilege that our lives have been infused with the self-giving nature of Christ's love and grace so that others may be drawn to His distinctive beauty through us (V. 16).

We bring Christ's presence to everyone we meet. May we gently dispel any darkness of fear or unbelief by shining His light into their lives, rather than seeking to focus on ourselves.   ANNE LE TISSIER

*How have other believers' good deeds drawn your attention
to God rather than to them? How can you keep the focus on
God when you serve others or stand out in some way?*

*Forgive me, Jesus, when I seek praise for myself. Inspire me
as Your light-bearer to turn other's attention to You.*

BIBLE IN A YEAR | PSALMS 72–73; ROMANS 9:1–15

There is neither Jew nor Gentile, neither
slave nor free. [GALATIANS 3:28]

DIFFERENT TOGETHER IN JESUS

Business analyst Francis Evans once studied 125 insurance
salesmen to find out what made them successful. Surprisingly, competence wasn't the key factor. Instead, Evans
found customers were more likely to buy from salesmen with the
same politics, education and even height as them. Scholars call
this *homophily*: the tendency to prefer people like us.

Homophily is at work in other areas of life too, with us tending to marry and befriend people similar to us. While natural,
homophily can be destructive when left unchecked. When we
only prefer 'our kind' of people, society can fracture along racial,
political and economic lines.

In the first century, Jews stuck with Jews, Greeks with Greeks,
and rich and poor never mingled. And yet, in Romans 16:1–16,
Paul could describe the church in Rome as including Priscilla and
Aquila (Jewish), Epenetus (Greek), Phoebe (a "benefactor of
many," so probably wealthy) and Philologus (a name common
for slaves). What had brought such different people together?
Jesus—in whom there's "neither Jew nor Gentile, neither slave
nor free" (GALATIANS 3:28).

It's natural to want to live, work and go to church with people
like us. Jesus pushes us beyond that. In a world fracturing along
various lines, He's making us a people who are different together—united in Him as one family.   *SHERIDAN VOYSEY*

> *How can you actively reach out to people who are
> different from you? What could you do this week to
> bridge ethnic or economic divides?*
>
> *Jesus, I praise You for working to bring our fractured
> world together.*

BIBLE IN A YEAR | PSALMS 74–76; ROMANS 9:16–33

How much more valuable is a person than
a sheep! [MATTHEW 12:12]

GOOD TROUBLE FOR GOD

One day, a high school student noticed a classmate cutting
his arm with a small razor. Trying to do the right thing,
she took it from him and threw it away. Surprisingly,
instead of being commended, she received a ten-day school
suspension. Why? She briefly had the razor in her possession—
something not allowed at school. Asked if she would do it again,
she replied: "Even if I got in trouble, . . . I would do it again." Just
as this girl's act of trying to do good got her into trouble (her suspension was later reversed), Jesus' act of kingdom intervention
got Him into good trouble with religious leaders.

The Pharisees interpreted Jesus' healing a man with a de-
formed hand as a violation of their rules. Christ told them if
God's people were allowed to care for animals in dire situations
on the Sabbath, "How much more valuable is a person than
a sheep!" (MATTHEW 12:12). Because He's Lord of the Sabbath,
Jesus could regulate what is and isn't permitted on it (VV. 6–8).
Knowing that it would offend the religious leaders, He restored
the man's hand to wholeness anyway (VV. 13–14).

Sometimes believers in Christ can get into 'good trouble'—doing what honours Him but what might not make certain people
happy—as they help others in need. When we do, as God guides
us, we imitate Jesus and reveal that people are more important
than rules and rituals.　　　　　　　　　　　*MARVIN WILLIAMS*

**How can you show kindness to others? Why should you
be willing to get into good trouble for God?**

*Dear Jesus, please keep me from rituals that prevent me
from loving others.*

I am he who will sustain you.
[ISAIAH 46:4]

THE GOD OF ALL OUR DAYS

After an unsuccessful surgery, Joan's doctor said she'd need to undergo another operation in five weeks. As time passed, anxiety built. Joan and her husband were senior citizens, and their family lived far away. They'd need to drive to an unfamiliar city and navigate a complex hospital system, and they'd be working with a new specialist.

Although these circumstances seemed overwhelming, God took care of them. During the trip, their car's navigation system broke down, but they arrived on time because they had a paper map. God supplied wisdom. At the hospital, a Christian pastor prayed with them and offered to help later that day. God provided support. After the operation, Joan received good news of a successful surgery.

While we won't always experience healing or rescue, God is faithful and always close to vulnerable people—whether young, old or otherwise disadvantaged. Centuries ago, when captivity in Babylon had weakened the Israelites, Isaiah reminded them that God had upheld them from birth and would continue to care for them. Through the prophet, God said, "Even to your old age and grey hairs I am he, I am he who will sustain you" (ISAIAH 46:4).

God will not abandon us when we need Him the most. He can supply our needs and remind us He's with us at every point in our lives. He's the God of all our days.   *JENNIFER BENSON SCHULDT*

> ***How has God sustained you during times of weakness?***
> ***How might He want to work through you to support others?***

> *Dear God, You're trustworthy and kind. Help me to lean on*
> *You as I experience uncertainty.*

BIBLE IN A YEAR | PSALMS 79-80; ROMANS 11:1-18

God demonstrates his own love for us in this:
while we were still sinners, Christ died for us.
[ROMANS 5:8]

TRUE SACRIFICE

The famous cyclist Gino Bartali used his bicycle to free persecuted people. A committed Christian, he wanted to act against Mussolini's fascists and the German Nazis during the Second World War. He'd ride to a church known as San Damiano in Assisi, where he'd take his bike inside, remove the seat and fill the tubes with false identity papers. Then he'd deliver these to the persecuted Jewish people living around Florence and in the Tuscan hills. Gino Bartali risked his life so that others might live.

Bartali took his inspiration from Jesus, who died to give life to others. Writing to the church at Rome, the apostle Paul spoke of Christ's sacrifice: "When we were still powerless, Christ died for the ungodly" (ROMANS 5:6). What a gift, that Jesus would die for those seeped in wrongdoing! Paul observed that very rarely would anyone die even for a righteous person (V. 7). Then how much rarer is the sacrifice of a perfect person for sinners!

We may not need to put our lives on the line, but with God's love, help and strength, we too can act sacrificially. Whether stopping to help someone in need, giving financially, providing a safe space for a displaced person, or simply by listening, we can show Christ's love for others through our actions. Who might God inspire you to help today?   *AMY BOUCHER PYE*

> *How does it feel to know that Jesus died for you even*
> *though you've done wrong? How can you spread the love*
> *of Jesus through your actions today?*

Sacrificial Jesus, thank You for paying the ultimate price on
the cross, that I have the assurance of life with You forever.
Help me to share Your love.

BIBLE IN A YEAR | PSALMS 81-83; ROMANS 11:19-36

The word of the LORD is right and true; he is
faithful in all he does. [PSALM 33:4]

FOREVER FAITHFUL GOD

When Xavier was in primary school, I drove him to and
from school. One day, things didn't go according to
plan. I was late to pick him up. I parked the car, praying
frantically as I ran towards his classroom. I found him hugging
his backpack as he sat on a bench next to a teacher. "I'm so sorry, Mijo. Are you okay?" He sighed. "I'm fine, but I'm mad at you
for being late." How could I blame him? I was mad at me too. I
loved my son, but I knew there would be many times when I'd
disappoint him. I also knew he might feel disappointed with God
one day. So I worked hard to teach him that God never has—and
never will—break a promise.

Psalm 33 encourages us to celebrate God's faithfulness with
joyful praises (VV. 1–3) because "the word of the LORD is right and
true; he is faithful in all he does" (V. 4). Using the world God created as tangible proof of His power and dependability (VV. 5–7), the
psalmist calls on the "people of the world" to worship God (V. 8).

When plans fail or people let us down, we can be tempted to
be disappointed in God. However, we can rely on God's trustworthiness because His plans "stand firm forever" (V. 11). We can
praise God, even when things go wrong because our loving Creator sustains everything and everyone. God *is* forever faithful.

XOCHITL DIXON

> **Why is it hard to praise God when your plans fail or
> people disappoint you? How has God used the world He
> created to prove His enduring trustworthiness?**
>
> *Dear God, please remind me of Your past faithfulness
> as I walk by faith today.*

BIBLE IN A YEAR | PSALMS 84–86; ROMANS 12

I have become all things to all people so that
by all possible means I might save some.
[1 CORINTHIANS 9:22]

A DIFFERENT APPROACH

When Scottish missionary Mary Slessor sailed to the African nation of Calabar (now Nigeria) in the late 1800s, she was enthusiastic to continue the work of the late David Livingstone. Her first assignment, teaching school while living among fellow missionaries, left her burdened for a different way to serve. So she did something rare in that region—she moved in with the people she was serving. Mary learned their language, lived their way and ate their food. She even took in dozens of children who'd been abandoned. For nearly forty years, she brought hope and the gospel to those who needed both.

The apostle Paul knew the importance of truly meeting the needs of those around us. He mentioned in 1 Corinthians 12:4–5 that there are "different kinds of gifts, but the same Spirit," and "different kinds of service, but the same Lord." So he served people in their area of need. For instance, "to the weak [he] became weak" (9:22).

One church I'm aware of recently announced the launch of an "all abilities" ministry approach complete with a barrier-free facility—making worship available for people with disabilities. This is the Paul-like kind of thinking that wins hearts and allows the gospel to flourish in a community.

As we live out our faith before those around us, may God lead us to introduce them to Jesus in new and fresh ways. *DAVE BRANON*

**What unique way to reach out to others has God placed
on your heart? How will you accomplish it?**

*Dear heavenly Father, please give me wisdom to find the
right way to help others.*

BIBLE IN A YEAR | PSALMS 87–88; ROMANS 13

The chief cupbearer, however, did not remember
Joseph; he forgot him. [GENESIS 40:23]

LONELY, BUT NOT FORGOTTEN

When you listen to their stories, it becomes clear that perhaps the most difficult part of being a prisoner is isolation and loneliness. In fact, one study revealed that regardless of the length of their incarceration, most prisoners receive only two visits from friends or loved ones during their time behind bars. Loneliness is a constant reality.

It's a pain I imagine Joseph felt as he sat in prison, unjustly accused of a crime. There had been a glimmer of hope. God helped Joseph correctly interpret a dream from a fellow inmate who happened to be a trusted servant of Pharaoh. Joseph told the man he would be restored to his position and asked the man to mention him to Pharaoh so Joseph could gain his freedom (GENESIS 40:14). But the man "did not remember Joseph; he forgot him" (V. 23). For *two more years*, Joseph waited. In those years of waiting, without any sign that his circumstances would change, Joseph was never completely alone because God was with him. Eventually, the servant of Pharaoh remembered his promise and Joseph was released after correctly interpreting another dream (41:9–14).

Regardless of circumstances that make us feel we've been forgotten, and the feelings of loneliness that creep in, we can cling to God's reassuring promise to His children: "I will not forget you!" (ISAIAH 49:15).　　　　　　　*LISA M. SAMRA*

*When have you experienced the pain of being forgotten?
How does the reminder of God's constant presence
provide comfort?*

*Heavenly Father, help me to reach out to You when I feel
forgotten and remember that You're always with me.*

BIBLE IN A YEAR | PSALMS 89-90; ROMANS 14

Jesus is not ashamed to call them brothers
and sisters. [HEBREWS 2:11]

JESUS OUR BROTHER

Bridger Walker was only six when a menacing dog lunged at his younger sister. Instinctively, Bridger jumped in front of her, shielding her from the dog's ferocious attack. After receiving emergency care and ninety stitches to his face, Bridger explained his actions. "If someone had to die, I thought it should be me." Thankfully, plastic surgeons have helped Bridger's face heal. And his brotherly love, evidenced in recent pictures where he's seen hugging his sister, remains as strong as ever.

Ideally, family members watch over us and care for us. True brothers step in when we're in trouble and come alongside us when we're afraid or alone. In reality, even our best brothers are imperfect; some even wound us. We have one brother, however, who's always on our side, Jesus. Hebrews tells us that Christ, as an act of humble love, joined the human family, sharing our "flesh and blood" and becoming like us, "fully human in every way" (HEBREWS 2:14, 17). As a result, Jesus is our truest brother, and He delights in calling us His "brothers and sisters" (V. 11).

We refer to Jesus as our Saviour, Friend and King—and each of these are true. However, Jesus is also our brother who has experienced every human fear and temptation, every despair or sadness. Our brother stands alongside us—always.   *WINN COLLIER*

What's been your experience with human brothers?
How do you see Jesus as your true brother?

Dear Jesus, I'm astounded to think of You as my brother.
Walk with me. Love me. Teach me. Show me Your way.

They should always pray and not give up.
[LUKE 18:1]

THE POWER OF PERSISTENCE

In 1917, a young seamstress was thrilled to get admitted to one of the most renowned fashion design schools. But when Ann Cone arrived to register for classes, the school director told her she wasn't welcome. "To be blunt, Mrs. Cone, we didn't know that you were Black," he said. Refusing to leave, she whispered a prayer: *Please let me stay here.* Seeing her persistence, the director let Ann stay, but segregated her from the whites-only classroom leaving the back door open "for [her] to hear".

Undeniably talented, Ann still graduated six months early and attracted high-society clients. She even designed a world-famous wedding gown. She made the gown twice, seeking God's help after a pipe burst above her sewing studio, ruining the first dress.

Persistence like that is powerful, especially in prayer. In Jesus' parable of the persistent widow, a widow pleads repeatedly for justice from a corrupt judge. At first, he refused her, but "because this widow keeps bothering me, I will see that she gets justice" (LUKE 18:5).

With far more love, "will not God bring about justice for His chosen ones, who cry out to him day and night?" (V. 7). He *will,* said Jesus (V. 8). As He inspires us, let's seek to persistently pray and never give up. In His time and perfect way, God will answer.

PATRICIA RAYBON

What helps you to be persistent in prayer?
What request will you keep pleading?

Dear Jesus, I thank You for answering my
persistent prayers.

BIBLE IN A YEAR | PSALMS 94-96; ROMANS 15:14-33

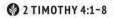

They will gather round them a great number of teachers
to say what their itching ears want to hear. [2 TIMOTHY 4:3]

ITCHY EARS

"**W**e all just have to believe what we're comfortable with," was my cheerful, sweet-natured colleague's conclusion to our lunchtime discussion. I
was working in a hotel at the time, surrounded by people with
this type of worldview. Whenever I talked about Jesus, it would
emerge like a brick wall.

The Apostle Paul once warned his friend Timothy that people
"will gather round them a great number of teachers to say what
their itching ears want to hear. They will turn their ears away from
the truth" (2 TIMOTHY 4:3–4). My colleague's ears only itched for
things that didn't make her—or anyone else—feel uncomfortable.

But one day every ear will have to hear and acknowledge the
truth: Jesus "will judge the living and the dead" (V. 1). He is King
and Judge; He alone defines good and evil.

It's not always comfortable to live for Jesus in a pleasure-driv-
en society. Like Paul, we may "endure hardship" (V. 5) when we
encourage others to submit to Him. Yet even though he was
about to be executed for his faith, Paul could enthuse: "there is
in store for me the crown of righteousness, which the Lord, the
righteous Judge, will award to me on that day" (V. 8).

Christ is the Judge, but He has a Saviour's heart. He has provided a way of salvation for all who will come to Him. That's the
message every ear needs to hear.　　　　　　　*DEBBI FRALICK*

***Have you encountered or struggled with your own 'itchy ears'?
How does the Word of God, including the uncomfortable bits,
soothe your soul?***

*Jesus, I thank You that You are the Judge and King over all the earth.
And I praise You for Your Saviour's heart which means I'm rescued
and promised my own crown of righteousness in heaven.*

BIBLE IN A YEAR | PSALMS 97–99; ROMANS 16

Rejoice before the LORD your God at the place
he will choose as a dwelling for his Name.
[DEUTERONOMY 16:11]

FESTIVALS OF WORSHIP

Attending a large event might change you in a surprising way. After interacting with more than 1,200 people at multi-day gatherings in the UK and other parts of the world, researcher Daniel Yudkin and his colleagues learned that large festivals can impact our moral compass and even affect our willingness to share resources with others. Their research found that 63 percent of attendees had a "transformative" experience at the festival that also left them feeling more connected to humanity and more generous towards friends, family and even complete strangers.

When we gather with others to worship God, however, we can experience more than merely the social transformation of a secular festival; we commune with God Himself. God's people undoubtedly experienced that connection to Him when they gathered in Jerusalem in ancient times for their sacred festivals throughout the year. They travelled—without modern conveniences—to be present at the temple three times a year for "the Festival of Unleavened Bread, the Festival of Weeks and the Festival of Tabernacles" (DEUTERONOMY 16:16). These gatherings were times of solemn remembrance, worship and rejoicing "before the LORD" with family, servants, foreigners and others (V. 11).

Let's gather with others for worship to help one another to continue to enjoy Him and trust in His faithfulness. *KIRSTEN HOLMBERG*

> **How have you experienced a sense of connection with God
> when gathering with others for worship? How has the
> presence of others helped?**
>
> *Thank You, God, for inviting Your people to worship You together.*

BIBLE IN A YEAR | PSALMS 100–102; 1 CORINTHIANS 1

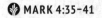

Who is this? Even the wind and the waves
obey him. [MARK 4:41]

THE POWER OF CHRIST

In 2013, about six hundred on-site spectators watched aer-
ialist Nik Wallenda walk on a tightrope across a 1500-foot-
wide gorge near the Grand Canyon. Wallenda stepped onto
the 2-inch-thick steel cable and thanked Jesus for the view as
his head camera pointed towards the valley below. He prayed
and praised Jesus as he walked across the gorge as calmly as if
he was strolling on a pavement. When the wind became treach-
erous, he stopped and crouched. He rose and regained his balance, thanking God for "calming that cable". With every step
on that tightrope, he displayed his dependence on the power
of Christ to everyone listening then and now as the video is
watched across the world.

When the winds of a storm caused waves to overtake the disciples on the sea of Galilee, fear seeped through their pleas for
help (MARK 4:35–38). After Jesus stilled the squall, they knew He
controlled the winds and everything else (VV. 39–41). Slowly they
learned to grow in their trust of Him. Their personal experiences
could help others recognise Jesus' intimate availability and extraordinary might.

As we experience life's storms or walk on the tightropes
of trust stretched over the deep valleys of affliction, we can
demonstrate confident faith in the power of Christ. God will use
our faith-walk to inspire others to hope in Him.　　*XOCHITL DIXON*

> ***How has witnessing Christ's power in the lives of others
> strengthened your faith? How can prayer help you walk
> with confident faith?***
>
> *Thank You, Father, for calming my heart as I trust You
> through life's stormy seasons.*

BIBLE IN A YEAR | PSALMS 103–104; 1 CORINTHIANS 2

The LORD would speak to Moses face to face,
as one speaks to a friend. [EXODUS 33:11]

FINDING OPEN SPACES

In his book *Margin,* Dr. Richard Swenson writes, "We must have some room to breathe. We need freedom to think and permission to heal. Our relationships are being starved to death by velocity. . . . Our children lay wounded on the ground, run over by our high-speed good intentions. Is God now pro-exhaustion? Doesn't He lead people beside the still waters anymore? Who plundered those wide-open spaces of the past, and how can we get them back?" Swenson says we need some quiet, fertile "land" in life where we can rest in God and meet with Him.

Does that resonate? Seeking open spaces is something Moses lived out well. Leading a nation of "stubborn and rebellious" people (EXODUS 33:5 NLT), he often withdrew to find rest and guidance in God's presence. And in his "tent of meeting" (V. 7), "the LORD would speak to Moses face to face, as one speaks to a friend" (V. 11). Jesus also "often withdrew to lonely places and prayed" (LUKE 5:16). Both He and Moses realised the importance of spending time alone with the Father.

We too need to build margin into our lives, some wide and open spaces spent in rest and in God's presence. Spending time with Him will help us make better decisions—creating healthier margins and boundaries in our life so we have the bandwidth available to love Him and others well.

Let's seek God in open spaces today.

TOM FELTEN

***Why do you need margin in your life? How will you build
some space into your schedule to spend time with God?***

Jesus, help me to seek some quiet moments with You each day.

Encourage one another and build each other up.
[1 THESSALONIANS 5:11]

THE GIFT OF ENCOURAGEMENT

"**Y**our bees are swarming!" My wife stuck her head inside the door and gave me news no beekeeper wants to hear. I ran outside to see thousands of bees flying up from the hive to the top of a tall pine, never to return.

I was a little behind in reading the clues that the hive was about to swarm; more than a week of storms had hampered my inspections. The morning the storms ended, the bees left. The colony was new and healthy, and the bees were actually dividing the colony to start a new one. "Don't be hard on yourself," an experienced beekeeper told me cheerfully after seeing my disappointment. "This can happen to anyone!"

Encouragement is a winsome gift. When David was disheartened because Saul was pursuing him to take his life, Saul's son Jonathan encouraged David. "Don't be afraid," Jonathan said. "My father Saul will not lay a hand on you. You will be king over Israel, and I will be second to you. Even my father Saul knows this" (1 SAMUEL 23:17).

Those are surprisingly selfless words from someone next in line to the throne. It's highly likely that Jonathan recognised God was with David, so he spoke out of a humble heart of faith.

All around us are people who need encouragement. God will help us help them as we humble ourselves before Him and ask Him to love them through us.　　　*JAMES BANKS*

Who do you know who needs encouragement?
How might you humbly serve them today?

Dear God, You give me eternal encouragement and good hope. Help me to show Your love to someone today.

BIBLE IN A YEAR | PSALMS 107–109; 1 CORINTHIANS 4

The gates of hell shall not prevail against it.
[MATTHEW 16:18 KJV]

GOD'S ETERNAL CHURCH

"Is church over?" asked a young mother arriving at our church with two children in tow just as the Sunday service was ending. But a greeter told her that a church nearby offered two Sunday services and the second would start soon. Would she like a ride there? The young mother said yes and seemed grateful to travel to the other church. Reflecting later, the greeter came to this conclusion: "Is church over? Never. God's church goes on forever."

The church isn't a fragile 'building'. It's the faithful family of God who are "members of his household," wrote Paul, "built on the foundation of the apostles and prophets, with Christ Jesus himself as the chief cornerstone. In him the whole building is joined together and rises to become a holy temple in the Lord. And in him you too are being built together to become a dwelling in which God lives by his Spirit" (EPHESIANS 2:19–22).

Jesus Himself established His church for eternity. He declared that despite challenges or troubles facing His church, "the gates of hell shall not prevail against it" (MATTHEW 16:18 KJV).

Through this empowering lens, we can see our local churches—all of us—as a part of God's universal church, being built "in Christ Jesus throughout all generations, for ever and ever!" (EPHESIANS 3:21).   *PATRICIA RAYBON*

What about your local church makes you grateful?
How can you help God's universal church grow?

As a part of Your church, dear Jesus, keep building me in You.

BIBLE IN A YEAR | PSALMS 110–112; 1 CORINTHIANS 5

Come, Lord Jesus.
[REVELATION 22:20]

COME, LORD JESUS

T he family's latest update was hopeful, yet desperately sad. "We know the road is still long, but our little knight is not giving up. His courage and his efforts are just incredible." Shockingly, someone had thrown their little boy from the tenth floor of London's Tate Modern gallery in 2019 while they were on holiday; an attack which left him with life-changing injuries.

While justice was served and the attacker went to prison, this boy still lives with the consequences. The family wrote of his many challenges, from memory to fine motor skills. His fatigue and limitations mean that "he also has a really hard time making friends".

In the end, earthly justice can only go so far. It can't give the boy or his family their lives back. It can't bring healing or the promise of a better future.

It's when life is at its most unfair, maybe unbearable even, that we need the Bible's final prayer: "Come, Lord Jesus" (REVELATION 22:20). Jesus' return is our hope: "Look, I am coming soon!" (V. 12). This is when true justice will be done (VV. 12–15). And those who trust Christ will know full healing from every kind of pain, sorrow and injustice (V. 2).

When life cruelly robs us of the things that matter most, our hope is not found in this world, but in the vision of Revelation 22. Strength and peace rise as we pray, "Come, Lord Jesus."

CHRIS WALE

How do the promises and visions of Revelation's last chapter give you hope when your heart is aching? In what circumstances do you most need to learn to pray, "Come, Lord Jesus"?

Come, Lord Jesus. And as I wait for You, please be my strength and my peace for every pain and injustice I suffer.

BIBLE IN A YEAR | PSALMS 113–115; 1 CORINTHIANS 6

The Spirit God gave us does not make us timid, but gives us power, love and self-discipline. [2 TIMOTHY 1:7]

OPENHEARTED GENEROSITY

N o one ever died saying, "I'm so glad for the self-centred, self-serving and self-protective life I lived," author Parker Palmer said in a commencement address, urging graduates to "offer [themselves] to the world . . . with openhearted generosity."

But, Parker continued, living this way would also mean learning "how little you know and how easy it is to fail." Offering themselves in service to the world would require cultivating a "beginner's mind" to "walk straight into your not-knowing, and take the risk of failing and failing, again and again—then getting up to learn again and again."

It's only when our lives are built on a foundation of grace that we can find the courage to choose such a life of fearless "openhearted generosity". As Paul explained to his protégé Timothy, we can confidently "fan into flame" (2 TIMOTHY 1:6) and live out of God's gifting when we remember that it's God's grace that saves and calls us to a life of purpose (V. 9). It's His power that gives us the courage to resist the temptation to live timidly in exchange for the Spirit's "power, love and self-discipline" (V. 7). And it's His grace that picks us up when we fall, so that we can continue a lifelong journey of grounding our lives in His love (VV. 13–14).

MONICA LA ROSE

How are you tempted to live timidly? How do God's grace and power help you live more boldly for Him?

Dear God, thank You that we don't have to live timidly, fearfully guarding ourselves from failure or hurt. Help us to lean into the courage You provide.

BIBLE IN A YEAR | PSALMS 116–118; 1 CORINTHIANS 7:1–19

Then the Jews said, "See how he loved him!"
[JOHN 11:36]

WHAT A FRIEND

I t had been a few years since my friend and I had seen one
another. During that time, he'd received a cancer diagnosis
and started treatments. An unexpected trip to his town af-
forded me the chance to see him again. I walked into the restaurant, and tears filled both of our eyes. It'd been too long since
we'd been in the same room, and now death crouched in the
corner reminding us of the brevity of life. The tears in our eyes
sprang from a long friendship filled with adventures and antics
and laughter and loss—and love. So much love that it spilled out
from the corners of our eyes at the sight of one another.

Jesus wept too. John's gospel records that moment, after the
Jews said, "Come and see, Lord" (11:34), and Jesus stood before
the tomb of His good friend Lazarus. Then we read those two
words that reveal to us the depths to which Christ shares our
humanity: "Jesus wept" (V. 35). Was there much going on in that
moment, things that John did and didn't record? Yes. Yet I also
believe the reaction of the Jews to Jesus is telling: "See how he
loved him!" (V. 36). That line is more than sufficient grounds for
us to stop and worship the Friend who knows our every weakness. Jesus was flesh and blood and tears. Jesus is the Saviour
who loves and understands. *JOHN BLASE*

*When did you last consider the humanity of Jesus? How
does knowing that Jesus understands and shares your
tears encourage you today?*

*Dear Jesus, thank You for being the One who saves and for
also being the One who shares my tears.*

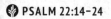

In the assembly I will praise you.
[PSALM 22:22]

HUMBLED BUT HOPEFUL

At the pastor's invitation at the end of the church service, Latrice made her way to the front. When she was invited to greet the congregation, no one was prepared for the weighty and wonderful words she spoke. She had been forced to relocate after devastating tornadoes had taken the lives of seven of her family members. "I can still smile because God's with me," she said. Though bruised by trial, her testimony was a powerful encouragement for those facing challenges of their own.

David's words in Psalm 22 (which point to the sufferings of Jesus) are those of a battered man who felt forsaken by God (V. 1), despised and mocked by others (VV. 6–8), and surrounded by predators (VV. 12–13). He felt weak and drained (VV. 14–18)—but he wasn't hopeless. "But you, LORD, do not be far from me. You are my strength; come quickly to help me" (V. 19). Your present challenge—even if it's not of the same variety as David's or Latrice's—is just as real. And the words of verse 24 are just as meaningful: "He has not despised or scorned the suffering of the afflicted one; . . . but has listened to his cry for help." And when we experience God's help, let's declare His goodness so others can hear of it (V. 22).   *ARTHUR JACKSON*

***What are the benefits of sharing stories of God's
kindness with others? Why is it vital to fellowship with
other brothers and sisters in Christ?***

*Heavenly Father, I bring my feelings of helplessness
to You. Breathe fresh hope into my heart and help me
praise Your name.*

BIBLE IN A YEAR | PSALM 119:89–176; 1 CORINTHIANS 8

I had it in my heart to build a house . . . for
the ark of the covenant. [1 CHRONICLES 28:2]

DEALING WITH DISAPPOINTMENT

After raising money all year for a "trip of a lifetime", a group of high school friends arrived at the airport to learn that many of them had purchased tickets from a bogus company posing as an airline. "It's heartbreaking," one school teacher said. Yet, even though they had to change their plans, the students decided to "make the most of it". They enjoyed two days at nearby attractions, which donated the tickets.

Dealing with failed or changed plans can be disappointing or even heartbreaking. Especially when we've invested time, money or emotion into the planning. King David "had it in [his] heart to build" a temple for God (1 CHRONICLES 28:2), but God told him: "You are not to build a house for my Name . . . . Solomon your son is the one who will build my house" (VV. 3, 6). David didn't despair. He praised God for choosing him to be king over Israel, and he gave the plans for the temple to Solomon to complete (VV. 11–13). As he did, he encouraged him: "Be strong and courageous, and do the work . . . for the LORD God . . . is with you" (V. 20).

When our plans fall through, no matter the reason, we can bring our disappointment to God who "cares for [us]" (1 PETER 5:7). He will help us handle our disappointment with grace.   *ALYSON KIEDA*

**When have you put a lot into plans that then
fell through? What helped you to deal with your
disappointment?**

*Dear God, thank You that Your promises and plans never
fail. Please help me when mine do.*

BIBLE IN A YEAR | PSALMS 120–122; 1 CORINTHIANS 9

The LORD gave and the LORD has taken away;
may the name of the LORD be praised. [JOB 1:21]

LOSING EVERYTHING

The timing couldn't have been worse. After making a small fortune engineering bridges, monuments and large buildings, Cesar had aspirations of starting a new endeavour. So he sold his first business and banked the money, planning to reinvest it soon. During that brief window, his government seized all assets held in private bank accounts. In an instant, Cesar's life-savings evaporated.

Choosing not to view the injustice as a cause to complain, Cesar asked God to show him the way forward. And then—he simply started over.

In one awful moment, Job lost far more than merely his possessions. He lost most of his servants and all his children (JOB 1:13–22). Then he lost his health (2:7–8). Job's response remains a timeless example for us. He prayed, "Naked I came from my mother's womb, and naked I will depart. The LORD gave and the LORD has taken away; may the name of the LORD be praised" (1:21). The chapter concludes, "In all this, Job did not sin by charging God with wrongdoing" (V. 22).

Like Job, Cesar chose to trust God. In just a few years he had built a new business more successful than the first. His story resembles the conclusion of Job's (SEE JOB 42). But even if Cesar had never recovered economically, he knew his real treasure wasn't on this earth anyway (MATTHEW 6:19–20). He would still be trusting God.   *TIM GUSTAFSON*

**How did you feel when you experienced your greatest loss?
What is the Holy Spirit showing you about your losses?**

*Dear God, please teach me something about Your love
today. There's so much I don't understand.*

BIBLE IN A YEAR | PSALMS 123–125; 1 CORINTHIANS 10:1–18

Come to me, all you who are weary
and burdened, and I will give you rest.
[MATTHEW 11:28]

WHEN YOU'RE WEARY

I sat in the stillness of a workday's end, my laptop in front of me. I should've been exhilarated about the work I'd finished that day, but I wasn't. I was tired. My shoulders ached because of my anxiety over a problem at work, and my mind was spent from thinking about a troubled relationship. I wanted to escape from it all—my thoughts wandered to watching TV that night.

But I closed my eyes. "Lord," I whispered. I was too tired to say more. All my weariness went into that one word. And somehow, I immediately knew that was where it should go.

"Come to me," Jesus tells us who are weary and burdened, "and I will give you rest" (MATTHEW 11:28). Not the rest from a good night's sleep. Not the break from reality that television offers. Not even the relief when a problem has been solved. Although these may be good sources of rest, the respite they offer is short-lived and dependent on our circumstances.

In contrast, the rest Jesus gives is lasting and guaranteed by His unchanging character. He's always good. He gives us true rest for our souls even amid trouble because we know that everything is in His control. We can trust and submit to Him, endure and even thrive in difficult situations because of the strength and restoration only He can give.

"Come to me," Jesus tells us. "Come to me."　　　*KAREN HUANG*

When your spirit is weary, where do you go for rest? How would you respond to Jesus, who invites you to go to Him?

Heavenly Father, remind me that true rest is found only in You.

You will seek me and find me when you seek
me with all your heart. [JEREMIAH 29:13]

TRUSTING GOD

As an emergency doctor in London, Laura felt called by God to serve in the war zone in Ukraine. She was privileged to help a man with severe facial scars, which he'd received as his home was burning down. And she was deeply moved by the eight-year-old boy who, whenever his mum felt overwhelmed by the thought of being a refugee, tenderly held her face in his hands. As Laura observed, "Many of the people we met were absolutely reliant on their faith that God was going to bring good days ahead and a good future, like it says in Scripture."

She was referring to this text: "'For I know the plans I have for you,' declares the LORD, 'plans to prosper you and not to harm you, plans to give you hope and a future'" (JEREMIAH 29:11).

People often quote this passage but sometimes overlook its particular historical context. Here, because of their sins, God's people had been exiled from the promised land. God wanted them to obey and trust Him, believing that He would bring them back from the place to which He had banished them (V. 14).

Whether we're living in times of bounty or feeling exiled and alone today, we can trust God's promises that we'll find Him when we seek Him with all our heart (V. 13). Whatever our circumstances, we will indeed be found by Him.　*AMY BOUCHER PYE*

*How do you think you'd react if you faced the conflicts of
war? What does being found by God mean to you?*

*Merciful God, please reveal Yourself to all those who are
suffering because of war. Bring peace and hope, and an
end to the atrocities.*

BIBLE IN A YEAR | PSALMS 129-131; 1 CORINTHIANS 11:1-16

When my spirit grows faint within me, it is you who watch over my way. [PSALM 142:3]

UNKNOWN ROUTE

Perhaps I shouldn't have agreed to join Brian on a run. I was in a foreign country, and I had no idea where or how far we would go or what the terrain would be like. Plus, he was a fast runner. Would I twist an ankle trying to keep up with him? What could I do but trust Brian because he knew the way? As we started, I got even more worried. The trail was rough, winding through a thick forest on uneven ground. Thankfully, Brian kept turning around to check on me and warn me of rough patches ahead.

Perhaps this was how some of the people in Bible times felt while entering unfamiliar territory—Abraham in Canaan, the Israelites in the wilderness, and Jesus' disciples on their mission to share the good news. They had no clue what the journey would be like, except that it would surely be tough. But they had Someone leading them who knew the way ahead. They had to trust that God would give them strength to cope and that He would take care of them. They could follow Him because He knew exactly what lay ahead.

This assurance comforted David when he was on the run. Despite great uncertainty, he said to God: "When my spirit grows faint within me, it is you who watch over my way" (PSALM 142:3). There will be times in life when we fear what lies ahead. But we know this: our God, who walks with us, knows the way.

LESLIE KOH

What worries you most in life? How can you remind yourself that God is walking with you and knows the way ahead?

Father, even though I don't know what may happen next, You do. I know You'll take care of me and guide my steps.

HOPE DEEPER THAN DEATH

I've been hearing conversations lately by church leaders realising the need for the church to regain a central focus on the cross and resurrection of Christ. The story of God's cosmic defeat of death and evil truly sustains hope. Sadly, some faith communities have lost this emphasis in exchange for a primarily individualistic emphasis on experiencing happiness.

But during the pandemic, many church leaders began to realise that—for those grieving the loss of loved ones or loss of a livable income, or those weighed down by the suffering they saw all around them—messages focused on individual happiness were ringing hollow.

We need hope that truly reckons with the full weight of sin and death's wounding of our world—hope that's deeper than death.

The gospel is the story of God's redemption of a wounded cosmos through the cross and resurrection of Jesus—an event that's changed the fabric of reality. One that, in God's grace, we've been invited to share with the world.

Only when we fully reckon with the *bad* news—the depth of sin and death's stranglehold over creation—can we grasp the wonder of the *good* news, that "creation itself will be liberated from its bondage to decay and brought into the freedom and glory of the children of God" (ROMANS 8:21).

Even as we lament honestly the "groaning" of creation (V. 22), we can experience the good news that *Jesus is alive!* Working through communities of people filled with the Spirit and with hope. Carrying us from death into glorious resurrection life.

Monica La Rose, *Our Daily Bread* author

★ How does the unfolding story found in the Bible help believers in Jesus understand their mission for Him? As believers, we're called to participate in God's grand mission in the world. This topic is addressed in the devotions for **September 1, 8** and **22**.

In this world you will have trouble. But take heart! I have overcome the world. [JOHN 16:33]

GOD'S EPIC STORY

A magazine cover displayed a horrifying photograph of starving children in a country devastated by civil war. A young boy, distressed, took a copy of the magazine to a pastor and asked, "Does God know about this?" The pastor replied, "I know you don't understand, but, yes, God knows about that." The boy walked out, declaring he was uninterested in such a God.

These questions disturb not only children but all of us. Alongside an affirmation of God's mysterious knowledge, I wish that boy had heard about the epic story God is continuing to write, even in the most desperate of places.

Jesus unfolded this story for His followers, those who assumed He would shield them from hardship. Christ told them instead that "in this world you will have trouble." What Jesus did offer, however, was His promise that these evils weren't the end. In fact, He'd already "overcome the world" (JOHN 16:33). And in God's final chapter, every injustice will be undone, every suffering healed.

Genesis to Revelation recounts the story of God destroying every unthinkable evil, making every wrong right. The story presents the loving One whose interest in us is unquestioned. Jesus said to His disciples, "I have told you these things, so that in me you may have peace" (V. 33). May we rest in His peace and presence today.   *WINN COLLIER*

How does the story you see feel tragic? How does Jesus' promise to write a good ending free you?

Dear God, it's hard for me to see how You'll right all the evils. But I trust You to do it.

BIBLE IN A YEAR | PSALMS 135-136; 1 CORINTHIANS 12

You are my Son, whom I love; with you I am
well pleased. [MARK 1:11]

TO KNOW GOD

On a visit to Ireland, I was overwhelmed by the abundance of decorative shamrocks. The little green, three-leafed plant could be found in every shop on seemingly everything—clothing, hats, jewellery and more!

More than just a prolific plant across Ireland, the shamrock was embraced for generations as a simple way to explain the Trinity, the historic Christian belief that God is One essence who eternally exists in three distinct persons: God the Father, God the Son and God the Holy Spirit. While all human explanations of the Trinity are inadequate, the shamrock is a helpful symbol because it's one plant made of the same substance with three distinct leaves.

The word *Trinity* isn't found in Scripture, but it summarises the theological truth we see explicit in passages where all three persons of the Trinity are present at the same time. When Jesus, God the Son, is baptised, God the Spirit is seen coming down from heaven "like a dove", and God the Father's voice is heard saying, "You are my Son" (MARK 1:10-11).

Irish believers in Jesus used the shamrock because they wanted to help people know God. As we more fully understand the beauty of the Trinity, it helps us know God and deepens our ability to worship Him "in the Spirit and in truth" (JOHN 4:24).

LISA M. SAMRA

> **What symbols help you understand the Trinity?**
> **Why is it essential to believe God is one?**
>
> *I worship You, Father, Son and Spirit, as one God acting*
> *together to extend love and salvation to all people.*

BIBLE IN A YEAR | PSALMS 137–139; 1 CORINTHIANS 13

You show that you are a letter from Christ . . .
written . . . with the Spirit of the living God.
[2 CORINTHIANS 3:3]

THE BLESSED MASK

As the mask mandate requirements during the pandemic loosened, I struggled to remember to keep a mask handy for where they were still required—like my daughter's school. One day when I needed a mask, I found just one in my car: the one I avoided wearing because it had BLESSED written across the front.

I prefer to wear masks without messages, and I believe that the word on the mask I found is overused. But I had no choice, so I reluctantly put the mask on. And when I nearly showed my annoyance with a new receptionist at the school, I caught myself, partly because of the word on my mask. I didn't want to look like a hypocrite, walking around with BLESSED scrawled across my mouth while showing impatience to a person trying to figure out a complicated system.

Though the letters on my mask reminded me of my witness for Christ, the words of Scripture in my heart should be a true reminder to be patient with others. As Paul wrote to the Corinthians, "You are a letter from Christ, . . . written not with ink but with the Spirit of the living God, not on tablets of stone but on tablets of human hearts" (2 CORINTHIANS 3:3). The Holy Spirit who "gives life" (V. 6), can help us live out "love, joy, peace" and, yes, "patience" (GALATIANS 5:22). We're truly *blessed* by His presence within us!   *KATARA PATTON*

**What are your words and actions saying to others?
How can you represent Christ in what you do today?**

*Dear Jesus, with each person I encounter today,
help me to share what it means to live for You.*

BIBLE IN A YEAR | PSALMS 140–142; 1 CORINTHIANS 14:1–20

You, LORD, preserve both people and
animals. [PSALM 36:6]

THE WONDERS OF CREATION

Having finished hosting a meeting at the vicarage, I was contemplating leaving the comfort of my sofa and heading up to bed. Out of the corner of my eye I spied something move. *I hope that's not what I think it is*, I thought. My heart sank when I realised that it was, indeed, a dreaded mouse.

The next morning I smiled wryly when I read a social-media post from a friend who wanted to share this wonderful truth: "Your tender care and kindness leave no one forgotten, not a man or even a mouse" (PSALM 36:6, TPT). *Even*, I wondered, *that mouse running around the vicarage?*

David may have written this song of love for God from a high place as he looked out at the horizon: "Your love, LORD, reaches to the heavens, your faithfulness to the skies" (PSALM 36:5). Probably he wasn't thinking of God's lovingkindness for even lowly creatures such as mice, but he was exalting God for preserving "both people and animals" (V. 6). Indeed, he continued, because of God's great love, we can take refuge in the shadow of His wings (V. 7) and find in Him the fountain of life (V. 9).

We can join David in worshipping God for the wonders of His creation, from the breath-taking views on top of a mountain to the lowly creatures we might find in unexpected places. He is most worthy of our praise!   *AMY BOUCHER PYE*

> **How does praising God for His creation change the way
> you view the earth and all that is in it? What could you
> do today to care for part of God's creation?**
>
> *Creator God, thank You for making the world in all of its
> beauty. Open my eyes to see the wonders You have made.*

BIBLE IN A YEAR | PSALMS 143–145; 1 CORINTHIANS 14:21–40

How unsearchable his judgements, and his
paths beyond tracing out! [ROMANS 11:33]

HIS PATHS

Victor Kiplangat became the first Ugandan to win a Commonwealth marathon during the 2022 Games, crossing the finishing line with an impressive lead time. Yet the race wasn't straightforward. Kiplangat got lost as he navigated Birmingham's streets. "The motorcycle riders were confusing me," he explained. "But I still made it to the finish."

Scripture compares our lives to a marathon; we're running "the race marked out for us" by God (HEBREWS 12:1). But, like Kiplangat, we often get confused about which way to go and how to navigate unexpected diversions. Sometimes we wish God would mark His paths more clearly!

Instead of getting frustrated by God's "unsearchable" ways, Paul rejoiced that "his paths [are] beyond tracing out!" (ROMANS 11:33). In his letter to the Christians in Rome, having explored God's salvation of sinners—and His mercy towards the disobedient (V. 32)—Paul admits that God's gracious ways defy human logic. Yet they are so much better; full of rich "wisdom and knowledge" (V. 33).

When we feel lost or confused in our own race, Paul reminds us that we run with the One who needs no counsellor (V. 34). "For from him and through him and for him are all things" (V. 36). His ways may be beyond understanding, but His goodness and power towards us are unmistakeable. We can trust Him to run with us, and when we go wrong, He will bring us back to His paths.

CHRIS WALE

What has disrupted your race for Jesus recently? How might rejoicing in God's wisdom and nearness bring you peace, even as you wait for His leading?

Father, Your awesome ways are far beyond my limited understanding. Help me to stay close to You today and trust Your leading.

BIBLE IN A YEAR | PSALMS 146–147; 1 CORINTHIANS 15:1–28

I consider everything a loss because of the surpassing worth of knowing Christ Jesus my Lord . . . that I may gain Christ and be found in him. [PHILIPPIANS 3:8–9]

I'M NOBODY! WHO ARE YOU?

In a poem that begins, "I'm nobody! Who are you?" Emily Dickinson playfully challenges all the effort people tend to put into being 'somebody', advocating instead for the joyful freedom of blissful anonymity. For "How dreary—to be—Somebody! How public—like a Frog—/ To tell one's name—the live-long June / To an admiring Bog!"

Finding freedom in letting go of the need to be 'somebody' in some ways echoes the testimony of the apostle Paul. Before he met Christ, Paul had a long list of seemingly impressive religious credentials, apparent "reasons to put confidence in the flesh" (PHILIPPIANS 3:4).

But encountering Jesus changed everything. When Paul saw how hollow his religious achievements were in light of Christ's sacrificial love, he confessed, "I consider everything a loss because of the surpassing worth of knowing Christ Jesus my Lord . . . . I consider them garbage, that I may gain Christ" (V. 8). His only remaining ambition was "to *know* Christ . . . the power of his resurrection and participation in his sufferings, becoming like him in his death" (V. 10).

It's dreary, indeed, to attempt on our own to become 'somebody'. But, to know Jesus, to lose ourselves in His self-giving love and life, is to find ourselves again (V. 9), finally free and whole.

MONICA LA ROSE

When have you experienced freedom from seeking your own self-worth? How can finding yourself "in Christ" free you from both pride and self-rejection?

Loving God, thank You that I don't need to try to be 'somebody' to be loved and accepted by You.

BIBLE IN A YEAR | PSALMS 148–150; 1 CORINTHIANS 15:29–58

He has not stopped showing his kindness
to the living and the dead. [RUTH 2:20]

ACTS OF KINDNESS

Months after suffering a miscarriage, Valerie decided to sell her baby things at a car boot sale. Gerald, a carpenter who lived a few miles away, eagerly bought the wooden cot she was selling. While there, his wife talked with Valerie and learned about her loss. After hearing of her situation on the way home, Gerald decided to use the cot to craft a keepsake for Valerie. A week later, he tearfully presented her with a beautiful bench. "There are good people out there, and here's proof," Valerie said.

Like Valerie, Ruth and Naomi suffered great loss. Naomi's husband and two sons had died. And now she and her bereft daughter-in-law Ruth had no heirs and no one to provide for them (RUTH 1:1–5). That's where Boaz stepped in. When Ruth went to a field to pick up leftover grain, Boaz—the owner—asked about her. When he learned who she was, he was kind to her (2:5–9). Amazed, Ruth asked, "Why have I found such favour in your eyes?" (V. 10). He replied, "I've been told all about what you have done for your mother-in-law since the death of your husband" (V. 11).

Boaz later married Ruth and provided for Naomi (CH. 4). Through their marriage, a forefather of David—and of Jesus—was born. Just as God used Gerald and Boaz to help transform the grief of another, He can work through us to show kindness and empathy to others in pain. 　　　　　　*ALYSON KIEDA*

> ***When have you been the giver or recipient of an act of kindness? What was the result?***
>
> *Dear God, thank You for sending Your Son to redeem me,
> the greatest kindness of all.*

BIBLE IN A YEAR | PROVERBS 1–2; 1 CORINTHIANS 16

At once they left their nets and followed him.
[MATTHEW 4:20]

THE GOD OF SURPRISES

The convention centre darkened, and thousands of us university students bowed our heads as the speaker led us in a prayer of commitment. As he welcomed those to stand who felt called to serve in overseas missions, I could feel my friend Lynette leave her seat and knew she was promising to live and serve in the Philippines. Yet I felt no urge to stand. Seeing the needs in the United States, I wanted to share God's love in my native land. But a decade later, I would make my home in Britain, seeking to serve God among the people He gave me as my neighbours. My ideas about how I would live my life changed when I realised that God invited me on an adventure different from what I had anticipated.

Jesus often surprised those He met, including the fishermen He called to follow Him. When Christ gave them a new mission to fish for people, Peter and Andrew left their nets "at once" and followed Him (MATTHEW 4:20), and James and John "immediately" left their boat (V. 22). They set off on this new adventure with Jesus, trusting Him, yet not knowing where they were going.

God, of course, calls many people to serve Him right where they are! Whether staying or going, we can all look to Him expectantly to surprise us with wonderful experiences and opportunities to live for Him in ways we might never have dreamed possible.   *AMY BOUCHER PYE*

> **How do you react when you hear stories of God at work? How has He surprised you?**
>
> *Loving Jesus, You call people to follow You in unique and amazing ways. Teach me to discern Your voice and respond to Your call.*

BIBLE IN A YEAR | PROVERBS 3–5; 2 CORINTHIANS 1

No human being can tame the tongue.
[JAMES 3:8]

ACCEPTING GUIDANCE

The air smelled of leather and oats as we stood in the barn where my friend Michelle was teaching my daughter to ride a horse. Michelle's white pony opened its mouth as she demonstrated how to place the bit behind its teeth. As she pulled the bridle over its ears, Michelle explained that the bit was important because it allowed the rider to slow the horse and steer it to the left or right.

A horse's bit, like the human tongue, is small but important. Both have great influence over something big and powerful—for the bit, it's the horse. For the tongue, it's our words (JAMES 3:3, 5).

Our words can run in different directions. "With the tongue we praise our Lord and Father, and with it we curse human beings" (V. 9). Unfortunately, the Bible warns that it's very hard to control our speech because words spring from our hearts (LUKE 6:45). Thankfully, God's Spirit, who indwells every believer, helps us grow in patience, goodness and self-control (GALATIANS 5:22–23). As we cooperate with the Spirit, our hearts change and so do our words. Profanity turns to praise. Lying gives way to truth. Criticism transforms into encouragement.

Taming the tongue isn't just about training ourselves to say the right things. It's about accepting the Holy Spirit's guidance so that our words generate the kindness and encouragement our world needs. *JENNIFER BENSON SCHULDT*

What inner attitudes come out through your words?
How might cooperation with the Spirit influence your speech?

*Dear God, please change my heart so that my words
encourage others and honour You.*

Blessed is she who has believed that the Lord
would fulfil his promises to her! [LUKE 1:45]

PROMISE FULFILLED

E ach summer when I was a child, I would travel two hundred
miles to enjoy a week with my grandparents. I wasn't aware
until later how much wisdom I soaked up from those two
people I loved. Their life experiences and walk with God had giv-
en them perspectives that my young mind couldn't yet imagine.
Conversations with them about the faithfulness of God assured
me that God is trustworthy and fulfils *every* promise He makes.

Mary, the mother of Jesus, was a teenager when an angel
visited her. The incredible news brought by Gabriel must have
been overwhelming, yet she willingly accepted the task with
grace (LUKE 1:38). But perhaps her visit with her elderly relative
Elizabeth—who was also in the midst of a miraculous pregnan-
cy (some scholars believe she may have been sixty years old)—
brought her comfort as Elizabeth enthusiastically confirmed Gabriel's words that she was the mother of the promised Messiah
(VV. 39–45).

As we grow and mature in Christ, as my grandparents did, we
learn that He keeps His promises. He kept His promise of a child
for Elizabeth and her husband Zechariah (VV. 57–58). And that
son, John the Baptist, became the harbinger of a promise made
hundreds of years before—one that would change the course of
humanity's future. The promised Messiah—the Saviour of the
world—was coming (MATTHEW 1:21–23).　　　　*CINDY HESS KASPER*

> **Why can you trust God to fulfil His promises?**
> **Which of His promises bring you the most joy?**

*Loving Father, thank You for being trustworthy and for
fulfilling Your promises.*

BIBLE IN A YEAR | PROVERBS 8-9; 2 CORINTHIANS 3

Who is wise and understanding among you? Let them show it by their good life, by deeds done in the humility that comes from wisdom. [JAMES 3:13]

WHICH WISDOM?

Just before Easter 2018, a terrorist entered a market, killing two people and taking a third woman hostage. When efforts to free the woman failed, a policeman made the terrorist an offer: release the woman and take him instead.

The offer was shocking because it went against popular wisdom. You can always tell a culture's 'wisdom' by the sayings it celebrates, like the celebrity quotes that get posted on social media. "The biggest adventure you can take is to live the life of your dreams," one popular quote reads. "Love yourself first and everything else falls into line," says another. "Do what you have to do, for you," states a third. Had the police officer followed such advice, he'd have put himself first and run.

The apostle James says there are two kinds of wisdom in the world: one "earthly", another "heavenly". The first is marked by selfish ambition and disorder (JAMES 3:14–16); the second, by humility, submission and peacemaking (VV. 13, 17–18). Earthly wisdom puts self first. Heavenly wisdom favours others, leading to a life of humble deeds (V. 13).

The terrorist accepted the police officer's offer. The hostage was released, the policeman was shot, and that Easter the world witnessed an innocent man dying for someone else.

Heavenly wisdom leads to humble deeds because it places God above self (PROVERBS 9:10). Which wisdom are you following today?

SHERIDAN VOYSEY

What 'wisdom' does the world offer? How can you best assess the wisdom you're offered?

All-wise God, please give me the kind of wisdom that leads to humble deeds done in love.

BIBLE IN A YEAR | PROVERBS 10–12; 2 CORINTHIANS 4

Be still before the LORD and wait
patiently for him. [PSALM 37:7]

BE STILL

After I'd got settled into the chamber, my body floating comfortably above the water, the room went dark and the gentle music that had been playing in the background went silent. I'd read that isolation tanks were therapeutic, offering relief for stress and anxiety. But this was like nothing I'd ever encountered. It felt like the chaos of the world had stopped, and I could clearly hear my innermost thoughts. I left the experience balanced and rejuvenated, reminded that there is power in stillness.

We can rest most comfortably in the stillness of the presence of God, who renews our strength and grants us the wisdom we need to tackle the challenges we face each day. When we're still, silencing the noise and removing distractions in our lives, He strengthens us so we can hear His gentle voice more clearly (PSALM 37:7).

While sensory deprivation chambers are certainly one form of stillness, God offers us a simpler way to spend uninterrupted time with Him. He says, "When you pray, go into your room, close the door and pray to your Father" (MATTHEW 6:6). God will guide our steps and allow His righteousness to shine brightly through us when we seek the answers to life's challenges in the stillness of His magnificent presence (PSALM 37:5–6). *KIMYA LODER*

What are some things that consume your time? How can you make more room for quiet time with God?

*Dear Father, I know I get caught up in the fast pace of life.
Help me to be still, making room for You in everything I do.*

[God] defends the cause of the fatherless
and the widow, and loves the foreigner.
[DEUTERONOMY 10:18]

WELCOMING THE FOREIGNER

As thousands of Ukrainian women and children arrived at Berlin's railway station fleeing war, they were met with a surprise—German families holding handmade signs offering refuge in their homes. "Can host two people!" one sign read. "Big room [available]," read another. Asked why she offered such hospitality to strangers, one woman said her mother had needed refuge in the past, and she wanted to help others in such need.

In Deuteronomy, God calls the Israelites to care for those far from their homelands. Why? Because He's the defender of the fatherless, the widow and the foreigner (DEUTERONOMY 10:18), and because the Israelites knew what such vulnerability felt like: "for you yourselves were foreigners in Egypt" (V. 19). Empathy was to motivate their care.

But there's a flip side to this too. When the widow at Zarephath welcomed the foreigner Elijah into her home, she was the one blessed (1 KINGS 17:9–24), just as Abraham was blessed by his three foreign visitors (GENESIS 18:1–15). God often uses hospitality to bless the host, not just the guest.

Welcoming strangers into your home is hard, but those German families may be the real beneficiaries. As we too respond to the vulnerable with God's empathy, we may be surprised at the gifts He gives us through them.   *SHERIDAN VOYSEY*

*Why do you think God cares so much for widows,
orphans and refugees? How could you 'welcome'
a vulnerable person this week?*

*Dear God, give me a heart as big as Yours for the widow,
the fatherless and the vulnerable.*

BIBLE IN A YEAR | PROVERBS 16–18; 2 CORINTHIANS 6

Be still, and know that I am God.
[PSALM 46:10]

LET GO

The owner of the bookshop where Keith worked had been away on holiday for only two days, but Keith, his assistant, was already panicking. Operations were smooth, but Keith was anxious that he wouldn't do a good job overseeing the shop. Frenetically, he micromanaged all he could.

"Stop it," his boss finally told him over a video call. "All you have to do is follow the instructions I email you daily. Don't worry, Keith. The burden isn't on you; it's on me."

In a time of conflict with other nations, Israel received a similar word from God: "Be still" (PSALM 46:10). "Stop striving," He said in essence, "just follow what I say. I will fight for you." Israel was not being told to be passive or complacent but to be actively still—to obey God faithfully while yielding control of the situation and leaving the results of their efforts to Him.

We're called to do the same. And we can do it because the God we trust is sovereign over the world. If "he lifts his voice [and] the earth melts," and if He can make "wars cease to the ends of the earth" (VV. 6, 9), then surely, we can trust in the security of His refuge and strength (V. 1). The burden of control over our life isn't on us—it's on God.　　*KAREN HUANG*

> ***How can you let go of situations that are out of your control and surrender them to God? What aspects of His character help you to surrender all to Him?***

> *Almighty God, You know what's troubling me.*
> *I don't know how to deal with it, but You do.*
> *Help me surrender to Your leading.*

BIBLE IN A YEAR | PROVERBS 19–21; 2 CORINTHIANS 7

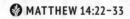

Peter got down out of the boat, walked
on the water and came towards Jesus.
[MATTHEW 14:29]

GOD OF THE WAVES

Irish missionary Amy Carmichael knew what it was to live
through life's storms: poverty, illness, chronic pain, persecution. Having weathered so many hardships with God's help,
she reflected, "God is the God of the waves and the billows, and
they are still His when they come over us; again and again we
have proved that the overwhelming thing does not overwhelm."

Perhaps Peter had a similar revelation when he stepped out
of his fishing boat and onto the stormy sea. Imagine being there
with him, blown about by the wind, buffeted by huge waves and
blinded by stinging spray (SEE MATTHEW 14:24). And then to see
Jesus calmly walking towards you—on the same swirling waters
that threaten to hurl you to the depths (V. 25).

If the storm terrified Peter, how much more awesome Jesus
must have suddenly seemed—He who couldn't be touched by
it. The overwhelming storm could not overwhelm its Creator.
Even when Peter then began to sink beneath the waves, Jesus
"reached out his hand and caught him" (V. 31).

If you are facing storms which feel far too big to handle, set
your gaze instead on Jesus, to Whom they must all submit.
You'll find the courage and perseverance for today's challenges
in His presence. Even if you feel you are sinking, know that Jesus
stands ready to hold you so that you will not be overcome.

CHRIS WALE

**What storms threaten to overwhelm you today? How can
you set your sights on the Lord, rather than the storm itself?**

*Dear Jesus, You reign over every thunderstorm and wave I
endure. Thank You for not allowing me to sink. May I feel
Your hand holding me tightly today.*

BIBLE IN A YEAR | PROVERBS 22–24; 2 CORINTHIANS 8

Do not conform to the pattern of this
world, but be transformed by the renewing
of your mind. [ROMANS 12:2]

JUST LIKE JESUS

In 2014, biologists captured a pair of orange pygmy seahorses in the Philippines. They collected the marine creatures, along with a section of the orange coral sea fan they called home, for further study. Scientists wanted to know if the pygmy seahorses were born to match the colour of their parents or their environment. When the pygmy seahorses gave birth to dull brown babies, scientists placed a purple coral sea fan into the tank. The babies, whose parents were orange, changed their colour to match the purple sea fan. Due to their fragility by nature, their survival depends on their God-given ability to blend into their environment.

Blending-in is a useful defence mechanism in nature. However, God invites all people to receive salvation and stand out in the world by how we live. The apostle Paul urges believers in Jesus to honour God in every aspect of our lives, to worship Him by offering our bodies as a "living sacrifice" (ROMANS 12:1). Due to our fragility as human beings affected by sin, our spiritual health as believers depends on the Holy Spirit "renewing" our minds and empowering us to avoid conforming to "the pattern of this world" that rejects God and glorifies sin (V. 2).

Blending into this world means living in opposition to the Scriptures. However, through the power of the Holy Spirit, we can look and love just like Jesus!   *XOCHITL DIXON*

> **How have you been blending into the world?**
> **How has God changed you?**

Dear God, please make me more like Jesus each day.

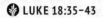

What do you want me to do for you?
[LUKE 18:41]

ANY QUESTIONS?

Ann was meeting with her oral surgeon—a doctor she'd known for many years—for a preliminary exam. He asked her, "Do you have any questions?" She said, "Yes. Did you go to church last Sunday?" Her question wasn't intended to be judgemental, but simply to initiate a conversation about faith.

The surgeon had a less-than-positive church experience growing up, and he hadn't gone back. Because of Ann's question and their conversation, he reconsidered the role of Jesus and church in his life. When Ann later gave him a Bible with his name imprinted on it, he received it with tears.

Sometimes we fear confrontation or don't want to seem too aggressive in sharing our faith. But there can be a winsome way to witness about Jesus—ask questions.

For a man who was God and knew everything, Jesus sure asked a lot of questions. While we don't know His purposes, it's clear His questions prompted others to respond. He asked his disciple Andrew, "What do you want?" (JOHN 1:38). He asked blind Bartimaeus, "What do you want me to do for you?" (MARK 10:51; LUKE 18:41). He asked the paralysed man, "Do you want to get well?" (JOHN 5:6). Transformation happened for each of these individuals after Jesus' initial question.

Is there someone you want to approach about matters of faith? Ask God to give you the right questions to ask.   DAVE BRANON

Why can questions be better conversation starters than direct statements? What questions can you ask those who need spiritual help?

Dear Jesus, please help me to reach out to others in a way that can lead to transformation.

BIBLE IN A YEAR | PROVERBS 27-29; 2 CORINTHIANS 10

Make sacred garments for your brother Aaron
to give him dignity and honour. [EXODUS 28:2]

THE RED DRESS PROJECT

The Red Dress project was conceived by British artist Kirstie Macleod and has become an exhibit in museums and galleries around the world. For thirteen years, eighty-four pieces of burgundy silk travelled across the globe to be embroidered upon by more than three hundred women (and a handful of men). The pieces were then constructed into a gown, telling the stories of each contributing artist—many of whom are marginalised and impoverished.

Like the Red Dress, the garments worn by Aaron and his descendants were made by many "skilled workers" (EXODUS 28:3). God's instructions for the priestly attire included details that told the collective story of Israel, including engraving the names of the tribes on onyx stones that would sit on the priests' shoulders "as a memorial before the LORD" (V. 12). The tunics, embroidered sashes and caps gave the priests "dignity and honour" as they served God and led the people in worship (V. 40).

As new covenant believers in Jesus, we—together—are a priesthood of believers, serving God and leading one another in worship (1 PETER 2:4–5, 9); Jesus is our high priest (HEBREWS 4:14). Though we don't wear any particular clothing to identify ourselves as priests, with His help, we "clothe [ourselves] with compassion, kindness, humility, gentleness and patience" (COLOSSIANS 3:12).   *KIRSTEN HOLMBERG*

> **Which of the attributes from Colossians do you most
> need to put on today? How else has God 'clothed' you for
> service to Him?**
>
> *Please clothe me, Jesus, in compassion, kindness, humility,
> gentleness and patience.*

BIBLE IN A YEAR | PROVERBS 30-31; 2 CORINTHIANS 11:1-15

These were all commended for their faith.
[HEBREWS 11:39]

FAITHFUL BUT NOT FORGOTTEN

As he was growing up, Sean knew little about what it meant to have a family. His mother had died and his father was hardly home. He often felt lonely and abandoned. A couple who lived nearby, however, reached out to him. They took him into their home and got their children to be 'big brother' and 'big sister' to him, which gave him assurance that he was loved. They also took him to church, where Sean, now a confident young man, is a youth leader today.

Although this couple played such a key role in turning a young life around, what they did for Sean isn't widely known to most people in their church family. But God knows, and I believe their faithfulness will be rewarded someday, as will those listed in the Bible's 'Hall of Faith'. Hebrews 11 starts with the big names of Scripture, but it goes on to speak of countless others we may never know, yet who "were all commended for their faith" (V. 39). And "the world," says the writer, "was not worthy of them" (V. 38).

Even when our deeds of kindness go unnoticed by others, God sees and knows. What we do might seem like a small thing—a kind deed or an encouraging word—but God can use it to bring glory to His name, in His time and in His way. He knows, even if others don't. 　　　　　　　　　　　*LESLIE KOH*

> **What is one simple thing you could do for someone today? How can you remind yourself that God knows your heart and the work of your hands?**

> *Heavenly Father, please continue to show me what good works You've prepared for me to do, and give me the faith to do it for You alone.*

"Teacher," they said, "we want you to do for us whatever we ask." [MARK 10:35]

SHOOTING OURSELVES IN THE FOOT

In 2021, an engineer with the ambition to shoot an arrow further than anyone in history took aim at the record of 2,028 feet. While lying on his back, he drew back the bowstring of his personally designed foot-operated bow and prepared to launch the projectile to what he hoped would be a new record distance of more than a mile (5,280 FEET). Taking a deep breath, he let the arrow fly. It didn't travel a mile. In fact, it travelled less than a foot—launching into *his* foot and causing considerable damage. Ouch!

Sometimes we can figuratively shoot ourselves in the foot with misguided ambition. James and John knew what it meant to ambitiously seek something good, but for the wrong reasons. They asked Jesus to "let one of us sit at your right and the other at your left in your glory" (MARK 10:37). Jesus had told the disciples they would "sit on twelve thrones, judging the twelve tribes of Israel" (MATTHEW 19:28), so it's easy to see why they made this request. The problem? They were selfishly seeking their own lofty position and power in Christ's glory. Jesus told them that their ambition was misplaced (MARK 10:38) and that "whoever wants to become great among you must be your servant" (V. 43).

As we aim to do good and great things for Christ, may we seek His wisdom and direction—humbly serving others as He did so well (V. 45). 　　　　　　　　　　　　　　　　　　*TOM FELTEN*

Why can ambition be both good and bad?
How can we make it our ambition to serve like Jesus?

Dear Jesus, I desire to do great things for You,
but for the right reasons.

BIBLE IN A YEAR │ ECCLESIASTES 4–6; 2 CORINTHIANS 12

"Neither do I condemn you," Jesus declared.
"Go now and leave your life of sin."
[JOHN 8:11]

GOD COVERS OUR SIN

When one single mother had to find work to take care of her family in the 1950s, she took on typing jobs. The only issue was that she wasn't a very good typist and kept making mistakes. She looked for ways to cover up her errors and eventually created what became known as Liquid Paper, a white correction fluid used to cover up typing errors. Once it dries, you can type over the cover-up as if there were no errors.

Jesus offers us an infinitely more powerful and important way to deal with our sin—no cover-up but complete forgiveness. A good example of this shows up in the beginning of John 8 in the story of a woman who was caught in adultery (VV. 3–4). The teachers of the law wanted Jesus to do something about the woman and her sins. The law said she should be stoned, but Christ didn't bother to entertain what the law did or didn't say. He simply offered a reminder that all have sinned (SEE ROMANS 3:23) and told anyone who hadn't sinned to "throw a stone at" the woman (JOHN 8:7). Not one rock was tossed.

Jesus offered her a fresh start. He said He didn't condemn her and instructed that she "leave [her] life of sin" (V. 11). Christ gave her the solution to forgive her sin and 'type' a new way of living over her past. That same offer is available to us by His grace.

KATARA PATTON

How has Jesus and the forgiveness of sin He provides written a new story in your life? How will this help you treat others who've sinned?

Dear Jesus, thank You for cleansing me of my sins. Help me to live a renewed life in You.

BIBLE IN A YEAR | ECCLESIASTES 7-9; 2 CORINTHIANS 13

The past troubles will be forgotten . . . . See,
I will create new heavens and a new earth.
[ISAIAH 65:16–17]

BEAUTIFUL RESTORATION

In his book *Art + Faith: A Theology of Making,* renowned artist Makoto Fujimura describes the ancient Japanese art form of Kintsugi. In it, the artist takes broken pottery (originally tea ware) and pieces the shards back together with lacquer, threading gold into the cracks. "Kintsugi," Fujimura explains, "does not just 'fix' or repair a broken vessel; rather, the technique makes the broken pottery even more beautiful than the original." Kintsugi, first implemented centuries ago when a warlord's favourite cup was destroyed and then beautifully restored, became art that's highly prized and desired.

Isaiah describes God artfully enacting this kind of restoration with the world. Though we're broken by our rebellion and shattered by our selfishness, God promises to "create new heavens and a new earth" (ISAIAH 65:17). He plans not merely to repair the old world but to make it entirely new, to take our ruin and fashion a world shimmering with fresh beauty. This new creation will be so stunning that "past troubles will be forgotten" and "former things will not be remembered" (VV. 16–17). With this new creation, God won't scramble to cover our mistakes but rather will unleash His creative energy—energy where ugly things become beautiful and dead things breathe anew.

As we survey our shattered lives, there's no need for despair. God is working His beautiful restoration.   *WINN COLLIER*

**What needs beautiful restoration? How does this
imagery of God's new creation stir hope in you?**

Dear God, please restore me and renew this world.

BIBLE IN A YEAR | ECCLESIASTES 10–12; GALATIANS 1

I have learned to be content whatever the
circumstances. [PHILIPPIANS 4:11]

CONTENT IN ALL CIRCUMSTANCES

The sign said, "The Elephant Man". It described an "exhibit" in Victorian circuses and "freak" shows. Shockingly, however, this popular exhibit was a human being: Joseph Merrick (1862-1890). He suffered from severe deformities and had escaped an abusive life in the workhouse only to endure the shrieks of horrified crowds as he sought to make a living.

But then he found refuge and friendship with surgeon Frederick Treves. Treves wondered at Merrick's gentleness and the way he never complained about his abusers or his condition. The answer lay in Merrick's deep faith. He knew the Bible intimately, not just in his head, but also in his heart and soul. He had the strength and transforming presence of Christ that the apostle Paul had experienced.

Paul faced hunger, beating, stoning and imprisonment, and suffered with a debilitating health condition too. But he had "learned to be content whatever the circumstances". His "secret of being content" (V.12) was his union with Jesus. "I can do all this," Paul said, "through him who gives me strength" (V. 13). Neither Paul nor Merrick relied on circumstances. Their resilience, assurance and character came from their living union with Christ through His Spirit and Word.

Upsetting, painful and difficult circumstances can overwhelm us, consuming our thoughts and emotions. But we can draw strength from God, who meets our needs or helps us to face them, "according to the riches of his glory in Christ Jesus" (V. 19).   ANNE LE TISSIER

*What promises of Scripture infuse your heart with peace
in challenging situations? Could you pause during today to
worship God, letting yourself focus on His love and power?*

*Ever-present Jesus, thank You that Your life in me reassures,
satisfies and strengthens me, despite the problems I face.*

BIBLE IN A YEAR | SONG OF SONGS 1-3; GALATIANS 2

Clothe yourselves with compassion.
[COLOSSIANS 3:12]

COMPASSION IN ACTION

Building benches isn't James Warren's job. He started building them, however, when he noticed a woman sitting on
the ground while waiting for a bus. *That's undignified*,
Warren worried. So, the twenty-eight-year-old workforce con-
sultant found some scrap wood, built a bench and placed it at
the bus stop. It quickly got used. Realising many of the bus stops
in his city lacked seating, he made another bench, then several
more, inscribing "Be Kind" on each one. His goal? "To make people's lives just a little bit better, in any way I can," Warren said.

Compassion is another way of describing such action. As practised by Jesus, compassion is a feeling so strong that it leads us
to take action to meet another's need. When crowds of desperate people pursued Jesus, "he had compassion on them,
because they were like sheep without a shepherd" (MARK 6:34).
He turned that compassion into action by healing their sick
(MATTHEW 14:14).

We too should "clothe [ourselves] with compassion," Paul
urged (COLOSSIANS 3:12). The benefits? As Warren says, "It fills me
up. It's air in my tyres."

All around us are needs, and God will bring them to our attention. Those needs can motivate us to put our compassion
into action, and those actions will encourage others as we show
them the love of Christ.   *PATRICIA RAYBON*

> **When did you see a need that, with compassion, you
> helped solve? How did your compassion make you feel?**
>
> *As I see pain and need, Loving God, soften my heart to act
> with Christ-like compassion.*

BIBLE IN A YEAR | SONG OF SONGS 4–5; GALATIANS 3

The LORD is with me; I will not be afraid.
What can mere mortals do to me?
[PSALM 118:6]

REASON FOR FEAR

When I was a boy, the school playground was where bullies threw their weight around and kids like me received that bullying with minimal protest. As we cowered in fear before our tormentors, there was something even worse: their taunts of "Are you scared? You're afraid of me, aren't you? There's no one here to protect you."

In fact, most of those times I really was frightened—and with good cause. Having been punched in the past, I knew I didn't want to experience that again. So, what could I do and who could I trust when I was stricken with fear? When you're eight years old and being bullied by a kid who is older, bigger and stronger, the fear is legitimate.

When the psalmist faced attack, he responded with confidence rather than fear—because he knew he didn't face those threats alone. He wrote, "The LORD is with me; I will not be afraid. What can mere mortals do to me?" (PSALM 118:6). As a boy, I'm not sure I would have been able to understand his level of confidence. As an adult, however, I've learned from years of walking with Christ that He's greater than any fear-inducing threat.

The threats we face in life are real. Yet we need not fear. The Creator of the universe is with us, and He's more than enough.

BILL CROWDER

***What are you fearing today? Ask God for His presence,
comfort and protection for whatever you're facing.***

*Father, thank You that You're with me and that I can trust
You in those moments to see me through by Your grace.*

BIBLE IN A YEAR | SONG OF SONGS 6-8; GALATIANS 4

How gracious [God] will be when you
cry for help! [ISAIAH 30:19]

A DISTINCT CRY

When babies cry, it's a signal that they're tired or hungry, right? Well, according to doctors at one university, subtle differences in a baby's cries can also provide important clues for other problems. Doctors have devised a computer programme that measures cry factors like pitch, volume and how clear the cry sound is to determine if something's wrong with the baby's central nervous system.

Isaiah prophesied that God would hear the distinct cries of His people, determine their hearts' condition and respond with grace. The people of Judah, rather than consulting God, had ignored His prophet and sought help in an alliance with Egypt (ISAIAH 30:1–7). God told them that if they chose to continue in their rebellion, He'd bring about their defeat and humiliation. However, He also longed "to be gracious to [them]; . . . to show [them] compassion" (V. 18). Rescue would come, but only through their cries of repentance and faith. If God's people did cry out to Him, He would forgive their sins and renew their spiritual strength and vitality (VV. 8–26).

The same holds true for believers in Jesus today. When our distinct cries of repentance and trust reach the ears of our heavenly Father, He hears them, forgives us and renews our joy and hope in Him.   *MARVIN WILLIAMS*

> *Why are you tempted to rebel against God and seek help apart from Him? How does repentance before Him lead to reconciliation and life?*
>
> *Dear God, forgive me for seeking safety, security and protection apart from You. Please restore my love for You.*

BIBLE IN A YEAR | ISAIAH 1–2; GALATIANS 5

He said, "Hagar, slave of Sarai, where have you come from, and where are you going?"
[GENESIS 16:8]

GOD CALLS YOUR NAME

Natalia went to a different nation with the promise of receiving an education. But soon the father in her new home began physically and sexually abusing her. He forced her to care for his home and children without pay. He refused to let her go outside or use the phone. She had become his slave.

Hagar was Abram and Sarai's Egyptian slave. Neither one used her name. They called her "my slave" or "your slave" (GENESIS 16:2, 5–6). They merely wanted to use her so they could have an heir.

How different is God! The angel of the Lord makes His first appearance in Scripture when He speaks to a pregnant Hagar in the desert. The angel is either God's messenger or God Himself. Hagar believes He is God, for she says, "I have now seen the One who sees me" (V. 13). If the angel is God, He could possibly be the Son—the One who reveals God to us—making an early, preincarnate appearance. He says her name, "Hagar, slave of Sarai, where have you come from, and where are you going?" (V. 8).

God saw Natalia and brought caring people into her life who rescued her. She's now studying to become a nurse. God saw Hagar and called her by name. And God sees you. You may be overlooked or worse, abused. Jesus calls you by name. Run to Him.   *MIKE WITTMER*

What does it mean to you that Jesus knows your name?
How might you similarly encourage others?

Thank You, Jesus, for knowing my name.
I rest in Your love for me.

Catch for us the foxes . . . that ruin the
vineyards. [SONG OF SONGS 2:15]

TEND YOUR GARDEN

I was so excited to plant fruit and veg in our back garden. Then
I started to notice small holes in the dirt. Before it had time to
ripen, our first fruit mysteriously disappeared. One day I was
dismayed to find our largest strawberry plant had been completely uprooted by a nesting rabbit and scorched to a crisp by
the sun. I wished I'd paid closer attention to the warning signs!

The beautiful love poem in Song of Songs records a conversation between a young man and woman. While calling to his
darling, the man sternly warned against animals who would
tear apart the lovers' garden, a metaphor for their relationship.
"Catch for us the foxes, the little foxes that ruin the vineyards,"
he said (Song of Songs 2:15). Perhaps he saw hints of 'foxes'
that could ruin their romance, like jealousy, anger, deceit or apathy. Because he delighted in the beauty of his bride (V. 14), he
wouldn't tolerate the presence of anything unwholesome. She
was as precious as "a lily among thorns" to him (V. 2). He was
willing to put in the work to guard their relationship.

Some of God's most precious gifts to us are family and friends,
although those relationships aren't always easy to maintain.
With patience, care and protection from "the little foxes", we
trust that God will grow beautiful fruit.   *KAREN PIMPO*

> ***Where have you become complacent in a close
> relationship? What foxes are you tolerating?***
>
> *Jesus, thank You for loving me so well.*

A generous person will prosper; whoever refreshes
others will be refreshed. [PROVERBS 11:25]

A GIVER'S HEART

O n our last day before we moved house, my friend brought
her four-year-old daughter Kinslee to say goodbye. "I
don't want you to move," said Kinslee. I hugged her and
gave her a canvas, hand-painted fan from my collection. "When
you miss me, use this fan and remember that I love you." Kinslee asked if she could have a different fan—a paper one from
my bag. "That one's broken," I said. "I want you to have my *best*
fan." I didn't regret giving Kinslee my favourite fan. Seeing her
happy made me happier. Later, Kinslee told her mother she was
sad because I kept the broken fan. They sent me a brand-new,
fancy purple fan. After giving generously to me, Kinslee felt happy again. So did I.

In a world that promotes self-gratification and self-preserva-
tion, we can be tempted to hoard instead of living with giving
hearts. However, the Bible says that a person who "gives freely
. . . gains even more" (PROVERBS 11:24). Our culture defines prosperity as having more and more and more, but the Bible says
that "a generous person will prosper" and "whoever refreshes
others will be refreshed" (V. 25).

God's unlimited and unconditional love and generosity continually recharge us. We can each have a giver's heart and create unending giving cycles because we know God—the Giver
of all good things—never gets tired of providing abundantly.

XOCHITL DIXON

> **How has the generosity of others helped you get closer to
> Jesus? How can you put someone else's needs above your
> own this week?**
>
> *Dear God, help me give as generously as You've given to me.*

BIBLE IN A YEAR | ISAIAH 7–8; EPHESIANS 2

I have put my words in your mouth.
[JEREMIAH 1:9]

THE POWER OF VOICE

The most powerful orators in history are often those leaders who've used their voices to bring about positive change. Consider William Wilberforce, whose speeches in parliament helped lead to the end of slavery in the British Empire in 1833. What if he'd chosen to be silent? We all possess the capacity to use our voice to inspire and help others, but the fear of speaking out can be paralysing. In the moments when we feel overwhelmed by this fear, we can look to God, our source of divine wisdom and encouragement.

When God called Jeremiah to be a prophet to the nations, he immediately began to doubt his own abilities. He cried out, "I do not know how to speak; I am too young" (JEREMIAH 1:6). But God wouldn't allow Jeremiah's fear to get in the way of his divine calling to inspire a generation through his voice. Instead, He instructed the prophet to simply trust God by saying and doing whatever He commanded (V. 7). In addition to affirming Jeremiah, He also equipped him. "I have put my words in your mouth" (V. 9), He assured him.

When we ask God to show us how He wants to use us, He'll equip us to carry out our purpose. With His help, we can boldly use our voice to make a positive impact on those around us.

KIMYA LODER

When have you been afraid to use your voice? How might you rely on God's strength and wisdom to speak up?

Heavenly Father, give me the strength to use the power of my words to influence those around me for the better.

WISDOM TO LIVE BEAUTIFULLY

We all experience days when we wish we were wiser. How do I handle that tricky email at work? What should I do when my child keeps misbehaving? Whether it's making decisions at work or dealing with personal trials, time and time again, we experience the pressing need for wisdom.

So we read books, consult others or take classes, hoping to gain some useful advice on how to manage our lives and relationships better. But while the acquired knowledge is helpful, often we still find something lacking. We need more than the wisdom the world offers; we need the wisdom only God provides.

Where can we find this wisdom? Scripture tells us that it begins with the "fear of the LORD" (PSALM 111:10; PROVERBS 1:7). To fear God is to revere and honour Him for His majesty and holiness. We can understand why acquiring wisdom begins here when we discover what true wisdom looks like.

James 3:17 lists seven marks of the wisdom God provides: it's pure, peace-loving, considerate, submissive, full of mercy and good fruit, impartial and sincere. The wisdom that all believers in Jesus should seek is connected to Christ-like character. It's the fruit of someone who walks with God, choosing to live in an upright, obedient way. In short, it's the result of someone who fears God.

Do you want to navigate life making decisions that will bring glory to God and benefit others? James says, "If you need wisdom, ask our generous God, and he will give it to you. He will not rebuke you for asking" (JAMES 1:5 NLT). Our generous God will help you fear Him so you may gain wisdom to live life beautifully for Him.

Poh Fang Chia, *Our Daily Bread* author

★ Wisdom is developed by reflecting on God's Word and submitting our lives to Him. So how can we further value and cultivate wisdom? This topic is addressed in the devotions for **October 1, 8** and **22**.

God said . . . "Let birds fly above the earth
across the vault of the sky." [GENESIS 1:20]

ELEGANT DESIGN

An international research team has created a flapping-wing drone that mimics the movements of a particular bird—the swift. Swifts can fly up to ninety miles per hour and are able to hover, plunge, turn quickly and stop suddenly. The ornithopter drone, however, is still inferior to the bird. One researcher said birds "have multiple sets of muscles which enable them to fly incredibly fast, fold their wings, twist, open feather slots and save energy". He admitted that his team's efforts were still only able to replicate about "10 percent of biological flight".

God has given the creatures in our world all kinds of amazing abilities. Observing them and reflecting on their know-how can be a source of wisdom for us. The ants teach us about gathering resources, badgers show us the value of dependable shelter and locusts teach us there's strength in numbers (PROVERBS 30:25–27).

The Bible tells us that "[God] founded the world by his wisdom" (JEREMIAH 10:12), and at the end of each step in the creation process, He confirmed that what He'd done was "good" (GENESIS 1:4, 10, 12, 18, 21, 25, 31). The same God who created birds to "fly above the earth across the vault of the sky" (V. 20), has given us the ability to combine His wisdom with our own reasoning. Today, consider how you might learn from His elegant designs in the natural world.　　　*JENNIFER BENSON SCHULDT*

> ***What part of God's creation do you admire the most?
> How does it speak to you about God's wisdom?***
>
> *Dear Father, open my eyes to Your wisdom as I consider
> Your creation.*

We are God's handiwork, created in Christ
Jesus to do good works. [EPHESIANS 2:10]

THE MASTERPIECE WITHIN

Author Arthur C. Brooks once told of his visit to the National Palace Museum in Taiwan, which contains one of the largest collections of Chinese art in the world. The museum guide asked, "What do you think of when I ask you to imagine a work of art yet to be started?" Brooks said, "An empty canvas, I guess." The guide replied, "There's another way to view it: the art already exists, and the job of artists is simply to reveal it."

In Ephesians 2:10, the word *handiwork*, sometimes translated as "workmanship" or "masterpiece", is from the Greek word *poiēma*, from which we derive our word *poetry*. God has created us as works of art, living poems. However, our art has become obscured: "As for you, you were dead in your transgressions and sins" (V. 1). To paraphrase the words of the museum guide, "The art [of us] is already there, and it's the job of the Divine Artist to reveal it." Indeed, God is restoring us, His masterpieces: "God, who is rich in mercy, made us alive" (VV. 4–5).

As we go through challenges and difficulties, we can take comfort in knowing that the Divine Artist is at work: "It is God who works in you to will and to act in order to fulfil his good purpose" (PHILIPPIANS 2:13). Know that God is working in you to reveal His masterpiece. *KENNETH PETERSEN*

*What are some of the ways that you, as God's artwork,
have become dimmed? How do you feel He's working in
your life these days?*

*Creator God, thank You for making me one of Your
masterpieces.*

Now we see only a reflection as in a
mirror; then we shall see face to face.
[1 CORINTHIANS 13:12]

I CAN SEE YOU!

The optometrist helped three-year-old Andreas adjust his first pair of glasses. "Look in the mirror," she said. Andreas glanced at his reflection, then turned to his father with a joyful and loving smile. Then Andreas' father gently wiped the tears that slipped down his son's cheeks and asked, "What's wrong?" Andreas wrapped his arms around his father's neck. "I can see you." He pulled back, tilted his head and gazed into his father's eyes. "I can see you!"

As we prayerfully study the Bible, the Holy Spirit gives us eyes to see Jesus, the "image of the invisible God" (COLOSSIANS 1:15). However, even with our vision cleared by the Spirit as we grow in knowledge through Scripture, we can still only see a glimpse of God's infinite immensity on this side of eternity. When our time on earth is done or when Jesus fulfils His promise to return, we'll see Him clearly (1 CORINTHIANS 13:12).

We won't need special glasses in that joy-filled moment when we see Christ face-to-face. We will know Him as He knows each of us, the beloved members of the body of Christ—the church. The Holy Spirit will infuse us with the faith, hope and love we need to stand firm, until we gaze at our loving and living Saviour and say, "I can *see* You, Jesus. I can see You!"   *XOCHITL DIXON*

> **What has the Holy Spirit revealed to you recently as
> you've read the Bible? How has your growth in the
> knowledge of God changed you?**

> *Jesus, please help me see You clearer and know You
> intimately as I walk with You faithfully now and until the
> day You call me home or come again.*

BIBLE IN A YEAR | ISAIAH 17-19; EPHESIANS 5:17-33

Everyone who believes that Jesus is the Christ is born of God. [1 JOHN 5:1]

FINDING LIFE

I t was a natural step for Brian to attend a Bible College. After all, he'd been around people who knew Jesus his whole life—at home, at school, at church. He was even gearing his college studies towards a career in 'Christian work'.

But at twenty-one years old, as he sat with the small congregation in an old village church and listened to a pastor preach from 1 John, he made a startling discovery. He realised that he was depending on knowledge and the trappings of religion, and that he'd never truly received salvation in Jesus. He felt that Christ was tugging at his heart that day with a sobering message: "You don't know Me!"

The apostle John's message is clear: "Everyone who believes that Jesus is the Christ is born of God" (1 JOHN 5:1). We can "overcome the world," as John puts it (V. 4) only by belief in Jesus. Not knowledge about Him, but deep, sincere faith—demonstrated by our belief in what He did for us on the cross. That day, Brian placed his faith in Christ alone.

Today, Brian's deep passion for Jesus and His salvation are no secret. It comes through loud and clear every time he steps behind the pulpit and preaches as a pastor—my pastor.

"God has given us eternal life, and this life is in his Son. Whoever has the Son has life" (VV. 11–12). For all who have found life in Jesus, what a comforting reminder this is! *DAVE BRANON*

What's your story of faith? What led you to understand you needed Jesus?

Jesus, thank You for the gift of salvation and for those who pointed me to faith in You.

I desire to depart and be with Christ . . .
but it is more necessary . . . that I remain.
[PHILIPPIANS 1:23–24]

READY TO GO

During the coronavirus pandemic, many suffered the loss of loved ones. On 27 November, 2020, our family joined their ranks when Bee Crowder, my ninety-five-year-old mum, died—though not from COVID-19. Like so many other families, we weren't able to gather to grieve Mum, honour her life or encourage one another. Instead, we used other means to celebrate her loving influence—and we found great comfort from her insistence that, if God called her home, she was ready and even eager to go. That confident hope, evidenced in so much of Mum's living, was also how she faced death.

Facing possible death, Paul wrote, "For to me, to live is Christ and to die is gain. . . . I am torn between the two: I desire to depart and be with Christ, which is better by far; but it is more necessary for you that I remain in the body" (PHILIPPIANS 1:21, 23–24). Even with his legitimate desire to stay and help others, Paul was drawn to his heavenly home with Christ.

Such confidence changes how we view the moment when we step from this life to the next. Our hope can give great comfort to others in their own season of loss. Although we grieve the loss of those we love, believers in Jesus don't grieve like those "who have no hope" (1 THESSALONIANS 4:13). True hope is the possession of those who know Him.   *BILL CROWDER*

How would you describe your response to the threatening realities in our world? How could the hope Jesus gives you change your outlook on the struggles of life?

*God of all hope, please remind me of Jesus'
death-conquering victory.*

BIBLE IN A YEAR | ISAIAH 23–25; PHILIPPIANS 1

That is why we labour and strive, because
we have put our hope in the living God.
[1 TIMOTHY 4:10]

WHAT COULD BE BETTER?

Eric heard about Jesus' love for him while in his early twenties. He started attending church where he met someone who helped him grow to know Christ better. It wasn't long before Eric's mentor assigned him to teach a small group of boys at church. Through the years, God drew Eric's heart to help at-risk youth in his city, to visit the elderly and to show hospitality to his neighbours—all for God's honour. Now in his late fifties, Eric explains how grateful he is that he was taught early to serve: "My heart overflows to share the hope I've found in Jesus. What could be better than to serve Him?"

Timothy was a child when his mother and grandmother influenced him in his faith (2 TIMOTHY 1:5). And he was probably a young adult when he met the apostle Paul, who saw potential in Timothy's service for God and invited him on a ministry journey (ACTS 16:1–3). Paul became his mentor in ministry and life. He encouraged him to study, to be courageous as he faced false teaching, and to use his talents in service to God (1 TIMOTHY 4:6–16).

Why did Paul want Timothy to be faithful in serving God? He wrote, "Because we have put our hope in the living God, who is the Saviour of all people" (V. 10). Jesus is our hope and the Saviour of the world. What could be better than to serve Him?

ANNE CETAS

***What have you learned about Christ that you want
someone else to know? Who could use your help and
whose help might you need?***

*Dear God, please give me a heart to bring Your hope to
those around me.*

BIBLE IN A YEAR | ISAIAH 26–27; PHILIPPIANS 2

I have set before you life and death,
blessings and curses. Now choose life.
[DEUTERONOMY 30:19]

A CHOICE

A few weeks after the death of a dear friend, I spoke with her mum. I was hesitant to ask how she was doing because I thought it was an inappropriate question; she was grieving. But I pushed aside my reluctance and simply asked how she was holding up. Her reply: "Listen, I choose joy."

Her words ministered to me that day as I struggled to push beyond some unpleasant circumstances in my own life. And her words also reminded me of Moses' edict to the Israelites at the end of Deuteronomy. Just before Moses' death and the Israelites' entrance into the promised land, God wanted them to know that they had a choice. Moses said, "I have set before you life and death . . . . Now choose life" (DEUTERONOMY 30:19). They could follow God's laws and live well, or they could turn away from Him and live with the consequences of "death and destruction" (V. 15).

We must choose how to live too. We can choose joy by believing and trusting in God's promises for our lives. Or we can choose to focus on the negative and difficult parts of our journeys, allowing them to rob us of joy. It will take practice and relying on the Holy Spirit for help, but we can choose joy—knowing that "in all things God works for the good of those who love him" (ROMANS 8:28).   *KATARA PATTON*

*How can you choose joy in spite of your circumstances
today? How is choosing joy similar to choosing life as God
described to the Israelites?*

*Dear God, giver of joy, please help me to choose to follow
You and believe and trust You this day.*

BIBLE IN A YEAR | ISAIAH 28-29; PHILIPPIANS 3

The way of the wicked is like deep darkness;
they do not know what makes them stumble.
[PROVERBS 4:19]

WISDOM WE NEED

In his monumental book *The Great Influenza*, John M. Barry recounts the story of the 1918 flu epidemic. Barry reveals how health officials, rather than being caught off guard, anticipated a massive outbreak. They feared that World War I, with hundreds of thousands of troops crammed into trenches and moving across borders, would unleash new viruses. But this knowledge was useless to stop the devastation. Powerful leaders, beating the drums of war, rushed towards violence. And epidemiologists estimate that fifty million people died in the epidemic, adding to the roughly twenty million killed in the war's carnage.

We've proven over and again that our human knowledge will never be enough to rescue us from evil (PROVERBS 4:14–16). Though we've amassed immense knowledge and present remarkable insights, we still can't stop the pain we inflict on one another. We can't halt "the way of the wicked", this foolish, repetitive path that leads to "deep darkness". Despite our best knowledge, we really have no idea "what makes [us] stumble" (V. 19).

That's why we must "get wisdom, get understanding" (V. 5). Wisdom teaches us what to do with knowledge. And true wisdom, this wisdom we desperately require, comes from God. Our knowledge always falls short, but His wisdom provides what we need. *WINN COLLIER*

Where do you see human knowledge falling short? How might God's wisdom instruct you in a better, truer way to live?

Dear God, I wrestle with pride. My human knowledge can't save me. Please teach me Your truth.

BIBLE IN A YEAR | ISAIAH 30–31; PHILIPPIANS 4

Clothe yourselves with compassion,
kindness, humility, gentleness and patience.
[COLOSSIANS 3:12]

SLOW-FASHIONED GRACE

Have you heard of #slowfashion? The hashtag captures a movement focused on resisting 'fast fashion'—an industry dominated by cheaply made and quickly disposed of clothes. In fast fashion, clothes are out of style nearly as quickly as they're in the shops—with some brands disposing of large quantities of their products every year.

The slow fashion movement encourages people to slow down and take a different approach. Instead of being driven by the need to always have the latest look, slow fashion encourages us to select fewer well-made and ethically sourced items that will last.

As I reflected on #slowfashion's invitation, I found myself wondering about other ways I fall into a 'fast fashion' way of thinking—always looking for fulfilment in the latest trend. In Colossians 3, however, Paul says finding true transformation in Jesus isn't a quick fix or a fad. It's a lifetime of quiet, gradual transformation in Christ.

Instead of needing to clothe ourselves with the world's latest status symbols, we can exchange our striving for the Spirit's clothing of "compassion, kindness, humility, gentleness and patience" (V.12). We can learn patience with each other on the slow journey of Christ transforming our hearts—a journey that leads to lasting peace (V. 15).   *MONICA LA ROSE*

How are you tempted to find security by keeping up with the latest trends? What helps you find contentment in Jesus?

Dear God, thank You that I can surrender my anxious strivings in exchange for the peace of a quiet walk with You.

BIBLE IN A YEAR | ISAIAH 32-33; COLOSSIANS 1

My soul is in deep anguish. How long,
LORD, how long? [PSALM 6:3]

HOPE FOR THE HURTING

"**M**ost people carry scars that others can't see or understand." Those deeply honest words came from a famous sports' star who opted out of part of his 2020 season due to mental health struggles. Reflecting on his decision, he felt he needed to share his story to encourage others facing similar challenges and to remind others to show compassion.

Invisible scars are those deep hurts and wounds that can't be seen but still cause very real pain and suffering. In Psalm 6, David wrote of his own deep struggle—writing painfully raw and honest words. He was "in agony" (V. 2) and "deep anguish" (V. 3). He was "worn out" from groaning, and his bed was drenched with tears (V. 6). While David doesn't share the cause of his suffering, many of us can relate to his pain.

We can also be encouraged by the way David responded to his pain. In the midst of his overwhelming suffering, David cried out to God. Honestly pouring out his heart, he prayed for healing (V. 2), rescue (V. 4) and mercy (V. 9). Even with the question "How long?" (V. 3) lingering over his situation, David remained confident that God "heard [his] cry for mercy" (V. 9) and would act in His time (V. 10).

Because of who our God is, there is always hope. *LISA M. SAMRA*

How can you express your struggle to God when experiencing deep emotional anguish? How have you experienced His healing, mercy and rescue?

Heavenly Father, give me courage to express my deepest pain and to welcome Your presence and healing into my situation.

BIBLE IN A YEAR | ISAIAH 34–36; COLOSSIANS 2

May [God] give you the Spirit of wisdom and
revelation, so that you may know him better.
[EPHESIANS 1:17]

OPEN THE EYES OF MY HEART

In 2001, a premature baby named Christopher Duffley surprised doctors by surviving. At five months old, he entered the foster care system until his aunt's family adopted him. A teacher realised four-year-old Christopher, though blind and diagnosed with autism, had perfect pitch. Six years later at church, Christopher stood onstage and sang, "Open the Eyes of My Heart." The video reached millions online. In 2020, Christopher shared his goals of serving as a disability advocate. He continues to prove that possibilities are limitless with the eyes of his heart open to God's plan.

The apostle Paul commended the church in Ephesus for their bold faith (EPHESIANS 1:15–16). He asked God to give them "the Spirit of wisdom and revelation" so they would "know him better" (V. 17). He prayed that their eyes would be "enlightened," or opened, so they would understand the hope and inheritance God promised His people (V. 18).

As we ask God to reveal Himself to us, we can know Him more and can declare His name, power and authority with confidence (VV. 19–23). With faith in Jesus and love for all God's people, we can live in ways that prove His limitless possibilities while asking Him to keep opening the eyes of our hearts.   *XOCHITL DIXON*

> *How has God helped you overcome obstacles or limitations?*
> *How does knowing His truth, character and love change the*
> *way you see challenges?*

Mighty and merciful God, please open the eyes of my heart
so that I can know, love and live for You with bold faith
that leads others to worship You.

BIBLE IN A YEAR | ISAIAH 37–38; COLOSSIANS 3

I will surely show you kindness for the sake
of your father Jonathan. [2 SAMUEL 9:7]

KNOWING AND LOVING

In the powerful article "Does My Son Know You?" sportswriter Jonathan Tjarks wrote of his battle with terminal cancer and his desire for others to care well for his wife and young son. The thirty-four-year-old wrote the piece just six months prior to his death. Tjarks, a believer in Jesus whose father had died when he was a young adult, shared Scriptures that speak of care for widows and orphans (EXODUS 22:22; ISAIAH 1:17; JAMES 1:27). And in words directed to his friends, he wrote, "When I see you in heaven, there's only one thing I'm going to ask—Were you good to my son and my wife? . . . Does my son *know* you?"

King David wondered if there was "anyone still left of the house of Saul to whom [he could] show kindness for [his dear friend] Jonathan's sake" (2 SAMUEL 9:1). A son of Jonathan, Mephibosheth, who was "lame in both feet" (V. 3) due to an accident (SEE 4:4), was brought to the king. David said to him, "I will surely show you kindness for the sake of your father Jonathan. I will restore to you all the land that belonged to your grandfather Saul, and you will always eat at my table" (9:7). David showed loving care for Mephibosheth, and it's likely that in time the king truly got to *know* him (SEE 19:24–30).

Jesus has called us to love others just as He loves us (JOHN 13:34). As He works in and through us, let's truly get to know and love them well.   *TOM FELTEN*

How can you know others more deeply? What will it look like for you to love them the way God loves you?

Heavenly Father, help me to honour You by striving to truly know and love others.

BIBLE IN A YEAR | ISAIAH 39–40; COLOSSIANS 4

Trust in the LORD forever.
[ISAIAH 26:4]

YIELDING TO TRUST

Opening the blinds one winter morning, I faced a shocking sight. A wall of fog. "Freezing fog", the weather forecaster called it. Rare for our location, this fog came with an even bigger surprise: a later forecast for blue skies and sunshine—"in one hour". "Impossible," I told my husband. "We can barely see one foot ahead." But sure enough, in less than an hour, the fog had faded, the sky yielding to a sunny, clear blue.

Standing at the window, I pondered my level of trust when I can only see fog in life. I asked my husband, "Do I only trust God for what I can already see?"

When King Uzziah died and some corrupt rulers came to power in Judah, Isaiah asked a similar question. *Who can we trust?* God responded by giving Isaiah a vision so remarkable that it convinced the prophet that the Lord can be trusted in the present for better days ahead. As Isaiah praised, "You will keep in perfect peace those whose minds are steadfast, because they trust in you" (ISAIAH 26:3). The prophet added, "Trust in the LORD forever, for the LORD, the LORD himself, is the Rock eternal" (V. 4).

When our minds are fixed on God, we can trust Him even during foggy and confusing times. We might not see it clearly now, but if we trust God, we can be assured His help is on the way.

PATRICIA RAYBON

When life looks foggy and confusing, where can you put your trust? How can you turn your mind from today's problems to our eternal God?

The world looks foggy and confusing today, dear God, so help me fix my mind on You, in whom I can forever trust.

BIBLE IN A YEAR | ISAIAH 41–42; 1 THESSALONIANS 1

Peace I leave with you; my peace I give you.
[JOHN 14:27]

AN IMPOSSIBLE GIFT

I was elated to find the perfect gift for my mother-in-law's birthday: the bracelet even contained her favourite gemstones! Finding that perfect gift for someone is always an utter delight. But what if the gift the individual needs is beyond our power to give? Many of us wish we could give someone peace of mind, rest or even patience. If only those could be purchased and wrapped with a bow!

These types of gifts are impossible for one person to give to another. Yet Jesus—God in human flesh—does give those who believe in Him one such 'impossible' gift: the gift of peace. Before ascending to heaven and leaving the disciples, Jesus comforted them with the promise of the Holy Spirit: He "will teach you all things and will remind you of everything I have said to you" (JOHN 14:26). He offered them peace—His peace—as an enduring, unfailing gift for when their hearts were troubled or when they were experiencing fear. He, Himself, is our peace with God, with others and within.

We may not have the ability to give our loved ones the extra measure of patience or improved health they desire. Nor is it within our power to give them the peace we all desperately need to bear up under the struggles of life. But we can be led by the Spirit to speak to them about Jesus, the giver and embodiment of true and lasting peace. 　　　　　*KIRSTEN HOLMBERG*

How has Christ brought peace to your life?
Who might you introduce to Him?

Jesus, thank You for the comfort of Your enduring,
unfailing peace in my life.

BIBLE IN A YEAR | ISAIAH 43–44; 1 THESSALONIANS 2

Why, my soul, are you downcast? . . . Put your
hope in God, for I will yet praise him, my Saviour
and my God. [PSALM 42:5]

CROSS WITH GOD

"I'm cross with God!" grumbled my eight-year-old as he
stomped home. He should have been playing his first af-
ter-school football match, but constant heavy rain had
flooded the pitch.

"God is in control of everything, so why did He let it rain *today*?"

It might sound strange, but I was encouraged that my son's
thoughts had gone straight to God. And he was asking the question that we all ask when things don't go as we'd hoped. If God
can do anything, why did He let *that* happen?

The psalmist too was full of questions and sorrow (PSALM 42:1–3).
For whatever reason, he was being mocked (V. 3) and was unable
to worship God at the temple (V. 4). "I say to God my Rock, 'Why
have you forgotten me?'" (V. 9). God could have transformed the
psalmist's situation in an instant—so why didn't He?

Yet the psalmist was then able to say to his own soul, "Put
your hope in God, for I will yet praise him" (VV. 5, 11). I gave similar encouragement to my son that day. God is always at work
for His people, even when we don't see or understand what He
is doing. He is achieving something far greater in our confusing
circumstances. And when we finally do see it, we will have even
more reason to praise Him.

Let's wait for Him with hope, for we "will yet praise him". *CHRIS WALE*

**When have you been frustrated with God recently? How does it
change your perspective to remember that you "will yet praise him"?**

*Father God, help me to trust Your work in my life, even when I
can't see what You are doing. Show me again today the many
reasons I have to praise You.*

BIBLE IN A YEAR | ISAIAH 45–46; 1 THESSALONIANS 3

God said, "I will be with you."
[EXODUS 3:12]

WHO AM I?

Kizombo sat watching the campfire, pondering the great questions of his life. *What have I accomplished?* he thought. Too quickly the answer came back: *Not much, really.* He was back in the land of his birth, serving at the school his father had started deep in the rainforest. He was also trying to write his father's powerful story of surviving two civil wars. *Who am I to try to do all this?*

Kizombo's misgivings sound like those of Moses. God had just given Moses a mission: "I am sending you to Pharaoh to bring my people the Israelites out of Egypt" (EXODUS 3:10). Moses replied, "Who am I?" (V. 11).

After some weak excuses from Moses, God asked him, "What is that in your hand?" It was a staff (4:2). At God's direction, Moses threw it on the ground. The staff turned into a snake. Against his instincts, Moses picked it up. Again, it became a staff (V. 4). In God's power, Moses could face Pharaoh. He literally had one of the 'gods' of Egypt—a snake—in his hand. Egypt's gods were no threat to the one true God.

Kizombo thought of Moses, and he sensed God's answer: *You have Me and My Word.* He thought too of friends who encouraged him to write his father's story so others would learn of God's power in his life. He wasn't alone.

On our own, our best efforts are inadequate. But we serve the God who says, "I will be with you" (3:12).　　　　　*TIM GUSTAFSON*

> **What do you have that God can use? How might it encourage you to consider what He might do with you?**
>
> *Father, with You I lack nothing, no matter the situation.*

BIBLE IN A YEAR | ISAIAH 47–49; 1 THESSALONIANS 4

We have this hope as an anchor for the soul,
firm and secure. [HEBREWS 6:19]

OUR ANCHOR OF HOPE

I held up a picture of people sleeping under pieces of cardboard in a dim alley. "What do they need?" I asked my Sunday school class. "Food," someone said. "Money," said another. "A safe place," a boy said thoughtfully. Then one girl spoke up: "Hope."

"Hope is expecting good things to happen," she explained. I found it interesting that she talked about "expecting" good things when, due to challenges, it can be easy not to expect good things in life. The Bible nevertheless speaks of hope in a way that agrees with my student. If "faith is confidence in what we hope for" (HEBREWS 11:1), we who have faith in Jesus *can* expect good things to happen.

What is this ultimate good that believers in Christ can hope for with confidence?—"the promise of entering his rest" (4:1). For believers, God's rest includes His peace, confidence of salvation, reliance on His strength and assurance of a future heavenly home. The guarantee of God and the salvation Jesus offers is why hope can be our anchor, holding us fast in times of need (6:18–20). The world needs hope, indeed: God's true and certain assurance that throughout good and bad times, He'll have the final say and won't fail us. When we trust in Him, we know that He'll make all things right for us in His time.   *KAREN HUANG*

> **How does the Bible encourage and give you hope and confidence? What are some things you can thank God for?**
>
> *Dear God, my hope in You is firm and secure, not because my faith is strong, but because You're faithful to do as You've promised.*

BIBLE IN A YEAR | ISAIAH 50–52; 1 THESSALONIANS 5

Religion . . . is this: to look after orphans and
widows in their distress and to keep oneself
from being polluted by the world. [JAMES 1:27]

BLESSING OTHERS

The Earl of Shaftesbury, the Victorian reformer and philan-
thropist, described his father as a "selfish and cold-heart-
ed bully", and his mother as a "fiend". But he found love
and acceptance through his mother's maid, Maria, who shared
with him the good news of Jesus.

He committed to following Jesus at the age of six. And God's
mercy and love would carry him through incredibly tough times.
For instance, at seven he was sent to a public school where "the
treatment was starvation and cruelty". Maria died when he was
only ten, leaving him heartbroken.

Having endured such a painful childhood, Shaftesbury later
used his political and social clout to implement changes in law
to protect children from being exploited. His social action was
borne out of his love for God and daily Bible reading and prayer.
He followed the instruction of James, writing to the Christians
scattered about, to "look after orphans and widows in their
distress and to keep oneself from being polluted by the world"
(JAMES 1:27). He was a keen proponent of both care for the vulnerable and seeking to be pure before God.

God used Shaftesbury greatly, redeeming the heartache of his
childhood as he lived out his faith and beliefs. We too can find
"blessing in what [we] do" (V. 25). We can trust that our merciful
God will multiply our efforts as we look out for those in need.

AMY BOUCHER PYE

**How have you seen God turn even the hard experiences of your life for
good? How can you trust Him when you face challenges and anguish?**

*Reforming God, You make all things new. You can take the hard
things I experience and redeem them. Use me for Your glory.*

BIBLE IN A YEAR | ISAIAH 53-55; 2 THESSALONIANS 1

Seek first his kingdom and his righteousness,
and all these things will be given to you as well.
[MATTHEW 6:33]

FIRST ON THE LIST

The morning commenced with efficiency and precision. I practically jumped out of bed, launching into the teeth of the day's deadlines. Get the kids to school. *Check.* Get to work. *Check.* I blasted full throttle into writing my "To Do" list, in which personal and professional tasks tumbled together in an avalanche-like litany:

" . . . 13. Edit article. 14. Clean office. 15. Strategic team planning. 16. Write tech blog. 17. Clean basement. 18. Pray."

By the time I got to number eighteen, I'd remembered that I needed God's help. But I'd got that far before it even *occurred* to me that I was going at it alone, trying to manufacture my own momentum.

Jesus knew. He knew our days would crash one into another, a sea of ceaseless urgency. So He instructs, "Seek first [God's] kingdom and his righteousness, and all these things will be given to you as well" (MATTHEW 6:33).

It's natural to hear Jesus' words as a *command.* And they are. But there's more here—*an invitation.* In Matthew 6, Jesus invites us to exchange the world's frantic anxiety (VV. 25–32) for a life of trust, day by day. God, by His grace, helps us all of our days—even when we get to number eighteen on our list before we remember to see life from His perspective. *ADAM R. HOLZ*

> **How can you turn to God first each day? On stressful days, what helps you trust Jesus with things demanding your immediate attention?**

Father, thank You for Your invitation to relinquish my anxiety and to embrace the life of abundant provision You offer me each day.

BIBLE IN A YEAR | ISAIAH 56–58; 2 THESSALONIANS 2

The LORD God had planted a garden in the
east, in Eden; and there he put the man he
had formed. [GENESIS 2:8]

IN THE GARDEN

My dad loved being outdoors in God's creation camping,
fishing and playing games. He also enjoyed working
in his garden. But it took lots of work! He spent hours
pruning, hoeing, planting seeds or flowers, pulling weeds and
mowing the lawn. The results were worth it—a landscaped
lawn, tasty tomatoes and beautiful roses. Every year he pruned
the roses close to the ground, and every year they grew back—
filling the senses with their fragrance and beauty.

In Genesis, we read of the garden of Eden where Adam and
Eve lived, thrived and walked with God. There, God "made all
kinds of trees grow out of the ground—trees that were pleasing
to the eye and good for food" (GENESIS 2:9). I imagine that perfect
garden also included beautiful, sweet-smelling flowers—perhaps even roses, minus the thorns!

After Adam and Eve's rebellion against God, they were ex-
pelled from the garden and needed to plant and care for their
own gardens, which meant breaking up hard ground, battling
with thorns and other challenges (3:17–19, 23–24). Yet God continued to provide for them (V. 21). And He didn't leave humanity
without the beauty of creation to draw us to Him (ROMANS 1:20).
The flowers in the garden remind us of God's continued love and
promise of a renewed creation—symbols of hope and comfort!

ALYSON KIEDA

> **When has creation drawn you to praise the Creator?**
> **How do you see God in creation?**
>
> *Dear God, thank You for the many reminders of You in Your*
> *creation. Thank You for beauty among thorns.*

BIBLE IN A YEAR | ISAIAH 59-61; 2 THESSALONIANS 3

I am the light of the world. Whoever follows
me will never walk in darkness. [JOHN 8:12]

CHRIST, OUR TRUE LIGHT

"**G**o to the light!" That's what my husband advised as
we struggled to find our way out of a big city hospital
on a recent Sunday afternoon. We'd visited a friend,
and when we exited an elevator, we couldn't find anyone during
weekend hours to point us to the front doors—and the brilliant
sunlight. Roaming around half-lit hallways, we finally encountered a man who saw our confusion. "These hallways all look
the same," he said. "But the exit's this way." With his directions,
we found the exit doors—leading, indeed, to the bright sunlight.

Jesus invited confused, lost unbelievers to follow Him out of
their spiritual darkness. "I am the light of the world. Whoever
follows me will never walk in darkness, but will have the light
of life" (JOHN 8:12). In His light, we can see stumbling blocks, sin
and blind spots, allowing Him to remove such darkness from our
lives as He shines His light into our hearts and on our path. Like
the pillar of fire that led the Israelites through the wilderness,
Christ's light brings us God's presence, protection and guidance.

As John explained, Jesus is "the true light" (JOHN 1:9) and
"the darkness has not overcome it" (V. 5). Instead of wandering
through life, we can seek Him for direction as He lights the way.

PATRICIA RAYBON

**What areas in your life need the purifying light of Christ?
When you seek His light, what stumbling blocks will you avoid?**

*In a world filled with darkness, shine Your true light, dear
Jesus, in my heart and on my path.*

A prudent person foresees danger and takes precautions.
The simpleton goes blindly on [towards danger] and
suffers the consequences. [PROVERBS 27:12 NLT]

HEADLONG INTO DANGER

In 1892, a resident with cholera accidentally transmitted the disease via the Elbe River to Hamburg, Germany, infecting the entire water supply. Within weeks, ten thousand citizens died. Eight years earlier, German microbiologist Robert Koch had made a discovery: cholera was waterborne. Koch's revelation prodded officials in large European cities to invest in filtration systems to protect their water. Hamburg authorities, however, had done nothing. Citing costs and alleging dubious science, they'd ignored clear warnings while their city spiralled towards catastrophe.

The book of Proverbs has a lot to say about those of us who see trouble yet refuse to act. "A prudent person foresees danger and takes precautions" (27:12 NLT). When God helps us see danger ahead, it's common sense to take action to address the danger. We wisely change course. Or we ready ourselves with appropriate precautions that He provides. But we do *something*. To do nothing is sheer lunacy. We can all fail to miss the warning signs, however, and spiral towards disaster. "The simpleton goes blindly on and suffers the consequences" (V. 12 NLT).

In Scripture and in the life of Jesus, God shows us the path to follow and warns us of trouble we'll surely face. If we're foolish, we'll barrel ahead, headlong into danger. Instead, as He leads us by His grace, may we heed His wisdom and change course.

WINN COLLIER

***When have you refused God's wisdom? How can you
better learn to respond to His warnings?***

Dear God, please help me listen to You and turn away from danger.

BIBLE IN A YEAR | ISAIAH 65–66; 1 TIMOTHY 2

Commit your way to the LORD; trust in him
and he will do this. [PSALM 37:5]

SURRENDERING TO GOD

God doesn't help those who help themselves; He helps those who trust in and rely on Him. Jonathan Roumie—the actor who plays Jesus in the successful TV series *The Chosen,* which is based on the Gospels—realised this in May of 2018. Roumie had been living in a big city for eight years, was nearly broke, had enough food just for the day, and had no work in sight. Not knowing how he would make it, the actor poured out his heart and surrendered his career to God. "I literally [prayed] the words, 'I surrender. I surrender.' " Later that day, he found four cheques in the post and three months later, he was cast for the role of Jesus in *The Chosen*. Roumie found that God will help those who trust in Him.

Rather than being envious of and fretting over those "who are evil" (PSALM 37:1), the psalmist invites us to surrender everything to God. When we centre our daily activities on Him, "trust in [Him] and do good", "take delight in [Him]" (VV. 3–4) and surrender to Him all our desires, problems, anxieties, and the daily events of our lives, God will direct us and give us peace (VV. 5–6). As believers in Jesus, it's vital for us to let Him determine what our lives should be.

Let's surrender and trust God. As we do, He'll take action and do what's necessary and best.

MARVIN WILLIAMS

What parts of your life are off-limits to God these days?
What will it mean for you to surrender your life to Him today?

*Dear God, please help me to surrender to You freely today
and experience Your life and peace.*

BIBLE IN A YEAR | JEREMIAH 1–2; 1 TIMOTHY 3

We do not lose heart. Though outwardly we are wasting away, yet inwardly we are being renewed day by day. [2 CORINTHIANS 4:16]

DON'T LOSE HEART

I don't remember a time when my mum Dorothy was in good health. For many years as a brittle diabetic, her blood sugar was wildly erratic. Complications developed and her damaged kidneys necessitated permanent dialysis. Neuropathy and broken bones resulted in the use of a wheelchair. Her eyesight began to deteriorate towards blindness.

But as her body failed her, Mum's prayer life grew more vigorous. She spent hours praying for others to know and experience the love of God. Precious words of Scripture grew sweeter to her. Before her eyesight faded, she wrote a letter to her sister Marjorie including words from 2 Corinthians 4: "We do not lose heart. Though outwardly we are wasting away, yet inwardly we are being renewed day by day" (V. 16).

The apostle Paul knew how easy it is to "lose heart". In 2 Corinthians 11, he describes his life—one of danger, pain and deprivation (VV. 23–29). Yet he viewed those "troubles" as temporary. And he encouraged us to think not only about what we see but also about what we can't see—that which is *eternal* (4:17–18).

Despite what's happening to us, our loving Father is continuing our inner renewal every day. His presence with us is sure. Through the gift of prayer, He's only a breath away. And His promises to strengthen us and give us hope and joy remain true.

CINDY HESS KASPER

What's causing you to be discouraged or "lose heart"?
Which Scriptures are especially encouraging to you?

Precious Father, thank You for Your faithful love for me and the assurance of Your presence.

BIBLE IN A YEAR | JEREMIAH 3–5; 1 TIMOTHY 4

Everyone who calls on the name of the Lord
will be saved. [ROMANS 10:13]

ONE DOOR FOR ALL

The protocols at the restaurant in my childhood neighbourhood were consistent with social and racial dynamics in
the late 1950s and early 1960s. The kitchen helpers—
Mary, the cook, and dishwashers like me—were Black; however,
the in-restaurant patrons were White. Black customers could
order food, but they had to pick it up at the back door. Such
policies reinforced the unequal treatment of Blacks in that era.
Though we've come a long way since then, we still have room
for growth in how we relate to each other as people made in the
image of God.

Passages of Scripture like Romans 10:8–13 help us to see that
all are welcome in the family of God; there's no back door. All
enter the same way—through belief in Jesus' death for cleansing and forgiveness. The Bible word for this transformative
experience is *saved* (VV. 9, 13). Your social situation and racial
status (or that of others) do not factor into the equation. "As
Scripture says, 'Anyone who believes in him will never be put to
shame.' For there is no difference between Jew and Gentile—
the same Lord is Lord of all and richly blesses all who call on
him" (VV. 11–12). Do you believe in your heart the Bible's message
about Jesus? Welcome to the family!   ARTHUR JACKSON

*What evidence is there in your life that you've believed
the Bible's message about forgiveness through Jesus?
Who do you know that needs to hear the good news
about Christ?*

*Father, my heart rejoices that You so loved the world that
You sent Jesus.*

BIBLE IN A YEAR | JEREMIAH 6–8; 1 TIMOTHY 5

They will be called oaks of righteousness, a planting of
the LORD for the display of his splendour. [ISAIAH 61:3]

PLANTED

Overnight on 15 October 1987, one hundred mile-per-hour winds ravaged the south of England. Around 15 million trees were uprooted or blown down, including six of the seven oaks that gave Sevenoaks its name. But later the magnificent trees were replanted to honour the name of the town.

"Oak trees" was one way that Isaiah, the Old Testament prophet, described the Israelites. God's people were called to uphold His name among neighbouring nations by yielding to His ways. But they rebelled, becoming instead like a fading oak (ISAIAH 1:30) and were uprooted by the Babylonian invasion.

How tender Isaiah's words must have seemed in their exile, as he promised they would once again "be called oaks of righteousness, a planting of the LORD" (61:3). God would heal their broken hearts (V. 1) and bring them comfort (VV. 2–3). He would replant them "for the display of his splendour" (V. 3). They received this promise when God restored them to Israel; we can receive the gift of this prophecy as fulfilled through Jesus.

When we feel displaced from secure circumstances or robbed of treasured relationships, we can know restoration and reassurance through Christ. He gives us "joy instead of mourning" and "praise instead of . . . despair" (ISAIAH 1:3). And He plants us where we live and work as spiritual oaks of righteousness, to influence others with His goodness, love and truth.   *ANNE LE TISSIER*

> *How does it encourage you that God has planted you to
> display His splendour and truth? How can you influence
> your environment with God's goodness?*
>
> *Dear God, help me deepen my roots in Your word through
> Your Spirit within me, so that I may help others to know
> You and to flourish in the goodness of Your presence.*

BIBLE IN A YEAR | JEREMIAH 9–11; 1 TIMOTHY 6

His people made no funeral fire in his
honour, as they had for his predecessors.
[2 CHRONICLES 21:19]

GOOD SOIL

In the hit musical *Hamilton,* England's King George III is humorously portrayed as a cartoonish, deranged villain. However, a new biography on King George said he was not the tyrant described in *Hamilton.* If George had been the brutal despot that some said he was, he would have probably attempted to stop the American nation's drive for independence with more extreme, scorched-earth measures. But he was restrained by his "civilized, good-natured" temperament.

Who knows if King George died with regret? Would his reign have been more successful if he'd been harsher and more ruthless?

Not necessarily. In the Bible we read of King Jehoram, who solidified his throne by putting "all his brothers to the sword along with some of the officials of Israel" (2 CHRONICLES 21:4). Jehoram "did evil in the eyes of the LORD" (V. 6). His ruthless reign alienated his people, who neither wept for his gruesome death nor made a "funeral fire in his honour" (V. 19).

Historians may debate whether George was too soft; Jehoram was surely too harsh. A better way is that of King Jesus, who is "full of grace and truth" (JOHN 1:14). Christ's expectations are firm (He demands truth), yet He embraces those who fail (He extends grace). Jesus calls us who believe in Him to follow His lead. Then, through the leading of His Holy Spirit, He empowers us to do so.   *MIKE WITTMER*

> **Who are you responsible to lead? How might you show
> both grace and truth to them?**
>
> *Dear Jesus, I aim to lead others by following You.*

BIBLE IN A YEAR | JEREMIAH 12–14; 2 TIMOTHY 1

Come to [Jesus], the living Stone—rejected by
humans but chosen by God and precious to him.
[1 PETER 2:4]

MORE PRECIOUS THAN GOLD

Have you ever looked through low-priced items at a car-
boot sale and dreamed that you might find something of
incredible value? It happened at one place when a floral
Chinese antique bowl, purchased for just £30, was sold at a 2021
auction for more than £575,000. The piece turned out to be a
rare, historically significant artefact from the fifteenth century.
It's a stunning reminder that what some people consider of little
worth can actually have great value.

Writing to believers scattered throughout the known world,
Peter explained that their faith in Jesus was belief in the One
who'd been rejected by the wider culture. Despised by most of
the religious Jewish leaders and crucified by the Roman government, Christ was deemed worthless by many because He didn't
fulfil their expectations and desires. But though others had dis-
missed Jesus' worth, He was "chosen by God and precious to
him" (1 PETER 2:4). His value for us is infinitely more precious than
silver or gold (1:18–19). And we have the assurance that whoever
chooses to trust Jesus will never be ashamed of their choice (2:6).

When others reject Jesus as worthless, let's take another
look. God's Spirit can help us see the priceless gift of Christ, who
offers to all people the invaluable invitation to become part of
the family of God (V. 10).   *LISA M. SAMRA*

*Why do people miss the true value of Jesus? How might
you share the blessings of trusting Him?*

*Dear Jesus, thank You for living a life of obedience so that I
could become part of the family of God.*

BIBLE IN A YEAR | JEREMIAH 15–17; 2 TIMOTHY 2

Those who know your name trust in you.
[PSALM 9:10]

YOU CAN TRUST GOD

When my cat Mickey had an eye infection, I put eye drops in his eyes daily. As soon as I placed him on the kitchen counter, he'd sit, look at me with frightened eyes and brace himself for the spurt of liquid. "Good boy," I'd murmur. Even though he didn't understand what I was doing, he never jumped off, hissed or scratched me. Instead, he would press himself closer against me—the person putting him through the ordeal. He knew he could trust me.

When David wrote Psalm 9, he'd probably already experienced much of God's love and faithfulness. He'd turned to Him for protection from his enemies, and God had acted on his behalf (vv. 3-6). During David's times of need, God hadn't failed him. As a result, David came to know what He was like—He was powerful and righteous, loving and faithful. And so, David trusted Him. He knew God was trustworthy.

I've cared for Mickey through several illnesses since the night I found him as a tiny, starving kitten on the street. He knows he can trust me—even when I do things to him that he doesn't understand. In a similar way, remembering God's faithfulness to us and His character helps us trust Him when we can't understand what He's doing. May we continue to trust God through the difficult times in life.

KAREN HUANG

***When has God showed you His love and faithfulness
in tough situations? What else did you learn about His
character? How can this encourage you today?***

*Father, You're always faithful. Help me trust You. Let
difficult times draw me closer to You.*

BIBLE IN A YEAR | JEREMIAH 18–19; 2 TIMOTHY 3

The LORD, the LORD, the compassionate and
gracious God, slow to anger, abounding in
love and faithfulness. [EXODUS 34:6]

SMARTPHONE COMPASSION

Was the driver late with your food? You can use your
phone to give him a one-star rating. Did the shop assistant treat you curtly? You can write her a critical
review. While smartphones enable us to shop, keep up with
friends and more, they have also given us the power to publicly
rate each other. And this can be a problem.

Rating each other this way is problematic because judgements
can be made without context. The driver gets rated poorly for a
late delivery due to circumstances out of his control. The shop
assistant gets a negative review when she'd been up all night with
a sick child. How can we avoid rating others unfairly like this?

By imitating God's character. In Exodus 34:6–7, God describes
Himself as "compassionate and gracious"—meaning He wouldn't
judge our failures without context; "slow to anger"—meaning
He wouldn't post a negative review after one bad experience;
"abounding in love"—meaning His correctives are for our good,
not to get revenge; and "forgiving [of] sin"—meaning our lives
don't have to be defined by our one-star days. Since God's character is to be the basis of ours (MATTHEW 6:33), we can avoid the
harshness smartphones enable by using ours as He would.

In the online age, we can all rate others harshly. May the Holy
Spirit empower us to bring a little compassion today.

SHERIDAN VOYSEY

**How can you show more compassion to others? What
characteristic of God do you most need to imitate when online?**

*Holy Spirit, please grow the fruit of godly character in me
today, especially when I'm online.*

BIBLE IN A YEAR | JEREMIAH 20–21; 2 TIMOTHY 4

I long to dwell in your tent forever and
take refuge in the shelter of your wings.
[PSALM 61:4]

UNDER GOD'S WINGS

There are several Canada goose families with baby geese at the pond near our home. The little goslings are so fluffy and cute; it's hard not to watch them when I go for a walk or run around the pond. But I've learned to avoid eye contact and give the geese a wide berth—otherwise, I risk a protective goose parent suspecting a threat and hissing and chasing me!

The image of a bird protecting her young is one that Scripture uses to describe God's tender, protective love for His children (PSALM 91:4). In Psalm 61, David seems to be struggling to experience God's care in this way. He'd experienced God as his "refuge, a strong tower" (V. 3), but now he called desperately "from the ends of the earth", pleading, "lead me to the rock that is higher than I" (V. 2). He longed to once more "take refuge in the shelter of [God's] wings" (V. 4).

And in bringing his pain and struggles to God, David took comfort in knowing that He'd heard him (V. 5). Because of God's faithfulness, he knew he would "ever sing in praise of [His] name" (V. 8).

Like the psalmist, when we feel distant from God's love, we can run back to His arms to be assured that even in our pain, He's with us, protecting and caring for us as fiercely as a mother bird guards her young.   *MONICA LA ROSE*

How does it encourage you to remember God's protective care for you? How have you experienced His care?

Dear God, thank You for Your fierce, protective love for me. Help me to rest securely in Your tender care.

BIBLE IN A YEAR | JEREMIAH 22–23; TITUS 1

GROWING IN JESUS TOGETHER

A new believer in Jesus asked Julie, "Would you disciple me?" Julie was uncertain about how to proceed. Should they have a study together? And if so, what topic would be best? She prayerfully picked out a resource to look at together and is finding joy in helping her new friend grow in her understanding of Christ.

New immigrants moved into Sue's neighbourhood. She befriended the young family of seven and invited the kids over to play with her children. Sue began talking with the mum about her Saviour and friend, Jesus, and invited the family to church.

Whenever he can, Alan brings up his faith in Christ when talking with his co-workers. He never pushes his beliefs but shares if someone seems curious. He even started a small discussion group during lunchtime for those wanting to know more about Jesus.

These individuals are following the example of Christ, who said about Himself: "The Son of Man came to seek and to save the lost" (LUKE 19:10). When Jesus met a woman at a well, their conversation prompted her to believe Jesus could be the Messiah (JOHN 4:4–26). And then she ran back to her village to tell others about Him (V. 29). As a result, "many Samaritans from that town believed in him" (V. 39).

Jesus pursued us in love. Now we have the privilege of continuing His mission of carrying His good news into the world (MATTHEW 28:19–20). We don't need to worry about whether we'll do a perfect job. God will help us to walk with others to discover more of Him. It's what He's called us to do.

Anne Cetas, *Our Daily Bread* author

★ Jesus commissioned His disciples to make disciples of all nations. But what does that mean, and how can we participate in this mission? This topic is addressed in the devotions for **November 1, 8** and **22**.

Those of you who do not give up everything
you have cannot be my disciples. [LUKE 14:33]

WORTH IT TO FOLLOW JESUS

Ronda came from a religious but non-Christian family. Their
discussions about spiritual matters were dry and academ-
ic. "I kept praying all the prayers," she said, "but I wasn't
hearing [from God]."

She began to study the Bible. Slowly, steadily, she inched towards faith in Jesus as the Messiah. Ronda describes the defining moment: "I heard a clear voice in my heart saying, 'You've
heard enough. You've seen enough. It's time to just believe.' "
But Ronda faced a problem: her father. "My dad responded as if
Mount Vesuvius erupted," she recalls.

When Jesus walked this earth, crowds followed Him (LUKE 14:25).
We don't know exactly what they were looking for, but He was
looking for disciples. And that comes with a cost. "If anyone
comes to me and does not hate father and mother, wife and children, brothers and sisters—yes, even their own life—such a person cannot be my disciple," Jesus said (V. 26). He told a story about
building a tower. "Won't you first sit down and estimate the cost
. . . ?" He asked (V. 28). Jesus' point wasn't that we're to literally
hate family; rather, it's that we must choose Him over everything
else. He said, "Those of you who do not give up everything you
have cannot be my disciples" (V. 33).

Ronda loves her family deeply, yet she concluded, "Whatever
the cost, I figured it's worth it." What might you need to give up
to follow Jesus as He guides you?   *TIM GUSTAFSON*

> **What's your story of the moment Jesus became real to
> you? What has it cost you to follow Him?**
>
> *Father, please help me choose Your Son over everything
> this world has to offer.*

BIBLE IN A YEAR | JEREMIAH 24–26; TITUS 2

People of Athens! I see that in every way you
are very religious. [ACTS 17:22]

EVERYBODY WORSHIPS

I recently visited Athens, Greece. Walking around its Ancient
Agora—the marketplace where philosophers taught and
Athenians worshipped—I found altars to Apollo and Zeus, all
in the shadow of the Acropolis, where a statue of the goddess
Athena once stood.

We may not bow to Apollo or Zeus today, but society is no less
religious. "Everybody worships," novelist David Foster Wallace
said, adding this warning: "If you worship money and things . . .
then you will never have enough. . . . Worship your body and
beauty. . . and you will always feel ugly. . . . Worship your intel-
lect . . . [and] you will end up feeling stupid." Our secular age has
its own gods, and they're not benign.

"People of Athens!" Paul said while visiting the Agora, "I see
that in every way you are very religious" (ACTS 17:22). The apostle
then described the one true God as the Creator of all (VV. 24–26)
who wants to be known (V. 27) and who has revealed Himself
through the resurrection of Jesus (V. 31). Unlike Apollo and Zeus,
this God isn't made by human hands. Unlike money, looks or
intelligence, worshipping Him won't ruin us.

Our 'god' is whatever we rely on to give us purpose and security. Thankfully, when every earthly god fails us, the one true
God is ready to be found (V. 27).   SHERIDAN VOYSEY

**What other 'gods' do you see society worshipping today?
What do you rely on to give you purpose and security?**

*Father, forgive me for placing wealth, beauty, politics or
other things first. I take them off the throne of my heart
and ask You to reign there instead.*

BIBLE IN A YEAR | JEREMIAH 27–29; TITUS 3

You are the light of the world.
[MATTHEW 5:14]

REFLECTING THE LIGHT OF THE SON

After I had a conflict with my mother, she finally agreed to meet with me more than an hour away from my home. But upon arriving, I discovered she'd left before I got there. In my anger, I wrote her a note. But I revised it after I felt God nudging me to respond in love. After my mother read my revised message, she called me. "You've changed," she said. God used my note to lead my mum to ask about Jesus and, eventually, receive Him as her personal Saviour.

In Matthew 5, Jesus affirms that His disciples are the light of the world (V. 14). He said, "let your light shine before others, that they may see your good deeds and glorify your Father in heaven" (V. 16). As soon as we receive Christ as our Saviour, we receive the power of the Holy Spirit. He transforms us so we can be radiant testimonies of God's truth and love wherever we go.

Through the power of the Holy Spirit, we can be joyful lights of hope and peace who look more and more like Jesus every day. Every good thing we do then becomes an act of grateful worship, which looks attractive to others and can be perceived as vibrant faith. Surrendered to the Holy Spirit, we can give honour to the Father by reflecting the Light of the Son—Jesus.

XOCHITL DIXON

When have you noticed the light of Jesus shining through another person? How has someone else's good deeds prompted you to praise God?

Jesus, please shine Your vibrant light of love in and through my life so I can give honour to the Father and encourage others to put their trust in You.

BIBLE IN A YEAR | JEREMIAH 30–31; PHILEMON

He lifted me out of the slimy pit, out of the
mud and mire; he set my feet on a rock and
gave me a firm place to stand. [PSALM 40:2]

GOD'S RESCUE

Acompassionate volunteer was called a "guardian angel"
for his heroic efforts. Jake Manna was installing solar pan-
els at a job site when he joined an urgent search to find
a missing five-year-old girl. While neighbours searched their ga-
rages and gardens, Manna took a path that led him into a nearby
wooded area where he spotted the girl waist-deep in a marsh.
He waded carefully into the sticky mud to pull her out of her
predicament and return her, damp but unharmed, to her grateful mother.

Like that little girl, David also experienced deliverance. The singer
"waited patiently" for God to respond to his heartfelt cries for
mercy (PSALM 40:1). And He did. God leaned in, paid close attention to his cry for help and responded by rescuing him from the
"mud and mire" of his circumstances (V. 2)—providing sure footing for David's life. The past rescues from the muddy marsh of
life reinforced his desire to sing songs of praise, to make God his
trust in future circumstances and to share his story with others
(VV. 3–4).

When we find ourselves in challenges such as financial difficulties, marital turmoil and feelings of inadequacy, let's cry out
to God and patiently wait for Him to respond (V. 1). He's there,
ready to help us in our time of need and give us a firm place to
stand.　　　　　　　　　　　　　　　　　　　*MARVIN WILLIAMS*

When has God delivered you from the 'muddy marsh'?
How do His past rescues encourage you to trust in Him?

When I'm stuck in the mud, I'll wait patiently for You,
my loving God.

BIBLE IN A YEAR | JEREMIAH 32–33; HEBREWS 1

To him be glory in the church and in Christ
Jesus throughout all generations, for ever
and ever! Amen. [EPHESIANS 3:21]

BAKING FOR GOD

❝ I t seems like a frivolous thing to ask the Lord to help my
gelatine to set, but . . . I had the attitude of this whole
experience [being] a gift from God," reflected Kevin Flynn
after his Great British Bake Off experience. "Whatever goes well
I thank the Lord for, and whatever doesn't go well I hold onto
with an open hand."

Kevin highlights Ephesians 3:20–21 on his social-media sites
as a key passage because he wants to pour out praise to God
as the One worthy of all the honour. To God "be glory in the
church and in Christ Jesus throughout all generations, for ever
and ever!" (V. 21). Kevin wants to use all his words and actions—
and all his bakes—to glorify God.

These verses from Paul's letter form part of a prayer for the
Ephesian Christians. Paul desires that they would be strength-
ened with the power of the Spirit (V. 16) so that, indwelt by
Christ, they would be "rooted and established in love" (V. 17).
After all, God can do "immeasurably more than all we ask or
imagine, according to his power that is at work within us" (V. 20).

We might not be able to bake like Kevin, but we can ask God
to help us serve Him in all our activities. He will fill us with His
grace through His Spirit, helping us to bring Him honour and
praise.   *AMY BOUCHER PYE*

***Why is it important that Christians such as Kevin take
part in cultural events such as Bake Off? How can you
lean on God today, asking Him to fill you with His power?***

*Creator God, You have made me in Your image and filled me
with Your Holy Spirit. Help me to find my strength in You.*

BIBLE IN A YEAR | JEREMIAH 34–36; HEBREWS 2

Let us not become weary in doing good.
[GALATIANS 6:9]

PERSISTENT PIZZA

At twelve years old, Ibrahim arrived in Italy from West Africa, not knowing a word of Italian, struggling with a stutter and forced to face anti-immigrant putdowns. None of that stopped the hardworking young man who, in his twenties, opened a pizza shop in Trento, Italy. His little business won over doubters to be listed as one of the top fifty pizzerias in the world.

His hope was then to help feed hungry children on Italian streets. So he launched a "pizza charity" by expanding a Neapolitan tradition—where customers buy an extra coffee (*caffè sospeso*) for those in need—to pizza (*pizza sospesa*). He also urges immigrant children to look past prejudice and not give up.

Such persistence recalls Paul's lessons to the Galatians on continually doing good to all. "Let us not become weary in doing good, for at the proper time we will reap a harvest if we do not give up" (GALATIANS 6:9). Paul continued, "Therefore, as we have opportunity, let us do good to all people, especially to those who belong to the family of believers" (V. 10).

Ibrahim, an immigrant who faced prejudice and language barriers, created an opportunity to do good. Food became a 'bridge' leading to tolerance and understanding. Inspired by such persistence, we too can look for opportunities to do good. God, then, gets the glory as He works through our steady trying.

PATRICIA RAYBON

How does your persistence glorify God? In your life, what deserves more godly persistence and loving charity from you?

When I consider giving up, dear God, inspire me to endure in You.

BIBLE IN A YEAR | JEREMIAH 37–39; HEBREWS 3

The LORD God called to the man,
"Where are you?" [GENESIS 3:9]

DESTRUCTION DESTROYED

"The baby birds will fly tomorrow!" My wife, Cari, was elated about the progress a family of wrens was making in a hanging basket on our front porch. She'd watched them daily, taking pictures as the mother brought food to the nest.

Cari got up early the next morning to look in on them. She moved some of the greenery aside covering the nest but instead of seeing baby birds, the narrow eyes of a serpent met hers. The snake had scaled a vertical wall, slithered into the nest, and devoured them all.

Cari was heartbroken and angry. I was out of town, so she called a friend to remove the snake. But the damage was done.

Scripture tells of another serpent who left destruction in his path. The serpent in the garden of Eden deceived Eve about the tree God had warned her against eating from: "You will not certainly die," he lied, "for God knows that when you eat from it your eyes will be opened, and you will be like God, knowing good and evil" (GENESIS 3:4–5).

Sin and death entered the world as a result of Eve and Adam's disobedience to God. The deception wrought by "that ancient serpent, who is the devil" continues today (REVELATION 20:2). But Jesus came "to destroy the devil's work" (1 JOHN 3:8), and through Him we're restored to relationship with God. One day, He'll make "everything new" (REVELATION 21:5).   *JAMES BANKS*

***How has Jesus destroyed the devil's work in your heart
and life? What do you look forward to in Him?***

*Please deliver me, Jesus, from the devil's deception.
Saving God, give me grace to live for You!*

BIBLE IN A YEAR | JEREMIAH 40-42; HEBREWS 4

His sheep follow him because they
know his voice. [JOHN 10:4]

KNOWING THE SHEPHERD'S VOICE

When I was a boy living on a farm in the countryside, I spent glorious afternoons roaming with my best friend. We'd hike into the woods, ride ponies and watch the farmhands tend the horses. But whenever I heard my dad's whistle—that clear sound slicing through the wind and all the other clatter—I'd immediately drop whatever I was doing and head home. The signal was unmistakable, and I knew I was being called by my father. Decades later, I'd still recognise that whistle.

Jesus told His disciples that He was the Shepherd, and His followers were the sheep. "The sheep listen to [the shepherd's] voice," He said. "He calls his own sheep by name and leads them out" (JOHN 10:3). In a time when numerous leaders and teachers sought to confuse Christ's disciples by asserting their authority, He declared that His loving voice could still be heard clearly, more distinct than all the others. "His sheep follow [the shepherd], because they know his voice" (V. 4).

May we be careful as we listen for Jesus' voice and avoid foolishly dismissing it, for the fundamental truth remains: the Shepherd speaks clearly, and His sheep hear His voice. Perhaps through a verse of Scripture, the words of a believing friend or the nudge of the Spirit—Jesus speaks, and we do hear.

WINN COLLIER

How do you think you might have overcomplicated hearing God's voice? What's the Shepherd saying to you today?

God, I need to be reminded that You're speaking, and that I do hear You. Help me pay attention. Help me to listen and respond.

BIBLE IN A YEAR | JEREMIAH 43–45; HEBREWS 5

As they began to sing and praise, the LORD
set ambushes . . . and they were defeated.
[2 CHRONICLES 20:22]

JESUS' ULTIMATE VICTORY

At some military camps across Europe during World War II, an unusual type of supply was air-dropped for homesick soldiers—upright pianos. They were specially manufactured to contain only ten percent of the normal amount of metal, and they received special water-resistant glue and anti-insect treatments. The pianos were rugged and simple but provided hours of spirit-lifting entertainment for soldiers who gathered around to sing familiar songs of home.

Singing—especially songs of praise—is one way that believers in Jesus can find peace in our battles too. King Jehoshaphat found this to be true when he faced vast invading armies (2 CHRONICLES 20). Terrified, the king called all the people together for prayer and fasting (VV. 3–4). In response, God told him to lead out soldiers to meet the enemy, promising that they'd "not have to fight this battle" (V. 17). Jehoshaphat believed God and acted in faith. He appointed singers to go ahead of the soldiers and sing praise to God for the victory they believed they would see (V. 21). And as their music began, the Lord miraculously defeated their enemies and saved His people (V. 22).

Victory doesn't always come when and how we want it to. But we can always proclaim Jesus' ultimate victory over sin and death that's already been won for us. We can choose to rest in a spirit of worship even in the middle of a war zone.   *KAREN PIMPO*

> **How can you praise God right where you are today? How
> can you press into the victory that Jesus has won for you?**

> *You are stronger than my enemies, dear God. I lift up
> Your name in faith today.*

BIBLE IN A YEAR | JEREMIAH 46–47; HEBREWS 6

Pray for those who mistreat you.
[LUKE 6:28]

LOVE THROUGH PRAYER

For years, John had been somewhat of an irritant at church. He was bad-tempered, demanding and often rude. He complained constantly about not being served well, and about volunteers and staff not doing their job. He was, honestly, hard to love.

So when I heard that he'd been diagnosed with cancer, I found it difficult to pray for him. Memories of his harsh words and unpleasant character filled my mind. But remembering Jesus' call to love, I was drawn to say a simple prayer for John each day. A few days later, I found myself beginning to think a bit less often about his unlikeable qualities. *He must be really hurting,* I thought. *Perhaps he's feeling really lost now*.

Prayer, I realised, opens ourselves, our feelings and our relationships with others to God, allowing Him to enter and bring His perspective into it all. The act of submitting our will and feelings to Him in prayer allows the Holy Spirit to change our hearts, slowly but surely. No wonder Jesus' call to love our enemies is bound up tightly with a call to prayer: "Pray for those who mistreat you" (LUKE 6:28).

I have to admit, I still struggle to think well of John. But with the Spirit's help, I'm learning to see him through God's eyes and heart—as a person to be forgiven and loved.　　　　*LESLIE KOH*

Why is it important to pray for even the difficult people in your life? What can you pray for them?

Loving God, You know how I feel about those who've hurt or irritated me. Please give me Your heart of grace and compassion to pray for them, for You love them.

BIBLE IN A YEAR | JEREMIAH 48–49; HEBREWS 7

I am the LORD; that is my name! I will not
yield my glory to another. [ISAIAH 42:8]

LUCKY BOOTS

Too late, Tom felt the chilling click beneath his combat boots. Instinctively, he bounded away in an adrenaline-fuelled leap. The deadly device hidden underground didn't detonate. Later, the explosive ordnance disposal team unearthed eighty pounds of high explosives from the spot. Tom wore those boots until they fell apart. "My lucky boots," he calls them.

Tom may have clung to those boots simply to commemorate his close call. But people are often tempted to consider objects lucky or to even give them the more spiritual label "blessed". Danger arrives when we credit an object—even a symbol—as a source of God's blessing.

The Israelites learned this the hard way. The Philistine army had just routed them in battle. As Israel reviewed the debacle, someone thought of taking the "ark of the LORD's covenant" into a rematch (1 SAMUEL 4:3). That seemed like a good idea (VV. 6–9). After all, the ark of the covenant was a holy object.

But the Israelites had the wrong perspective. By itself, the ark couldn't bring them anything. Putting their faith in an object instead of in the presence of the one true God, the Israelites suffered an even worse defeat, and the enemy captured the ark (VV. 10–11).

Mementos that remind us to pray or to thank God for His goodness are fine. But they're never the source of blessing. That is God—and God alone.   *TIM GUSTAFSON*

How do you show evidence of your faith in God? When you're faced with a crisis, what do you focus on to help you?

Loving Father, forgive me when I'm tempted to put my faith in anything but You.

BIBLE IN A YEAR | JEREMIAH 50; HEBREWS 8

She said to herself, "If I only touch [Jesus'] cloak, I will be healed." [MATTHEW 9:21]

CLING TO JESUS

Dizziness struck me in the stairwell of the office building. Overwhelmed, I gripped the banister because the stairs seemed to spin. As my heart pounded and my legs buckled, I clung onto the banister, thankful for its strength. Medical tests showed I had anaemia. Although its cause wasn't serious and my condition was resolved, I'll never forget how weak I felt that day.

That's why I admire the woman who touched Jesus. She not only moved through the crowd in her weakened state, but she also showed faith in venturing out to approach Him (MATTHEW 9:20–22). She had good reason to be afraid: Jewish law defined her as unclean and by exposing others to her uncleanness, she could face serious consequences (LEVITICUS 15:25–27). But the thought *If I only touch His cloak* kept her going. The Greek word that is translated as "touch" in Matthew 9:21 is not mere touching but has the stronger meaning of "to hold on to" or "to attach oneself". The woman tightly held on to Jesus. She believed He could heal her.

Jesus saw, in the midst of a crowd, the desperate faith of one woman. When we too venture out in faith and cling to Christ in our need, He welcomes us and comes to our aid. We can tell Him our story without fear of rejection or punishment. Jesus tells us today, "Cling to Me."   *KAREN HUANG*

> **What's caused you suffering and fear? To what or whom have you turned for help and healing? How can you cling to Jesus today?**
>
> *Dear God, thank You for Your love. I don't have to feel ashamed and afraid. You accept me and call me Your child.*

BIBLE IN A YEAR | JEREMIAH 51–52; HEBREWS 9

Hezekiah turned his face to the wall and prayed to the LORD. [2 KINGS 20:2]

A CARD AND PRAYER

The recently widowed woman was growing concerned. To collect some vital funds from an insurance policy, she needed key information about the accident that had taken her husband's life. She had talked to a police officer who said he'd help her, but then she lost his business card. So she prayed, pleading with God for help. A short time later, she was at her church when she walked by a window and saw a card—the policeman's card—on a windowsill. She had no idea how it got there, but she knew *why*.

She took prayer seriously. And why not? Scripture says that God is listening for our requests. "The eyes of the Lord are on the righteous," Peter wrote, "and his ears are attentive to their prayer" (1 PETER 3:12).

The Bible gives us examples of how God responded to prayer. One is Hezekiah, the king of Judah, who became ill. He'd even received word from Isaiah, a prophet, saying he was going to die. The king knew what to do: he "prayed to the LORD" (2 KINGS 20:2). Immediately, God told Isaiah to give the king this message from Him: "I have heard your prayer" (V. 5). Hezekiah was granted fifteen more years of life.

God doesn't always answer prayers with things like a card on a windowsill, but He assures us that when difficult situations arise, we don't face them alone. God sees us, and He's with us— attentive to our prayers.　　　　　*DAVE BRANON*

> **What tops your list of concerns? How can you give them to God, asking for His guidance and help?**
>
> *Father, thank You for being there and hearing my prayers.*

BIBLE IN A YEAR | LAMENTATIONS 1-2; HEBREWS 10:1-18

I will forgive their wickedness and
will remember their sins no more.
[JEREMIAH 31:34]

SINS REMEMBERED NO MORE

I never saw the ice. But I felt it. The back end of the van I was
driving—my grandfather's—spun out. One swerve, two,
three—and I was airborne, flying off a fifteen-foot embank-
ment. I remember thinking, *This would be awesome if I wasn't
going to die*. A moment later, the van crunched into the steep
slope and rolled to the bottom. I crawled out of the crushed
vehicle, unscathed.

The van was utterly ruined that December morning in 1992.
God had spared me. But what about my grandfather? What
would *he* say? In fact, he never said a single word about the van.
Not one. There was no scolding, no repayment plan, nothing.
Just forgiveness. And a grandfather's smile that I was okay.

My grandfather's grace reminds me of God's grace in Jeremiah 31. There, despite their tremendous failings, God promises a
restored relationship with His people, saying, "I will forgive their
wickedness and will remember their sins no more" (V. 34).

I'm sure my grandfather never *forgot* that I'd wrecked his van.
But he acted just like God does here, not *remembering* it, not
shaming me, not making me work to repay the debt I rightfully
owed. Just as God says He'll do, my grandfather chose to remember it no more, as if the destructive thing I'd done had never happened.   *ADAM R. HOLZ*

> **How should God's forgiveness affect how you see your
> failures? How can you show others grace?**

> *Father, thank You for Your forgiveness. When I cling
> to my shame, help me to recall that, in Christ, You
> remember my sins no more.*

BIBLE IN A YEAR | LAMENTATIONS 3-5; HEBREWS 10:19-39

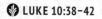
You are worried and upset about many things, but few things are needed—or indeed only one. [LUKE 10:41–42]

ONE THING NEEDED

One weekend in March, I led a retreat on the theme of Mary and Martha, the sisters in Bethany whom Jesus loved along with their brother Lazarus (JOHN 11:5). We were in a remote spot along the English coastline. When we were snowed in unexpectedly, many of the participants remarked how the extra day together meant they could practise sitting at Christ's feet as Mary did. They wanted to pursue the "one thing . . . needed" (LUKE 10:42 NKJV) that Jesus lovingly told Martha she should embrace, which was choosing to draw close and learn from Him.

When Jesus visited the home of Martha, Mary and Lazarus, Martha wouldn't have known He was coming in advance, so we can understand how she could have been upset with Mary for not helping with the preparations to feed Him and His friends. But she lost sight of what really mattered—receiving from Jesus as she learned from Him. Christ wasn't scolding her for wanting to serve Him, but rather reminding her that she was missing the most important thing.

When interruptions make us irritable or we feel overwhelmed about the many things we want to accomplish, we can stop and remind ourselves what really matters in life. As we slow ourselves down, picturing ourselves sitting at the feet of Jesus, we can ask Him to fill us with His love and life. We can revel in being His beloved disciple. *AMY BOUCHER PYE*

What distractions keep you from receiving from Jesus? How can you sit at His feet today?

Dear Jesus, thank You for loving to instruct me in Your ways. Help me not to get distracted by my activities, but to focus on You.

BIBLE IN A YEAR | EZEKIEL 1–2; HEBREWS 11:1–19

Let me tell you what he has done for me.
[PSALM 66:16]

TELL OF GOD'S GOODNESS

"**T**estimony Time" was the segment in our church service when people shared how God had been at work in their lives. Auntie—or Sister Langford as she was known by others in our church family—was known for packing lots of praise into her testimonies. On the occasions when she shared her personal conversion story, one could expect her to take up a good bit of the service. Her heart gushed with praise to God who had graciously changed her life!

Similarly, the testimony of the writer of Psalm 66 is packed with praise as he testifies about what God had done for His people. "Come and see what God has done, his awesome deeds for mankind" (V. 5). His deeds included miraculous rescue (V. 6), preservation (V. 9) and discipline that resulted in His people being brought to a better place (VV. 10–12). While there are God-experiences that we have in common with other believers in Jesus, there are also things unique to our individual journeys. Have there been times in your life when God has particularly made Himself known to you? Those are worth sharing with others who need to hear how He's worked in your life. "Come and hear, all you who fear God; let me tell you what he has done for me" (V. 16).   *ARTHUR JACKSON*

How can you more readily share your experiences of God's goodness with others? How have you been inspired to trust Him more when you've heard others share His awesome deeds?

Heavenly Father, I rejoice in the varied expressions of Your kindness to me. Help me not to keep these things to myself.

BIBLE IN A YEAR | EZEKIEL 3–4; HEBREWS 11:20–40

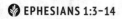

In him we were also chosen . . . that we
. . . might be for the praise of his glory.
[EPHESIANS 1:11–12]

THE ADVENTURE

"**C**hristianity is not for me. It's boring. One of my values I hold on to is adventure. That's life to me," a young woman told me. It saddened me that she hadn't yet learned the incredible joy and excitement that comes with following Jesus—an adventure like no other. I excitedly shared with her about Jesus and how real life is found in Him.

Mere words are inadequate to describe the adventure of knowing and walking with Jesus, God's Son. But in Ephesians 1, the apostle Paul gives us a small but powerful glimpse of life with Him. God gives us spiritual blessings directly from heaven (V. 3), holiness and blamelessness in God's eyes (V. 4) and adoption as His own into the King's royal family (V. 5). He blesses us with the lavish gift of His forgiveness and grace (VV. 7–8), understanding of the mystery of His will (V. 9) and a new purpose of living "for the praise of his glory" (V. 12). The Holy Spirit comes to live in us to empower and lead us (V. 13) and He guarantees eternity in God's presence forever (V. 14).

When Jesus Christ enters our life, we discover that getting to know Him more and following Him closely is the greatest of adventures. Seek Him now and every day for real life.   *ANNE CETAS*

*How would you describe the life of knowing and walking
with Jesus? Who might God want you to share this with?*

*Dear Jesus, thank You for loving me and always walking by my
side. You've given me more than I could have imagined. I love
being known and loved by You and sharing You with others.*

BIBLE IN A YEAR | EZEKIEL 5-7; HEBREWS 12

Then the LORD said to Cain,
"Why are you angry?" [GENESIS 4:6]

CONFRONTING IN LOVE

He did many things well, but there was a problem. Everyone saw it. Yet because he was so effective in accomplishing most of his role, his anger issue wasn't adequately addressed. He was never truly confronted. Sadly, this resulted in many people being hurt over the years. And, in the end, it led to the premature close of a career that could have been something so much more for this brother in Christ. If only I'd chosen to confront him in love long ago.

In Genesis 4, God provides the perfect picture of what it means to confront someone's sin in love. Cain was infuriated. Being a farmer, he'd presented "some of the fruits of the soil as an offering to the LORD" (V. 3). But God made it clear that what he brought Him wasn't acceptable. Cain's offering was rejected, and he was "very angry, and his face was downcast" (V. 5). So, God confronted him and said, "Why are you angry?" (V. 6). He then told Cain to turn from his sin and pursue what was good and right. Sadly, Cain ignored God's words and committed a horrific act (V. 8).

While we can't force others to turn from sinful behaviours, we can compassionately confront them. We can "speak the truth in love" so that we both become "more and more like Christ" (EPHESIANS 4:15 NLT). And, as God gives us ears to listen, we can also receive hard words of truth from others.   *TOM FELTEN*

Why is it vital for us to confront others in love?
How do you receive hard but helpful words?

Father, help me to have the courage to confront others in
love and to receive hard but true words with grace.

BIBLE IN A YEAR | EZEKIEL 8-10; HEBREWS 13

My grace is sufficient for you, for my
power is made perfect in weakness.
[2 CORINTHIANS 12:9]

GATHERING STRENGTH IN GOD

Grainger McKoy is an artist who studies and sculpts birds, capturing their grace, vulnerability and power. One of his pieces is titled *Recovery*. It shows the single right wing of a pintail duck, stretched high in a vertical position. Below, a plaque describes the bird's recovery stroke as "the moment of the bird's greatest weakness in flight, yet also the moment when it gathers strength for the journey ahead." Grainger includes this verse: "My grace is sufficient for you, for my power is made perfect in weakness" (2 CORINTHIANS 12:9).

The apostle Paul wrote these words to the church at Corinth. Enduring a season when he was overwhelmed with personal struggle, Paul begged God to remove what he described as "a thorn in my flesh" (V. 7). His affliction might have been a physical ailment or spiritual opposition. Like Jesus in the garden the night before His crucifixion (LUKE 22:39–44), Paul repeatedly asked God to remove his suffering. The Holy Spirit responded by assuring him that He'd provide the strength needed. Paul learned, "When I am weak, then I am strong" (2 CORINTHIANS 12:10).

Oh, the thorns we experience in this life! Like a bird gathering its strength for the journey ahead, we can gather up God's strength for what we're facing. In His strength, we find our own.

ELISA MORGAN

**Where are you experiencing weakness today? How can
you—in that exact weakness—gather God's strength
for your journey?**

*Dear Father, help me gather my strength from You as I
face what's ahead in my life today.*

BIBLE IN A YEAR | EZEKIEL 11–13; JAMES 1

A cheerful heart is good medicine.
[PROVERBS 17:22]

PRICELESS RESULTS

O n every school day for three years, Colleen has been dressing up in a different costume or mask to greet her children as they arrived back home at the end of each day. It brightens the day of everyone—including the bus driver who drops them home: "[She] bring[s] so much joy to the kids, it's amazing. I love that." Colleen's children agree.

It all started when Colleen began fostering children. Knowing how difficult it was to be separated from parents and to attend a new school, she began greeting the kids in a costume. After three days of doing so, the kids didn't want her to stop. So Colleen continued. It was an investment of time and money, but, as one reporter describes, it brought a "priceless result: happiness".

One little verse amid a book of wise and witty advice, largely by King Solomon to his son, sums up the results of this mum's antics: "A cheerful heart is good medicine, but a crushed spirit dries up the bones" (PROVERBS 17:22). By bringing cheer to all her kids (biological, adopted and foster), she hoped to prevent crushed spirits.

The source of true and lasting joy is God through the Holy Spirit (LUKE 10:21; GALATIANS 5:22). The Spirit enables us to shine God's light as we strive to bring joy to others, a joy that offers hope and strength to face trials.   *ALYSON KIEDA*

When has someone done something to bring you joy?
What was the result?

Dear Father, thank You for giving me joy.
Help me to spread it to others.

BIBLE IN A YEAR | EZEKIEL 14–15; JAMES 2

You are precious and honoured in my sight.
[ISAIAH 43:4]

PRECIOUS TO GOD

A s a boy, Ming found his father harsh and distant. Even when Ming was ill and had to see the doctor, his father grumbled that it was troublesome. Once, he overheard a quarrel and learned his father had wanted him aborted. The feeling of being an unwanted child followed him into his adult years. When Ming became a believer in Jesus, he found it difficult to relate to God as Father, even though he knew Him as Lord of his life.

If, like Ming, we haven't felt loved by our earthly fathers, we may face similar doubts in our relationship with God. We may wonder, *Am I a burden to Him? Does He care about me?* But while our earthly fathers may have been silent and distant, God our heavenly Father comes close and says, "I love you" (ISAIAH 43:4).

In Isaiah 43, God speaks as our Creator and as a Father. If you wonder whether He wants you to live under His care as part of His family, hear what He said to His people: "Bring my sons from afar and my daughters from the ends of the earth" (V. 6). If you wonder what you're worth to Him, hear His affirmation: "You are precious and honoured in my sight" (V. 4).

God loves us so much that He sent Jesus to pay the penalty of sin so that we who believe in Him can be with Him forever (JOHN 3:16). Because of what He says and what He's done for us, we can have full confidence that He wants us and loves us.

JASMINE GOH

What's your experience of relating to God as a Father? How can you remind yourself that you're precious to Him?

Father, I want to live each day as Your child, precious and honoured in Your sight.

BIBLE IN A YEAR | EZEKIEL 16–17; JAMES 3

You will shine among them like stars in the
sky as you hold firmly to the word of life.
[PHILIPPIANS 2:15–16]

SHINING STARS

The first thing I noticed about the city was its gambling outlets. Next, its cannabis shops, 'adult' stores and giant billboards for opportunistic lawyers making money off others' mishaps. While I had visited many shady cities before, this one seemed to reach a new low.

My mood brightened, however, when I spoke to a taxi driver the next morning. "I ask God every day to send me the people He wants me to help," he said. "Gambling addicts, prostitutes, people from broken homes—they all tell me their problems in tears. I stop the car. I listen. I pray for them. This is my ministry."

After describing Jesus' descent into our fallen world (PHILIPPIANS 2:5–8), the apostle Paul gives believers in Christ a calling. As we pursue God's will (V. 13) and hold to the "word of life"—the gospel (V. 16)—we'll be "children of God without fault in a warped and crooked generation" who "shine . . . like stars in the sky" (V. 15). Like that taxi driver, we're to bring Jesus' light into the darkness.

A believer in Christ has only to live faithfully in order to change the world, historian Christopher Dawson said, because in that very act of living "there is contained all the mystery of divine life". Let's ask God's Spirit to empower us to live faithfully as Jesus' people, shining His light in the world's darkest places.

SHERIDAN VOYSEY

*How can you focus on Christ today, rather than the
world's evil? How can you shine His light today in your
neighbourhood?*

*Jesus, thank You for being the Light of the World who
brings me out of darkness.*

BIBLE IN A YEAR | EZEKIEL 18-19; JAMES 4

When you give a banquet, invite the poor,
the crippled, the lame, the blind, and you
will be blessed. [LUKE 14:13–14]

A STRANGER FOR DINNER

I n 2016, Wanda Dench sent a text inviting her grandson to dinner, not knowing he'd recently changed his phone number.
The text instead went to a stranger, Jamal. Jamal didn't have
plans, and so, after clarifying who he was, asked if he could still
come to dinner. Wanda said, "Of course you can." Jamal joined
the family dinner in what has since become a yearly tradition for
him. A mistaken invitation became an annual blessing.

Wanda's kindness in inviting a stranger to dinner reminds me
of Jesus' encouragement in Luke's gospel. During a dinner party
at a "prominent" Pharisee's house (LUKE 14:1), Jesus noticed who
was invited and how the guests jostled for the best seats (V. 7).
Jesus told His host that inviting people based on what they could
do for him in return (V. 12) meant the blessing would be limited.
Instead, Jesus told the host that extending hospitality to people
without the resources to repay him would bring even greater
blessing (V. 14).

For Wanda, inviting Jamal to join her family for dinner resulted in the unexpected blessing of a lasting friendship that was a
great encouragement to her after her husband's death. When
we reach out to others, not because of what we might receive,
but because of God's love flowing through us, we receive far
greater blessing and encouragement.   *LISA M. SAMRA*

When has an unexpected invitation encouraged you?
What blessings did you experience?

*Heavenly Father, may my invitations reflect a heart that
wants to bless others as You lead me.*

BIBLE IN A YEAR | EZEKIEL 20–21; JAMES 5

I love you, LORD, my strength.
[PSALM 18:1]

WORTHY OF ALL PRAISE

Many consider Ferrante and Teicher to be the greatest piano duet team of all time. Their collaborative presentations were so precise that their style was described as four hands but only one mind. Hearing their music, one can begin to grasp the amount of effort required to perfect their craft.

But there's more. They loved what they did. In fact, even after they had retired in 1989, Ferrante and Teicher would occasionally show up at a local piano shop just to play an impromptu concert. They simply loved making music.

David also loved making music—but he teamed up with God to give his song a higher purpose. His psalms affirm his struggle-filled life and his desire to live in deep dependence upon God. Yet, in the midst of his personal failures and imperfections, his praise expressed a kind of spiritual 'perfect pitch', acknowledging the greatness and goodness of God even in the darkest of times. The heart behind David's praise is simply stated in Psalm 18:1, which reads, "I love you, LORD, my strength."

David continued, "I called to the LORD, who is worthy of praise" (V. 3) and turned to Him "in my distress" (V. 6). Regardless of our situation, may we likewise lift our hearts to praise and worship our God. He's worthy of all praise! *BILL CROWDER*

In what ways do you share your love for God with Him and with others? What might be standing in the way of your worship?

Heavenly Father, You've put a new song in my mouth. Please help my worship to express Your true goodness and greatness.

BIBLE IN A YEAR | EZEKIEL 22–23; 1 PETER 1

Faith is confidence in what we hope for
and assurance about what we do not see.
[HEBREWS 11:1]

SEEING BY FAITH

During my morning walk, the sun hit the waters of the lake at a perfect angle to produce a stunning view. I asked my friend to stop and wait for me as I positioned my camera to take a pic. Because of the position of the sun, I couldn't see the image on my phone's screen before I snapped the shot. But having done this before, I sensed it would be a great picture. I told my friend, "We can't see it now, but pictures like this always come out good."

Walking by faith through this life is often like taking that picture. You can't always see the details on the screen, but that doesn't mean the stunning picture isn't there. You don't always see God working, but you can trust that He's there. As the writer of Hebrews wrote, "Faith is confidence in what we hope for and assurance about what we do not see" (HEBREWS 11:1). By faith we place our confidence and assurance in God—especially when we can't see or understand what He's doing.

With faith, not seeing doesn't prevent us from 'taking the shot'. It just might make us pray more and seek God's direction. We can also find encouragement in the stories of faith that have come before us (VV. 4–12), as well as remembering God's faithfulness to us in our own stories. What God has done before, He can do again.

KATARA PATTON

What are you trusting God to do even though you may not see it clearly right now? How has He delivered you or your family in the past?

Heavenly Father, thank You for all the ways You've provided for me in the past. Help me to walk by faith even if I can't see all You're doing.

BIBLE IN A YEAR | EZEKIEL 24–26; 1 PETER 2

But who am I, and who are my people, that
we should be able to give as generously as
this? [1 CHRONICLES 29:14]

WHO AM I?

As a member of the leadership team for a local ministry, part of my job was to invite others to join us as group discussion leaders. My invitations described the time commitment required and outlined the ways leaders would need to engage with their small group participants, both in meetings and during regular phone calls. I was often reluctant to impose on other people, being aware of the sacrifice they'd be making to become a leader. And yet sometimes their reply would completely overwhelm me: "I'd be honoured." Instead of citing legitimate reasons to decline, they described their gratitude to God for all He'd done in their lives as their reason for being eager to give back.

When the time came to give resources towards building a temple for God, David had a similar response: "Who am I, and who are my people, that we should be able to give as generously as this?" (1 CHRONICLES 29:14). David's generosity was driven by gratitude for God's involvement in his life and that of the people of Israel. His response speaks of his humility and his acknowledgment of God's goodness towards "foreigners and strangers" (V. 15).

Our giving to God's work—whether in time, talent or treasure—reflects our gratitude to the One who gave to us to begin with. All that we have comes from His hand (V. 14); in response, we can give gratefully to Him.   *KIRSTEN HOLMBERG*

> **How has God been involved in your life?**
> **How can you give in response?**

> *Dear Father, please help me to respond to Your*
> *love and care with a generous heart.*

BIBLE IN A YEAR | EZEKIEL 27-29; 1 PETER 3

They are to . . . [fulfil] the obligations of
the Israelites by doing the work of the
tabernacle. [NUMBERS 3:8]

SERVING FOR GOD'S SAKE

When England's Queen Elizabeth passed away in September 2022, thousands of soldiers were deployed to march in the funeral procession. Their individual roles must have been almost unnoticeable in the large crowd, but many saw it as the greatest honour. One soldier said it was "an opportunity to do our last duty for Her Majesty". For him, it was not *what* he did, but *whom* he was doing it for that made it an important job.

The Levites assigned to take care of the tabernacle furnishings had a similar aim. Unlike the priests, the Gershonites, Kohathites and Merarites were assigned seemingly mundane tasks: cleaning the furniture, lampstands, curtains, posts, tent pegs and ropes (NUMBERS 3:25–26, 28, 31, 36–37). Yet their jobs were specifically assigned by God, constituted "doing the work of the tabernacle" (V. 8) and are recorded in the Bible for posterity.

What an encouraging thought! Today, what many of us do at work, at home or in church may seem insignificant to a world that values titles and salaries. But God sees it differently. If we work and serve for *His* sake—seeking excellence and doing so for *His* honour, even in the smallest task—then our work is important because we're serving our great God. 　　*LESLIE KOH*

> *How might knowing that you're ultimately serving God change the way you work? How can you do it with pride and excellence for His sake?*
>
> *Father, thank You for giving me this opportunity to serve You. Help me to be faithful with the talents and strength You've given me to work for You.*

BIBLE IN A YEAR | EZEKIEL 30–32; 1 PETER 4

Be devoted to one another in love . . .
joyful in hope, patient in affliction,
faithful in prayer. [ROMANS 12:10–12]

THE SKILL OF COMPASSION

"A thorn has entered your foot—that is why you weep at times at night," wrote Catherine of Sienna in the fourteenth century. She continued, "There are some in this world who can pull it out. The skill that takes they have learned from [God]." Catherine devoted her life to cultivating that "skill", and is still remembered today for her remarkable capacity for empathy and compassion for others in their pain.

That image of pain as a deeply embedded thorn that requires tenderness and skill to remove lingers with me. It's a vivid reminder of how complex and wounded we are, and of our need to dig deeper to develop true compassion for others and ourselves.

Or, as the apostle Paul describes it, it's an image that reminds us that loving others like Jesus does requires more than good intentions and well-wishes—it requires being "*devoted* to one another" (ROMANS 12:10), "joyful in hope, patient in affliction, faithful in prayer" (V. 12). It requires being willing to not only "rejoice with those who rejoice" but to "mourn with those who mourn" (V. 15). It requires all of us.

In a broken world, none of us escape unwounded—pain and scars are deeply embedded in each of us. But deeper still is the love we find in Christ; love tender enough to draw out those thorns with the balm of compassion, willing to embrace both friend and enemy (V. 14) to find healing together.   *MONICA LA ROSE*

***When have you experienced the healing power of compassion?
How can you cultivate a community of healing?***

*Loving God, thank You for Your compassion.
Help me to love others like that.*

BIBLE IN A YEAR | EZEKIEL 33–34; 1 PETER 5

This is love: not that we loved God, but that
he loved us and sent his Son as an atoning
sacrifice for our sins. [1 JOHN 4:10]

THIS IS LOVE

When Zac was two, he tripped and fell, banging his head
against our front doorstep. The deep gash along his
eyebrow was serious enough to require a hospital visit
and stitches.

Even though the nurses gave him ketamine to numb the pain
and sooth him, Zac still wriggled and cried as they applied the
stitches. I felt helpless as I watched my son, wishing I could swap
places and save him from the pain.

I later realised that my desire to swap with Zac is essentially
how John describes love in his first letter. "This is love: not that
we loved God, but that he loved us and sent his Son as an atoning sacrifice for our sins" (1 JOHN 4:10). God saw our pain, caused
by our sin and the broken world we live in. But rather than just
wish He could do something about it, He sent Jesus—His one
and only Son—to take our place and bring us into new life.

On the cross, Jesus died the death that our sin deserved. He
paid for every wrong and bore all our shame in His body so that
we would never have to face the eternal consequences. Now we
can "live through him" (V. 9).

If we ever doubt God's love for us, we don't need look any
further than the cross. For John describes that costly sacrifice
with these powerful words: "This is love."   *CHRIS WALE*

> **How does it humble and encourage you to think that
> Jesus took your place on the cross? How does this deepen
> your understanding of what love is?**

*Dear Jesus, I am so thankful that You not only saw me lost in
sin, but You came to save me from it. Thank You for this love.*

BIBLE IN A YEAR | EZEKIEL 35-36; 2 PETER 1

Some trust in chariots and some in horses,
but we trust in the name of the LORD our God.
[PSALM 20:7]

TRUSTING GOD

I needed two medications urgently. One was for my mum's allergies and the other for my niece's eczema. Their discomfort was worsening, but the medicines were no longer available in pharmacies. Desperate and helpless, I prayed repeatedly, *Lord, please help them.*

Weeks later, their conditions became manageable. God seemed to be saying: "There are times when I use medicines to heal. But medicines don't have the final say; I do. Don't place your trust in them, but in Me."

In Psalm 20, King David took comfort in God's trustworthiness. The Israelites had a powerful army, but they knew that their biggest strength came from "the name of the LORD" (V. 7). They placed their trust in God's name—in who He is, His unchanging character and His unfailing promises. They held on to the truth that He who is sovereign and powerful over all situations would hear their prayers and deliver them from their enemies (V. 6).

While God may use the resources of this world to help us, ultimately, victory over our problems comes from Him. Whether He gives us a resolution or the grace to endure, we can trust that He'll be to us all that He says He is. We don't have to be overwhelmed by our troubles, but we can face them with His hope and peace.

KAREN HUANG

In your personal battles, where or in what do you place your trust? How might trusting in God's name change the way you cope with these challenges?

Heavenly Father, give me the courage to trust in You. Help me to believe that You're all that You promise to be.

BIBLE IN A YEAR | EZEKIEL 37–39; 2 PETER 2

WARM HEARTS AND OPEN ARMS

The night air in Caracas, Venezuela, was warm and thick. The jammed streets smelled of *panaderies* (local bakeries), street food and petrol fumes. My friend and I arrived at the flat where we'd been invited for dinner, and a gregarious man with a smile as wide as a sunrise opened the door and embraced us.

We sat with his family at a long wooden table holding massive platters of beef, rice and plantain. My friend knew Spanish, but I could only listen as the others swapped stories and laughed. Sometimes they made gestures for me so I could try to follow along. Occasionally, my friend paused to offer a summary or to translate a question they'd posed. Although for hours I understood almost nothing, I never felt like an outsider. Just the opposite; their loving welcome enveloped me. I was in a city I'd never visited before, meeting people of a completely different history and ethnicity with whom I couldn't even verbally communicate. And yet, because they offered me warm hearts and open arms, I felt like I belonged.

Paul reminds us that if we believe in Jesus, we're called to always live out this kind of radical welcome. We're to "accept one another . . . just as Christ accepted [us]" (ROMANS 15:7). We're to welcome one another, to open our hearts wide, and gather others in. This should be our posture towards everyone—even those who are different from us. Paul addressed conflict between Jews and gentiles, but it's the same for any differences in ethnicity or social class, any supposed barrier. Cultural differences shouldn't be obstacles but rather opportunities to demonstrate the same radical welcome Jesus extends to us.

Winn Collier, *Our Daily Bread* author

★ By God's design we live in a diverse, multicultural world. As believers in Jesus, how can we live in loving relationship with those of different races and cultures? This topic is addressed in the devotions for **December 1, 8, 15** and **22**.

Come to me, all you who are weary.
[MATTHEW 11:28]

GOD'S HEART FOR ALL

Nine-year-old Dan Gill arrived with his best friend Archie at their classmate's birthday party. When the mother of the birthday boy saw Archie, however, she refused him entry. "There aren't enough chairs," she insisted. Dan offered to sit on the floor to make room for his friend, who was Black, but the mother said no. Dejected, Dan left their presents with her and returned home with Archie, the sting of his friend's rejection searing his heart.

Now, decades later, Dan is a schoolteacher who keeps one empty chair in his classroom. When students ask why, he explains it's his reminder to "always have room in the classroom for anyone".

A heart for all people can be seen in Jesus' welcoming life: "Come to me, all you who are weary and burdened, and I will give you rest" (MATTHEW 11:28). This invitation may seem to contradict the "first to the Jew" scope of Jesus' ministry (ROMANS 1:16). But the gift of salvation is for all people who place their faith in Jesus. "This is true for everyone who believes," Paul wrote in his letter to the Romans, "no matter who we are" (3:22 NLT).

We rejoice then at Christ's invitation to all: "Take my yoke upon you and learn from me, for I am gentle and humble in heart, and you will find rest for your souls" (MATTHEW 11:29). For all seeking His rest, His open heart awaits.   *PATRICIA RAYBON*

> *What was your situation when you accepted God's gift of salvation? Who in your life still needs to accept Jesus' invitation?*

> *Jesus, You called me when others didn't. Thank You for offering me salvation and love.*

BIBLE IN A YEAR | EZEKIEL 40–41; 2 PETER 3

From [Christ] the whole body . . . grows and
builds itself up in love, as each part does its
work. [EPHESIANS 4:16]

BUILDING UP GOODWILL

When we think of best business practices, what first comes to mind probably aren't qualities like kindness and generosity. But according to entrepreneur James Rhee, they should. In Rhee's experience as CEO at a company on the brink of financial ruin, prioritising what he calls "goodwill"—a "culture of kindness" and a spirit of giving—saved the company and led to its flourishing. Putting these qualities at centre stage gave people the hope and motivation they needed to unify, innovate and problem-solve. Rhee explains that "goodwill . . . is a real asset that can compound and be amplified."

In daily life too, it's easy to think of qualities like kindness as vague and intangible, afterthoughts to our other priorities. But, as the apostle Paul taught, such qualities matter most of all.

Writing to new believers, Paul emphasised that the purpose of believers' lives is transformation through the Spirit into mature members of the body of Christ (EPHESIANS 4:15). To that end, every word and every action has value only if it builds up and benefits others (V. 29). Transformation in Jesus can only happen through daily prioritising kindness, compassion and forgiveness (V. 32).

When the Holy Spirit draws us to other believers in Christ, we grow and mature as we learn from one another.   *MONICA LA ROSE*

> *Why do you think we often fail to see the tangible
> impact of goodwill? How can you make a habit of
> prioritising kindness?*
>
> *Dear God, teach me daily what truly matters—the love
> poured out through Your Son.*

BIBLE IN A YEAR | EZEKIEL 42–44; 1 JOHN 1

Out of Egypt I called my son. [MATTHEW 2:15]

A WARM WELCOME

Winter 2022 was impossibly tough in the UK. Soaring costs meant that the elderly, low-income families and millions of others were faced with the choice of heating their homes or putting food on the table.

In response, thousands of churches joined The Warm Welcome Campaign, offering their buildings as "warm spaces" to anyone in need.

"In the Christmas story we remember that Jesus was born in a primitive shelter and then fled to Egypt as a refugee," explains the campaign's founder. "His active ministry was amongst the poorest people in society. Churches are living this story today by stepping up across the UK to serve people in need and provide a Warm Welcome."

The campaign rooted itself in Jesus' own experience of suffering and His love for those who suffer. Even during His early years, God told Joseph, Jesus' earthly father, "Escape to Egypt. Stay there until I tell you, for Herod is going to search for the child to kill him" (MATTHEW 2:13). It wasn't until sometime later that Jesus could return to Israel, thereby fulfilling the prophecy: "Out of Egypt I called my son" (V. 15). It was an ancient revelation that, right from the start, Jesus would suffer.

The trials and deprivations in the Christmas story remind us that our Saviour knows what it is to be poor and in need. When we suffer similarly, we can be sure we will always receive a "warm welcome" from Him.   *CHRIS WALE*

How does it help you to know Jesus truly understands suffering? How might you be able to offer His "warm welcome" to others this winter?

Dear Jesus, when life is unbearably hard, it comforts me to know You truly understand. Thank You that I am always welcome to bring everything to You in prayer.

BIBLE IN A YEAR | EZEKIEL 45-46; 1 JOHN 2

Blessed are those who . . . walk in the light of
your presence, LORD. [PSALM 89:15]

SHADOW AND GOD'S LIGHT

When Elaine was diagnosed with advanced cancer, she
and her husband, Charles, knew it wouldn't be long until she'd be with Jesus. They had always treasured the
promise of Psalm 23 that God would be with them as they jour-
neyed through the deepest and most difficult valley of their fifty-four years together. After the diagnosis, they took hope in the
fact that Elaine was ready to meet Jesus, having placed her faith
in Him decades before.

At his wife's memorial service, Charles shared that he was
still travelling "through the valley of the shadow of death"
(PSALM 23:4 NKJV). His wife's life in heaven had already begun. But
the "shadow of death" was still with him and with others who'd
greatly loved Elaine.

As we travel through the valley of shadows, where can we
find our source of light? The apostle John declares that "God is
light; in him there is no darkness at all" (1 JOHN 1:5). And in John
8:12, Jesus proclaimed: "I am the light of the world. Whoever
follows me will never walk in darkness, but will have the light
of life."

As believers in Jesus, we "walk in the light of [His] presence"
(PSALM 89:15). Our God has promised to be with us and to be
our source of light, even when we travel through the darkest of
shadows.   *CINDY HESS KASPER*

What valley have you been walking through?
Which of God's promises provide light for your journey?

Loving God, thank You for Your promise to never leave
me. I trust You to be my strength, my provision and my
joy throughout my life.

BIBLE IN A YEAR | EZEKIEL 47–48; 1 JOHN 3

For when I am weak, then I am strong.
[2 CORINTHIANS 12:10]

STRIPPING AWAY THE RUBBISH

Tim Campbell, the first winner of the BBC programme, "The Apprentice", shared how failing in business became a turning point in his life—and in his faith in God. He chased a dream of success but when he lost £50,000, he despaired. While "crying on Brighton beach, into a bowl of mussels," he realised, "I had to be very, very quiet and actually listen to the Lord about what I was supposed to do next." That moment stripped "away all the rubbish" as he surrendered to God. Tim sensed that God was calling him to help others avoid the mistakes he'd made.

Another who experienced a major surrender to God is the Apostle Paul, who came to believe in Jesus dramatically (SEE ACTS 9:1–19). He delighted in his brokenness and weakness (2 CORINTHIANS 12:10) because he knew that through it, Christ's power rested on him (V. 9). He shared how God gave him a "thorn in [his] flesh" to keep him from being conceited (V. 7). And how God told him: "My grace is sufficient for you, for my power is made perfect in weakness" (V. 9).

We might not think that anything good could come from failure, but God can use these experiences to help us dedicate our lives to honouring Him. Through trials and brokenness He helps us trust Him instead of relying so much on ourselves. And that is truly winning.

AMY BOUCHER PYE

***How have you changed after experiencing hard times?
How can you more fully trust in God, whatever you face
just now?***

*Saving God, You can turn weakness into strength.
Help me to rely on You for all of my needs.*

BIBLE IN A YEAR | DANIEL 1-2; 1 JOHN 4

"The virgin will conceive and give birth to a son, and they will call him Immanuel" (which means "God with us"). [MATTHEW 1:23]

SAINT NICK

The person we know as Saint Nicholas (Saint Nick) was born around AD 270 to a wealthy Grecian family. Tragically, his parents died when he was a boy, so he lived with his uncle who loved him and taught him to follow God. When Nicholas was a young man, legend says that he heard of three sisters who didn't have a dowry for marriage and would soon be destitute. Wanting to follow Jesus' teaching about giving to those in need, he took his inheritance and gave each sister a bag of gold coins. Over the years, Nicholas gave the rest of his money away, feeding the poor and caring for others. In the following centuries, Nicholas was honoured for his lavish generosity, and he inspired the character we know as Santa Claus.

While the glitz and advertising of the season may overshadow our celebrations, the gift-giving tradition connects to Nicholas. And his generosity was based on his devotion to Jesus. Nicholas knew that Christ enacted unimaginable generosity, bringing the most profound gift: *God*. Jesus is "God with us" (MATTHEW 1:23). And He brought us the gift of life. In a world of death, He "save[s] his people from their sins" (V. 21)

When we believe in Jesus, sacrificial generosity unfolds. We tend to others' needs, and we joyfully provide for them as God provides for us. This is Saint Nick's story; but far more, this is God's story.   *WINN COLLIER*

What's your experience with gift-giving—is it forced or free and joyful? How does Jesus' life change your notions of generosity?

God, I want to be generous, but I don't always feel it. Help me to practise true generosity.

BIBLE IN A YEAR | DANIEL 3–4; 1 JOHN 5

Ezra had devoted himself to the study and observance of the Law of the LORD . . . and to teaching its decrees. [EZRA 7:10]

EFFECTIVE WITNESS

"**H**ard-hearted! Barbaric! Unreachable!"

It was a harsh description of the seventh-century Northumbrians, but one that stirred Aidan's heart. Sensing God's call to love them, he walked the lanes and talked with peasants, gently explaining the Christian faith and living a sacrificial life.

Aidan was a man of deep prayer, spending hours meditating on Scripture on the barren island of Lindisfarne. Cut off from the Northumbrian mainland twice daily by tides, he equipped himself in the stillness for his witness and work. His ministry became so effective that Christian communities blossomed among the formerly stubborn Northumbrians.

I wonder if Aidan was following the example of Ezra the priest. Did he learn a vital principle from him? Returning to Jerusalem from Babylonian exile, Ezra met with a people who had lapsed in their commitment to God. But "the hand of the LORD his God was on him" (EZRA 7:6), a striking description of God's favour on the influence of his teaching. Like Aidan, his effective ministry to instruct, edify and reform others was empowered first through what he studied in Scripture, and then put into practice himself (V. 10).

We don't need to be a priest, church leader or modern-day theologian to enhance the effectiveness of our witness. As we listen with open hearts while reading God's Word, and actively let it shape our attitudes and behaviour, His "gracious hand" (V. 9) of favour will enhance our influence too.　　*ANNE LE TISSIER*

How have you put into practice what God has shown you in His Word this week? How have you seen this impacting others who aren't yet in a relationship with God?

Loving God, please teach me how to live the life of Your Word so that the authenticity of what I say and do may lead others to You.

BIBLE IN A YEAR | DANIEL 5–7; 2 JOHN

Nazareth! Can anything good come
from there? [JOHN 1:46]

PREJUDICE AND GOD'S LOVE

"**Y**ou're not what I expected. I thought I'd hate you, but I don't." The young man's words seemed harsh, but they were actually an effort to be kind. I was studying abroad in his country, a land that decades earlier had been at war with my own. We were participating in a group discussion in class together, and I noticed he seemed distant. When I asked if I'd offended him somehow, he responded "Not at all . . . . And that's the thing. My grandfather was killed in that war, and I hated your people and your country for it. But now I see how much we have in common, and that surprises me. I don't see why we can't be friends."

Prejudice is as old as the human race. Two millennia ago, when Nathanael first heard about Jesus living in Nazareth, his bias was evident: "Nazareth! Can anything good come from there?" he asked (JOHN 1:46). Nathanael lived in the region of Galilee, like Jesus. He probably thought God's Messiah would come from another place; even other Galileans looked down on Nazareth because it seemed to be an unremarkable little village.

This much is clear. Nathanael's response didn't stop Jesus from loving him, and he was transformed as he became Jesus' disciple. "You are the Son of God!" Nathanael later declared (V. 49). There is no bias that can stand against God's transforming love.　　　　　　　　　　　　　　　　　　*JAMES BANKS*

What biases have you faced or wrestled with?
How does Jesus' love help you deal with them?

*Help me, loving God, to overcome any biases I may have
and to love others with the love You alone can give.*

BIBLE IN A YEAR | DANIEL 8–10; 3 JOHN

If one part suffers, every part suffers with it; if
one part is honoured, every part rejoices with it.
[1 CORINTHIANS 12:26]

ONE BODY

Richard Wurmbrand, a Romanian pastor, was imprisoned
for his Christian faith for over a decade, including three
years in solitary confinement. "When I was beaten on
the bottom of my feet, my tongue cried out," he remembered.
"Why? . . . Because the tongue and feet are both part of the
same body." He referred to Paul's letter to the church at Corinth,
in which the apostle addressed the many problems of this new
body of believers. For instance, some were suing each other,
and others were tolerating sexual immorality.

Paul noted that there "should be no division in the body", but
each part "should have equal concern for each other. If one part
suffers, every part suffers with it; if one part is honoured, every part
rejoices with it" (1 CORINTHIANS 12:25–26). Paul sought unity among
the believers; he wanted them to show concern for each other.

Wumbrand endured beatings and imprisonment half a century ago, but believers still face persecution today. And if we
are free to worship God, we too will suffer with them, in the
language of Paul. We can commit to praying for these sisters and
brothers, crying out to our God who makes us all one body. As
we ask Him for their release, for strength and hope amid their
suffering, we trust that He will hear and answer our prayers.

AMY BOUCHER PYE

*How does learning about the suffering and pain of fellow
Christians affect you? How could you pray for someone
who is imprisoned for their faith today?*

*Saving Lord, thank You that You have the power and ability
to bring freedom and release, even in what may seem to
be an impossible situation.*

BIBLE IN A YEAR | DANIEL 11–12; JUDE

I will not forget you!
[ISAIAH 49:15]

GOD WON'T FORGET YOU

As a child, I collected postage stamps. When my *angkong* (Fukienese for "grandfather") heard of my hobby, he started saving stamps from post deliveries to his office every day. Whenever I visited my grandparents, Angkong would give me an envelope filled with a variety of beautiful stamps. "Even though I'm always busy," he told me once, "I won't forget you."

Angkong wasn't given to overt displays of affection, but I felt his love deeply. In an infinitely deeper way, God demonstrated His love towards Israel when He declared, "I will not forget you" (ISAIAH 49:15). Suffering in Babylon for idolatry and disobedience in days past, His people lamented, "The Lord has forgotten me" (V. 14). But God's love for His people hadn't changed. He promised them forgiveness and restoration (VV. 8–13).

"I have engraved you on the palms of my hands," God told Israel, as He also tells us today (V. 16). As I ponder His words of reassurance, it reminds me so deeply of Jesus' nail-scarred hands—stretched out in love for us and for our salvation (JOHN 20:24–27). Like my grandfather's stamps and his tender words, God holds out His forgiving hand as an eternal token of His love. Let's thank Him for His love—an unchanging love. He will never forget us.

KAREN HUANG

When were you clearly reminded that God never forgets you? How can His unchanging love give you hope and security in your present situation?

Father, thank You for Your constant love and presence.

The women living there said, "Naomi has a son!"
And they named him Obed. [RUTH 4:17]

GOD IS MORE THAN ENOUGH

Ellen was on a tight budget, so she was glad to receive a Christmas bonus. That would have been enough, but when she deposited the money, she received another surprise. The teller said that as a Christmas present the bank had deposited her January mortgage payment into her account. Now she and Trey could pay other bills and bless someone else with a Christmas surprise!

God has a way of blessing us beyond what we expect. Naomi was bitter and broken by the death of her husband and sons (RUTH 1:20–21). Her desperate situation was rescued by Boaz, a relative who married her daughter-in-law and provided a home for her and Naomi (4:10).

That might have been all Naomi could hope for. But then God blessed Ruth and Boaz with a son. Now Naomi had a grandson to "renew [her] life and sustain [her] in [her] old age" (V. 15). *That* would have been enough. As the women of Bethlehem put it, "Naomi has a son!" (V. 17). Then little Obed grew—and became "the father of Jesse, the father of David" (V. 17). Naomi's family belonged to Israel's royal line, the most important dynasty in history! *That* would have been enough. David, however, became the ancestor of . . . Jesus.

If we believe in Christ, we're in a similar position to Naomi. We had nothing until He redeemed us. Now we're fully accepted by our Father, who blesses us to bless others. That's so much more than enough.　　　　　*MIKE WITTMER*

> ***When has God blessed you beyond what you imagined?
> How has He shown you that He's more than enough?***
>
> *Jesus, You're more than enough for me.*

BIBLE IN A YEAR | HOSEA 5–8; REVELATION 2

The name of the LORD is a strong tower;
The righteous run to it and are safe.
[PROVERBS 18:10 NKJV]

LEAN ON GOD

While at a water park with some friends, we attempted to navigate a floating obstacle course made of inflatable platforms. The bouncy, slippery platforms made walking straight almost impossible. As we wobbled our way across ramps, cliffs and bridges, we found ourselves yelping as we fell unceremoniously into the water. After completing one course, my friend, completely exhausted, leaned on one of the 'towers' to catch her breath. Almost immediately, it buckled under her weight, sending her hurtling into the water.

Unlike the flimsy towers at the water park, in Bible times, a tower was a stronghold for defence and protection. Judges 9:50–51 describes how the people of Thebez fled to "a strong tower" to hide from Abimelek's attack on their city. In Proverbs 18:10, the writer used the image of a strong tower to describe who God is—the One who saves those who trust Him.

Sometimes, however, rather than lean on the strong tower of God when we're tired or beaten down, we seek other things for safety and support—a career, relationships or physical comforts. We're no different from the rich man who looked for strength in his wealth (V. 11). But just as the inflatable tower couldn't support my friend, these things can't give us what we really need. God—who's all-powerful and in control of all situations—provides true comfort and security.   *JASMINE GOH*

What 'towers' do you lean on? How can you remind yourself to run to God, the strong tower?

Dear God, help me to run to You instead of turning to other things for comfort and security.

BIBLE IN A YEAR | HOSEA 9–11; REVELATION 3

In the same way . . . there is rejoicing in the presence of the angels of God over one sinner who repents. [LUKE 15:10]

MUCH REJOICING

The cuddly monkey lay in a tree, dirty, dishevelled and sodden. Spotting the lost toy, Rachel was determined to find its young owner. She posted pictures on social media— Monkey eating sweets with Mr Elephant, taking a bath, and being tucked up in bed. "Monkey has been a great house guest so far," reported Rachel. Monkey's adventures soon went viral.

Distraught, fourteen-month-old Amalia hadn't slept well since her beloved companion had gone missing in the park. But after a few days, her mum spotted the posts, made contact with Rachel, and returned the monkey to a delighted Amalia. "They're now both fast asleep, cuddling tightly," reported Mum.

Jesus tells two parables about individuals who rejoice when they find what was lost. God, as shepherd, "joyfully puts [the lost sheep] on his shoulders" (LUKE 15:5). It's an image of tenderness and intimacy, of a God who cares deeply for us. Likewise, the woman who finds her lost coin is so excited that she invites her friends to a party. "Rejoice with me," she enthuses (V. 9). That's how much God loves us and how precious we are to him. There is a celebration "in the presence of the angels of God over one sinner who repents" (V. 10).

Sometimes we forget this. If you're feeling low or abandoned today, meditate on God's unbridled joy at being reconciled with you. *TANYA MARLOW*

To what extent do you see yourself as deeply loved and precious? What difference does it make to remember that God rejoices over you?

Loving God, thank You that You rejoice when anyone is reconciled with You. Please help me experience Your exuberant love today.

BIBLE IN A YEAR | HOSEA 12-14; REVELATION 4

I have calmed and quieted myself, . . .
I am content. [PSALM 131:2]

APPETITE FOR DISTRACTION

I set my phone down, weary of the constant bombardment of images, ideas and notifications that the little screen broadcasted. Then, I picked it up and turned it on again. *Why?*

In his 2013 book *The Shallows*, Nicholas Carr describes how the internet has shaped our relationship with stillness: "What the Net seems to be doing is chipping away my capacity for concentration and contemplation. Whether I'm online or not, my mind now expects to take in information the way the Net distributes it: in a swiftly moving stream of particles. Once I was a scuba diver in the sea of words. Now I zip along the surface like a guy on a Jet Ski."

Living life on a mental jet ski doesn't sound healthy. But how do we begin to slow down, to dive deeply into still spiritual waters?

In Psalm 131, David writes, "I have calmed and quieted myself" (V. 2). David's words remind me that I have responsibility. Changing habits starts with *my choice* to be still—even if I must make that choice over and over again. Slowly, though, we experience God's satisfying goodness. Like a little child, we rest in contentment, remembering that He alone offers hope (V. 3)— soul-satisfaction that no smartphone app can touch and no social media site can deliver.   *ADAM R. HOLZ*

**How does technology influence your ability to rest
quietly before God? Does your phone contribute to your
contentment? Why or why not?**

*Father, the world is awash in distraction that doesn't
satisfy my soul. Help me trust You to fill me with
genuine contentment.*

BIBLE IN A YEAR | JOEL 1–3; REVELATION 5

Rich and poor have this in common: the LORD
is the Maker of them all. [PROVERBS 22:2]

EQUAL BEFORE GOD

While on holiday, my wife and I enjoyed some early morning bike rides. One route took us through a neighbourhood of multi-million-pound homes. We saw a variety of people—residents walking their dogs, fellow bike riders and numerous workers building new homes or tending well-kept landscapes. It was a mixture of people from all walks of life, and I was reminded of a valuable reality. There was no true distinction between us. Rich or poor. Wealthy or working-class. Known or unknown. All of us on that street that morning were the same. "Rich and poor have this in common: the LORD is the Maker of them all" (PROVERBS 22:2). Regardless of differences, we were all made in God's image (GENESIS 1:27).

But there's more. Being equal before God also means that no matter our economic, social or ethnic situation, we're all born with a sin condition: "all have sinned and fall short of the glory of God" (ROMANS 3:23). We're all disobedient and equally guilty before Him, and we need Jesus.

We often divide people into groups for a variety of reasons. But, in reality, we're all part of the human race. And though we're all in the same situation—sinners in need of a Saviour—we can be "justified freely" (made right with God) by His grace (V. 24).

DAVE BRANON

**How does it help you to love others better by recognising
we're all equal before God? How has Jesus met your
deepest need?**

*Dear God, thank You for sending Jesus to earth to live a perfect
life and to willingly give His life as a sacrifice for my sins.*

BIBLE IN A YEAR | AMOS 1–3; REVELATION 6

They devoted themselves . . . to fellowship.
[ACTS 2:42]

COMMUNITY IN CHRIST

In the southern Bahamas lies a small piece of land called Ragged Island. In the nineteenth century it had an active salt industry, but because of a decline in that industry, many people emigrated to nearby islands. In 2016, when fewer than eighty people lived there, the island featured three religious denominations, yet the people all gathered together in one place for worship and fellowship each week. With so few residents, a sense of community was especially vital for them.

The people of the early church felt a crucial need and desire for community as well. They were excited about their newfound faith that was made possible by Jesus' death and resurrection. But they also knew He was no longer physically with them, so they knew they needed each other. They devoted themselves to the apostles' teachings, to fellowship and to sharing Communion together (ACTS 2:42). They gathered in homes for worship and meals and cared for others' needs. The church is described in this way: "All the believers were one in heart and mind" (4:32). Filled with the Holy Spirit, they praised God continually and brought the church's needs to Him in prayer.

Community is essential for our growth and support. Don't try to go it alone. God will develop that sense of community as you share your struggles and joys with others and draw near to Him together.

ANNE CETAS

> **How might you commit to spending time with fellow believers? Where and when will you do this?**
>
> *I need You and Your people, God, to help me live the fullest life for You.*

BIBLE IN A YEAR | AMOS 4–6; REVELATION 7

For the LORD detests the perverse but takes the
upright into his confidence. [PROVERBS 3:32]

CHRISTMAS DILEMMA

David and Angie had felt called to move overseas, and the
fruitful ministry that followed seemed to confirm it. But
there was one downside to their move. David's elderly
parents would now spend Christmases alone.

David and Angie tried to mitigate his parents' Christmas Day
loneliness by posting gifts early and calling on Christmas morning. But what his parents really wanted was *them*. With David's
income only permitting an occasional trip home, what else
could they do? David needed wisdom.

Proverbs 3 is a crash course in wisdom-seeking, showing
us how to receive it by taking our situations to God (VV. 5–6),
describing its various qualities such as love and faithfulness
(VV. 3–4, 7–12), and its benefits such as peace and longevity
(VV. 13–18). In a touching note, it adds that God gives such wisdom by taking us "into his confidence" (V. 32). He whispers His
solutions to those who are close to Him.

Praying about his problem one night, David had an idea. On the
next Christmas Day, he and Angie put on their Christmas jumpers,
decorated the table with tinsel and brought in the roast dinner.
David's parents did the same. Then, placing a laptop on each table, they ate together via video link. It almost felt like they were in
the same room. It's become a family tradition ever since.

God took David into His confidence and gave him wisdom. He
loves to whisper creative solutions to our problems. *SHERIDAN VOYSEY*

***What dilemma are you facing? What loving solution
might God have for you?***

*Father God, please whisper to my heart Your creative
solution to my problem.*

BIBLE IN A YEAR | AMOS 7–9; REVELATION 8

The Lord is near. Do not be anxious about
anything, but . . . present your requests to God.
[PHILIPPIANS 4:5–6]

MY GOD IS NEAR

For more than thirty years, Lourdes, a voice teacher in Manila, had taught students face to face. When she was asked to conduct classes online, she was anxious. "I'm not good with computers," she recounted. "My laptop is old, and I'm not familiar with video conferencing platforms."

While it may seem a small thing to some, it was a real stress for her. "I live alone, so there is no one to help," she said. "I'm concerned that my students will quit, and I need the income."

Before each class, Lourdes would pray for her laptop to work properly. "Philippians 4:5–6 was the wallpaper on my screen," she said. "How I clung to those words."

Paul exhorts us to not be anxious about anything, because "the Lord is near" (PHILIPPIANS 4:5). God's promise of His presence is ours to hold on to. As we rest in His nearness and commit everything to Him in prayer—both big and small—His peace guards our "hearts and . . . minds in Christ Jesus" (V. 7).

"God led me to websites about fixing computer glitches," Lourdes said. "He also gave me patient students who understood my technological limitations." God's presence, help and peace are ours to enjoy as we seek to follow Him all the days of our life. We can say with confidence: "Rejoice in the Lord always. I will say it again: Rejoice!" (V. 4).   *KAREN HUANG*

> **How can knowing that God is near change your
> reaction of worry to one of peace? What specific
> requests can you present to Him?**

> *Dear God, thank You for being near me. Because of Your
> loving presence, help and peace, I don't have to be anxious.*

BIBLE IN A YEAR | OBADIAH; REVELATION 9

The sun rose above him as he passed Peniel,
and [Jacob] was limping because of his hip.
[GENESIS 32:31]

LEARNING FROM SCARS

Faye touched the scars on her abdomen. She had endured
another surgery to remove oesophageal-stomach cancer.
This time doctors had taken part of her stomach and left a
jagged scar that revealed the extent of their work. She told her
husband, "Scars represent either the pain of cancer or the start
of healing. I choose my scars to be symbols of healing."

Jacob faced a similar choice after his all-night wrestling match
with God. The divine assailant wrenched Jacob's hip out of its
socket, so that Jacob was left exhausted and with a noticeable
limp. Months later, when Jacob massaged his tender hip, I wonder what he reflected on?

Was he filled with regret for his years of deceit that forced this
fateful match? The divine messenger had wrestled the truth out
of him, refusing to bless him until Jacob owned up to who he was.
He confessed he was Jacob, the "heel grabber" (SEE GENESIS 25:26).
He'd played tricks on his brother Esau and father-in-law Laban,
deceiving them to gain advantage. The divine wrestler said Jacob's new name would be "Israel, because you have struggled
with God and with humans and have overcome" (V. 28).

Jacob's limp represented the death of his old life of deceit and
the beginning of his new life with God. The end of Jacob and the
start of Israel. His limp led him to lean on God, who now moved
powerfully in and through him.   *MIKE WITTMER*

> **What spiritual scars do you have? How might they
> symbolise the end of something bad and the start of
> something new?**

Father, my limp is a sign of Your love.

BIBLE IN A YEAR | JONAH 1-4; REVELATION 10

I am he who blots out your transgressions . . . and remembers your sins no more. [ISAIAH 43:25]

FORGIVENESS AND FORGETTING

Jill Price was born with the condition of hyperthymesia: the ability to remember in extraordinary detail everything that ever happened to her. She can replay in her mind the exact occurrence of any event she's experienced in her lifetime.

The TV show *Unforgettable* was premised on a female police officer with hyperthymesia—to her a great advantage in trivia games and in solving crimes. For Jill Price, however, the condition isn't so much fun. She can't forget the moments of life when she was criticised, experienced loss or did something she deeply regretted. She replays those scenes in her head over and over again.

Our God is omniscient (perhaps a kind of divine hyperthymesia); the Bible tells us that His understanding has no limit. And yet we discover in Isaiah a most reassuring truth: "I, even I, am he who blots out your transgressions . . . and remembers your sins no more" (ISAIAH 43:25). The book of Hebrews reinforces this: "We have been made holy through . . . Jesus Christ . . . [and our] sins and lawless acts [God] will remember no more" (HEBREWS 10:10, 17).

As we confess our sins to God, we can stop playing them over and over in our minds. We need to let them go, just as He does: "Forget the former things; do not dwell on the past" (ISAIAH 43:18). In His great love, God chooses to not remember our sins against us. Let's remember *that*.   *KENNETH PETERSEN*

What regrets do you harbour in your memory and play over and over again? How can you give them to God and release the past?

Dear God, thank You for forgiving and forgetting my sins.

BIBLE IN A YEAR | MICAH 1–3; REVELATION 11

Put your hope in God, for I will yet praise
him, my Saviour and my God. [PSALM 42:11]

THE LIGHT OF HOPE

My mother's shiny red cross should have been hanging next to her bed at the cancer care centre. And I should have been preparing for holiday visits between her scheduled treatments. All I wanted for Christmas was another day with my mum. Instead, I was home . . . hanging her cross on a fake tree.

When my son Xavier plugged in the lights, I whispered, "Thank You." He said, "You're welcome." My son didn't know I was thanking God for using the flickering bulbs to turn my eyes towards the ever-enduring Light of Hope—Jesus.

The writer of Psalm 42 expressed his raw emotions to God (VV. 1–4). He acknowledged his "downcast" and "disturbed" soul before encouraging readers: "Put your hope in God, for I will yet praise him, my Saviour and my God" (V. 5). Even though he was overcome with waves of sorrow and suffering, the psalmist's hope shone through the remembrance of God's past faithfulness (VV. 6–10). He ended by questioning his doubts and affirming the resilience of his refined faith: "Why, my soul, are you downcast? Why so disturbed within me? Put your hope in God, for I will yet praise him, my Saviour and my God" (V. 11).

For many of us, the Christmas season stirs up both joy and sorrow. Thankfully, even these mixed emotions can be reconciled and redeemed through the promises of the true Light of Hope—Jesus.   *XOCHITL DIXON*

How has Jesus helped you process grief while celebrating Christmas? How can you support someone who's grieving this season?

Dear Jesus, thank You for carrying me through times of grief and joy all year round.

BIBLE IN A YEAR | MICAH 4–5; REVELATION 12

[Jesus] broke down the wall of hostility that separated us. [EPHESIANS 2:14 NLT]

WALLS TORN DOWN, UNITY FOUND

Since 1961, families and friends had been separated by the Berlin Wall. Erected that year by the East German government, the barrier kept its citizens from fleeing to West Germany. In fact, from 1949 to the day the structure was built, it's estimated that more than 2.5 million East Germans had bolted to the West. One world leader stood at the wall in 1987 and famously said, "Tear down this wall." Those words reflected a groundswell of change that culminated with the wall being torn down in 1989—leading to Germany's joyous reunification.

Paul wrote of a "wall of hostility" torn down by Jesus (EPHESIANS 2:14). The wall had existed between Jews (God's chosen people) and gentiles (all other people). And it was symbolised by the dividing wall (the soreg) in the ancient temple erected by Herod the Great in Jerusalem. It kept gentiles from entering beyond the outer courts of the temple, though they could see the inner courts. But Jesus brought "peace" and reconciliation between the Jews and gentiles and between God and all people. He did so by "[breaking] down the wall . . . that separated us" by "his death on the cross" (VV. 14, 16 NLT). The "Good News of peace" made it possible for all to be united by faith in Christ (VV. 17–18 NLT).

Today, many things can divide us. As God provides what we need, let's strive to live out the peace and unity found in Jesus (VV. 19–22).   *TOM FELTEN*

> **What dividing walls do you see? How can you help remove them in Jesus' strength?**
>
> *Jesus, please help me tear down walls that deny Your truth and love.*

BIBLE IN A YEAR | MICAH 6–7; REVELATION 13

Encourage one another and build each
other up. [1 THESSALONIANS 5:11]

FELLOWSHIP IN JESUS

'm not sure who's responsible for turning out the lights and
locking up the church after our Sunday morning service, but I
know one thing about that person: Sunday dinner is going to
be delayed. That's because so many people love to hang around
after church and talk about life decisions, heart issues and struggles, and more. It's a joy to look around twenty minutes after
the service and see so many people still enjoying each other's
company.

Fellowship is a key component of the Christ-like life. Without
the connectivity that comes from spending time with fellow believers, we'd miss out on many benefits of being a believer.

For instance, Paul says we can "encourage one another and
build each other up" (1 THESSALONIANS 5:11). The author of Hebrews agrees, telling us not to neglect getting together, because
we need to be "encouraging one another" (HEBREWS 10:25). And
the writer also says that when we're together, we "spur one another on towards love and good deeds" (V. 24).

As people dedicated to living for Jesus, we prepare ourselves
for faithfulness and service as we "encourage the disheartened"
and are "patient with everyone" (1 THESSALONIANS 5:14). Living
that way, as He helps us, allows us to enjoy true fellowship and
"to do what is good for each other and for everyone else" (V. 15).

DAVE BRANON

What benefits do you gain from being with believers?
How can you help others experience fellowship in Christ?

Dear God, please help me to be someone who generously
encourages others in love and compassion.

BIBLE IN A YEAR | NAHUM 1-3; REVELATION 14

When they saw the star, they were overjoyed. [MATTHEW 2:10]

THE CHRISTMAS STAR

"If you find that star, you can always find your way home." Those were my father's words when he taught me how to locate the North Star as a child. Dad had served in the armed forces during wartime, and there were moments when his life depended on being able to navigate by the night sky. So he made sure I knew the names and locations of several constellations, but it was being able to find Polaris that mattered most of all. Knowing that star's location meant I could gain a sense of direction wherever I was and find where I was supposed to be.

Scripture tells of another star of vital importance. "Magi from the east," well-educated men (from an area encompassed by Iran and Iraq today) had been watching for signs in the sky of the birth of the One who was to be God's king for His people. They came to Jerusalem asking "Where is the one who has been born king of the Jews? We saw his star when it rose and have come to worship him" (MATTHEW 2:1–2).

Astronomers don't know what caused the star of Bethlehem to appear, but the Bible reveals that God created it to point the world to Jesus—"the bright Morning Star" (REVELATION 22:16). Christ came to save us from our sins and guide us back to God. Follow Him, and you'll find your way home.   *JAMES BANKS*

***In what practical way will you follow Jesus today?
What can you do this week to share His love with others?***

Jesus, thank You for being the Way to my forever-home in heaven. Please help guide me by Your light today!

You, Bethlehem Ephrathah, . . . out of you will
come . . . one who will be ruler over Israel.
[MICAH 5:2]

THE PROMISE OF CHRIST'S BIRTH

In November 1962, physicist John W. Mauchly said, "There is
no reason to suppose the average boy or girl cannot be master of a personal computer." Mauchly's prediction seemed remarkable at the time, but it proved astonishingly accurate. Today,
using a computer or handheld device is one of the earliest skills
a child learns.

While Mauchly's prediction has come true, so too have much
more important promises—those made in Scripture about the
coming of Christ. For example, Micah 5:2 declared, "But you,
Bethlehem Ephrathah, though you are small among the clans of
Judah, out of you will come for me one who will be ruler over
Israel, whose origins are from of old, from ancient times." God
sent Jesus, who arrived in tiny Bethlehem—marking him as from
the royal line of David (SEE LUKE 2:4–7).

The same Bible that accurately prophesied the first coming
of Jesus also promises His return (ACTS 1:11). Jesus promised His
first followers that He would come back for them (JOHN 14:1–4).

This Christmas, as we ponder the accurately promised facts
surrounding the birth of Jesus, may we also consider His promised return, and allow Him to prepare us for that majestic moment when we see Him face to face!   *BILL CROWDER*

> **How might you respond in worship to the truth of the
> prophecies of Christ's birth? How does His promise to
> return for us impact your decision-making?**
>
> *Loving Father, I'm so grateful for the birth of Jesus and
> His mission of rescue and redemption. Thank You for His
> certain return for me.*

BIBLE IN A YEAR | ZEPHANIAH 1–3; REVELATION 16

Mary treasured up all these things and pondered them in her heart. [LUKE 2:19]

THE DAY AFTER CHRISTMAS

After all the joy of Christmas Day, the following day felt like a let-down. We'd stayed overnight with friends but hadn't slept well. Then our car broke down as we were driving home. Then it started to snow. We had abandoned the car and taxied home in the snow and sleet feeling *blah*.

We're not the only ones who've felt low after Christmas Day. Whether it's from excessive eating, the way carols suddenly disappear from the radio, or the fact that the gifts we bought last week are now on sale half price, the magic of Christmas Day can quickly dissipate!

The Bible never tells us about the day after Jesus' birth. But we can imagine that after walking to Bethlehem, scrambling for accommodation, Mary's pain in giving birth, and having shepherds drop by unannounced (LUKE 2:4–18), Mary and Joseph were exhausted. Yet as Mary cradled her new-born, I can imagine her reflecting on her angelic visitation (1:30–33), Elizabeth's blessing (VV. 42–45) and her own realisation of her baby's destiny (VV. 46–55). Mary "pondered" such things in her heart (2:19), which must have lightened the tiredness and physical pain of that day.

We'll all have 'blah' days, perhaps even the day after Christmas. Like Mary, let's face them by pondering the One who came into our world, forever brightening it with His presence.

SHERIDAN VOYSEY

When are you prone to feeling low after a high? How can you ponder today all that Jesus has brought into the world?

Dear Jesus, I praise You for entering our dark world, forever brightening my days with Your presence.

BIBLE IN A YEAR | HAGGAI 1–2; REVELATION 17

The fruit of the righteous is a tree of life, and the one who is wise saves lives. [PROVERBS 11:30]

GOD'S WISDOM SAVES LIVES

Apostal worker became concerned after seeing one of her customers' post pile up. The postal worker knew the elderly woman lived alone and usually picked up her letters every day. Making a wise choice, the worker mentioned her concern to one of the woman's neighbours. This neighbour alerted yet another neighbour, who had a spare key to the woman's home. Together they entered their friend's home and found her lying on the floor. She had fallen four days earlier and couldn't get up or call for help. The postal worker's wisdom, concern and decision to act probably saved her life.

Proverbs says, "the one who is wise saves lives" (PROVERBS 11:30). The discernment that comes from doing right and living according to God's wisdom can bless not only ourselves but those we encounter too. The fruit of living out what honours Him and His ways can produce a good and refreshing life. And our fruit also prompts us to care about others and to look out for their well-being.

As the writer of Proverbs asserts throughout the book, wisdom is found in reliance on God. Wisdom is considered "more precious than rubies, and nothing you desire can compare with her" (8:11). The wisdom God provides is there to guide us throughout our lives. It just might save a life for eternity.

KATARA PATTON

How can you use wisdom to help someone today?
How much do you value wisdom?

Heavenly Father, please give me wisdom to follow Your path and directions. Help me to look out for others as You guide me.

BIBLE IN A YEAR | ZECHARIAH 1–4; REVELATION 18

If you take your neighbour's cloak as a
pledge, return it by sunset. [EXODUS 22:26]

MEETING THE NEEDS OF OTHERS

Phillip's father suffered from severe mental illness and had
left home to live on the streets. After Cyndi and her young
son Phillip spent a day searching for him, Phillip was rightly concerned for his wellbeing. He asked his mother whether
his father and other people without homes were warm. In response, they launched an effort to collect and distribute blan-
kets and cold-weather gear to homeless people in the area. For
more than a decade, Cyndi has considered it her life's work,
crediting her son and her deep faith in God for awakening her to
the hardship of being without a warm place to sleep.

The Bible has long taught us to respond to the needs of others.
In the book of Exodus, Moses records a set of principles to guide
our interaction with those who lack plentiful resources. When
we're moved to supply the needs of another, we're to "not treat
it like a business deal" and should make no gain or profit from it
(EXODUS 22:25). If a person's cloak was taken as collateral, it was
to be returned by sunset "because that cloak is the only covering
your neighbour has. What else can they sleep in?" (V. 27).

Let's ask God to open our eyes and hearts to see how we can
ease the pain of those who are suffering. Whether we seek to
meet the needs of many—as Cyndi and Phillip have—or those
of a single person, we honour Him by treating them with dignity
and care.   *KIRSTEN HOLMBERG*

How has God supplied your needs through others?
Whose needs might you be able to meet?

Heavenly Father, please open my eyes to the needs of others.

BIBLE IN A YEAR | ZECHARIAH 5-8; REVELATION 19

God blesses those who patiently endure
testing and temptation. [JAMES 1:12 NLT]

THE CROWN OF LIFE

Twelve-year-old LeeAdianez Rodriguez-Espada was worried that she'd be late for a 5K run (just over 3 miles). Her anxiety led her to take off with a group of runners fifteen minutes earlier than her start time. She didn't realise it, but they were participants of the half-marathon (more than 13 miles!). LeeAdianez fell in pace with other runners and put one foot in front of the other. At mile four, with the finish line nowhere in sight, she realised that she was in a longer and more difficult race. Instead of dropping out, she simply kept running. The accidental half-marathoner completed the race and placed 1,885th out of 2,111 finishers. Now that's perseverance!

While undergoing persecution, many first-century believers in Jesus wanted to drop out of the race for Christ, but James encouraged them to keep running. If they patiently endured testing, God promised a double reward (JAMES 1:4, 12). Firstly, "perseverance [would] finish its work" so they could be "mature and complete, not lacking anything" (V. 4). Secondly, God would give them the "crown of life"—life in Jesus on earth and the promise of being in His presence in the life to come (V. 12).

Some days the Christian race feels like it's not the one we signed up for—it's something longer and more difficult than we expected. But as God provides what we need, we can persevere and keep on running.   *MARVIN WILLIAMS*

> **What difficulty are you enduring right now? What can
> you do to remain faithful to God as you undergo testing?**
>
> *Dear God, my legs are tired, and I feel like giving up.
> Please strengthen me.*

> When I consider your heavens, . . . the moon and the
> stars, which you have set in place, what is mankind
> that you are mindful of them? [PSALM 8:3–4]

SEEING STARS

Amy Carmichael's ministry in India placed her in frequent danger as she rescued enslaved girls and, to help them experience the love of Christ, gave them a safe home. Despite opposition and her own battle with crippling aches and pains, she never lost either her resolve or her joy. As she explained, "Two men looked through prison bars. The one saw mud, the other stars." She continued, "There is always something to be happy about if we look for it."

Unlike Amy, we often let our daily problems and responsibilities fix our eyes to the earth. Yet perhaps when we're busiest we most need to follow the example of the psalmist who paused and looked up at God's "glory in the heavens" (PSALM 8:1). His awe and joy was revitalised as he basked in the revelation of creation. "When I consider . . . the moon and the stars, which you have set in place, what is mankind that you are mindful of them?" (VV. 3–4).

The vastness of the stars reminds us both of our smallness in God's universe and of His infinite rule. Yet God has crowned us "with glory and honour" as His masterpieces (V. 5). Every bit of creation—including the stars—has been "set in place" (V. 3) to display God's loving reign on our behalf.

Where do you look when you need joy or reassurance? Why not try drinking in the sight of the stars; they are a nightly reminder of God's unrivalled majesty (V. 9). 　　　*CHRIS WALE*

> ***Where in creation do you think God's glory is most clearly
> displayed? How can you take a moment to reflect on this
> when you are busy or stressed?***
>
> *Creator God, the whole world is full of Your glory. I thank
> You for the constant reminders in creation—including the
> stars—of Your mighty power and wonderful love.*

BIBLE IN A YEAR │ ZECHARIAH 13–14; REVELATION 21

May he produce in you . . . every good thing
that is pleasing to him. [HEBREWS 13:21 NLT]

THE RIGHTEOUS CITY

On New Year's Eve 2000, officials in one major city carefully opened a hundred-year-old time capsule. Nestled inside the copper box were hopeful predictions from some leaders who expressed visions of prosperity. The mayor's message, however, offered a different approach. He wrote, "May we be permitted to express one hope superior to all others . . . [that] you may realise as a nation, people and city, you have grown in righteousness, for it is this that exalts a nation."

More than success, happiness or peace, the mayor wished that future citizens would grow in what it means to be truly just and upright. Perhaps he took his cue from Jesus, who blessed those who long for His righteousness (MATTHEW 5:6). But it's easy to get discouraged when we consider God's perfect standard.

Praise God that we don't have to rely on our own effort to grow. The author of Hebrews said it this way: "May the God of peace . . . equip you with everything good for doing his will, and may he work in us what is pleasing to him, through Jesus Christ" (HEBREWS 13:20–21). We who are in Christ are made holy by His blood the moment we believe in Him (V. 12), but He actively grows the fruit of righteousness in our hearts throughout a lifetime. We'll often stumble on the journey, yet still we look forward to "the city that is to come" where God's righteousness will reign (V. 14). *KAREN PIMPO*

For what Christ-like attributes would you like to be known?
How can you encourage others to seek God's righteousness?

Dear God, work in me what's pleasing to You.

BIBLE IN A YEAR | MALACHI 1–4; REVELATION 22

ABOUT THE PUBLISHER

Our Daily Bread Ministries

In 1938, our ministry started with a radio programme called the Detroit Bible Class. Since then, our audience has grown from a small group of dedicated radio listeners to millions of people around the world who use our Bible-based resources. Over the years, our focus has remained the same: reaching out to people all around the world with the message of God's love.

Our Daily Bread Ministries is a non-denominational, non-profit organisation with staff and volunteers in over 37 offices working together to distribute more than 60 million resources annually in 150 countries. Regardless of whether it's a radio broadcast, DVD, podcast, book, mobile app or website, we provide materials to help people grow in their relationship with God.

Our Daily Bread Publishing

Our Daily Bread Publishing was founded in 1988 as an extension of Our Daily Bread Ministries. Our goal is to produce resources that feed the soul with the Word of God, and we do this through books, music, video, audio, software, greeting cards and downloadable content. All our materials focus on the never-changing truths of Scripture, so everything we produce shows reverence for God and His wisdom, demonstrates the relevance of vibrant faith, and equips and encourages people in their everyday lives.

OUR DAILY BREAD MINISTRIES OFFICES

Europe Offices

For information on our resources, visit **ourdailybread.org**. Alternatively, please contact the regional United Kingdom office, or go to **ourdailybread.org/locations** for the complete list of offices.

United Kingdom

Our Daily Bread Ministries, PO Box 1, Millhead, Carnforth, LA5 9ES europe@odb.org, +44 (0) 15395 64149

ourdailybread.org

TOPIC INDEX

JANUARY – DECEMBER 2025

TOPIC INDEX

JANUARY – DECEMBER 2025

TOPIC INDEX

JANUARY – DECEMBER 2025